22 Keys to Freedom

"UNLOCKING YOUR DESTINY WITHIN"

KRISTIN TAYLOR

<u>Endorsement</u>

I love this book! *22 Keys to Freedom* by Kristin Taylor is exactly what it claims to be—a book with keys. But keys are only good if they're used properly. Just holding them in your hand is not enough. They're meant to open doors, allowing you to walk into new places with new rooms. That's what this book does. So many books are storybooks, and that's not wrong. Others are filled with "how-tos," and that's not bad either. However, when combined, they form a very powerful combination.

Kristin unveils an extraordinary life story so full of hardships that it could be mistaken for a bad movie plot; yet, she has emerged as a truly remarkable and compassionate person. She uses her personal experience as seeds to bring forth wisdom, wisdom that is now available for all of us. That's the heart and strength of this book. It's not just a story, and it's not just information. It's a one-two punch that brings life and truth together, offering more than just hope. It brings keys! Keys that unlock closed or hidden doors that allow you to explore the depths of your heart and bring you into destiny.

Kristin has a unique way of pulling each chapter together, incorporating prayer, scriptures to meditate on, reflections, and declarations. She includes one of my favorite parts throughout the book, entitled "Applying wisdom to your daily life." She puts a spotlight on how to live and walk into greater freedom. *22 Keys to Freedom* by Kristin Taylor is a book you'll want to keep handy so you can pick it up and read it again and again. You'll be glad you did.

—Chris DuPré

Writer, Pastor, and Speaker

Author of *The Wild Love of God*

<u>Dedication</u>

This book is dedicated to every beloved who reads it.
I understand deeply the challenges life presents and the many layers
within the soul that we must face.
Healing takes time, so be gentle with yourself and your heart
as you navigate through life's journey. True freedom and healing come
from finding your identity in Christ

"I pray that the Father of glory, the God of our Lord Jesus Christ, would impart to you the riches of the Spirit of wisdom and the Spirit of Revelation to know Him through you, deepening intimacy with Him. I pray that the light of God will illuminate the eyes of your imagination, flooding you with light, until you experience the full revelation of hope of His calling, that is, the wealth of God's glorious inheritances that he finds in us, his holy ones! I pray that you will continually experience the immeasurable greatness of God's power made available to you through faith. Then your lives will be an advertisement of this immense power as it works through you! This is the mighty power that was released when God raised Christ from the dead and exalted him to the place of highest honor and supreme authority in the heavenly realm."

~ Ephesians 1:17-20 ~

Acknowledgements

First, I would like to express my deepest gratitude to my bestest friend
in the whole wide world, my precious husband, John Taylor. You have been my greatest supporter
through every challenge and triumph; your unwavering love, encouragement, and patience have
been a blessing beyond what words can say. Thank you for always fighting by my side.
You have stood by me as I have navigated my own healing journey
and through this process of writing my first book.
You have always affirmed me with love and truth. Thank you
for never giving up on me, us, or God, and thank you for
always believing in me every step of the way.
I have become the woman I am today because of your love
and faithfulness to me, our marriage, and the call that is upon our lives.

Lastly, I am eternally grateful to those of you who have supported me
throughout the process of writing this book. This includes all of you who contributed their time
and expertise in reading, editing, and offering me such endearing encouragement along this
journey. I also want to acknowledge those of you who have supported me
in the ministry of helping people heal from soul wounds. It is one of my greatest privileges
to lead people into a loving relationship with Christ and witness the lives of so many
become transformed, delivered, healed, and set free.
You are all amazing! I love you and I thank you for your support and dedication:

Christine Sheehan, Burt Casey, Carleen Taylor, Karen Daugherty,
Shannon Hardin, Chris Dupre (Author of *The Wild Love of God & The Lost Art of Pure Worship*),
Darlene Underwood (Author of *Destiny's Journey*),
Kris Monegato (Author of *Breakthrough Leadership*), Lauren McQueen (Author of *A New Day: 31 daily devotions*), and Angelise Shrader (Author of *Live out Love*).

Contents

Preface

I have tried to write this book several times; however, here I am, going through yet another grueling process in life to finally follow through with this vision that God put in me years ago. Isn't it interesting when we find ourselves at yet another crossroads in life that we finally push to take the next step to embark on the right course, even amid our pain? I just recently went through another miscarriage, and it has been gut-wrenching to walk through this now for the 2nd time within seven months. We have been trying for a baby for four years and still choose to trust God for our family. I do not share this with you for sympathy. I share this with you because life is not easy, but we have a choice. A choice to keep moving forward in this challenging journey with love, acceptance, and faith. ***Pain with perseverance and choosing love can birth you into your purpose if you allow it to.***

This book is all about extremely difficult circumstances that I have had the privilege of walking through and truly coming out on the other side, completely healed. I have gone through all of these things to share the wisdom I have learned along the way. My goal is to help people break free from the prisons we choose to put ourselves in. I use the words 'we choose' because, over the years, I have learned that our minds are an extremely powerful tool that we can use to keep our freedom no matter what situation we find ourselves in.

I was unjustly sentenced to three years in federal prison, and I was able to maintain my peace and happiness during that time, but I had to train myself. I consistently worked at keeping my focus on things that were true, lovely, noble, worthy of praise, and of good report. I had to filter every negative thought into a positive by allowing my heart to feel, yet not be overcome by the evil and negativity that surrounded me.

There are several keys throughout this book that I will share with you to begin implementing into your life. As you do this, I believe these keys will help you become free in any situation you face. I can say this with the utmost confidence because I am living proof that applying God's Word to your life works. I have overcome death five times in my life. I have won the battle over suicidal thoughts and attempts. I have won the battle over addiction. I have learned how to overcome debilitating pain both emotionally and physically. I am a survivor and now a thriver from years of sexual molestation and perversion. I have learned how to forgive the unforgivable by most standards. I survived the abusive, chaotic prison system, and I am now flourishing because of it. Those are just a few things I have gotten through on this beautiful journey we call life. I truly believe if you read this book with an open heart and are diligent to do the work I give you daily, you will come out on the other side as a changed human being.

Action is power! If you keep going around the same mountain in life, you have to ask yourself, what should I learn from this? Otherwise, you are walking out Albert Einstein's definition of insanity: doing the same thing and expecting different results. Nothing will change in our lives if we do not change our actions. I delve into deeper keys of the meaning of all of this, that will empower you to get back into the driver's seat of your life with the Holy Spirit as your GPS. I hope and desire to see every person who reads this book find true freedom and begin to believe that there is an amazing plan and purpose in your life!

Christians need to start walking in this power and truth! I have watched too many people be turned off by the Church and "so-called Christians," due to self-righteousness. As Christians, we need to humble ourselves and learn what it means to be truly Christ-like, so that people can see God's righteousness in us. The last thing people need is religion being thrown at them. They need actual encounters with the love of Jesus so they can understand His message. It is my heart's desire for people to embrace the words on the pages of this book through the heart of the Holy Spirit and receive it in love. I hope that none of what appears on these pages will lead to any condemnation in any way. I firmly believe that change happens only through true conviction and repentance. It is time for us, as believers in Christ, to face hard truths, walk in humility, and mature into all that God is leading us into. You are chosen for a time as this beloved!

22 Keys to Freedom
UNLOCKING YOUR DESTINY WITHIN

~ Isaiah 60~The time is now to arise and shine ~

I firmly believe that we are all on our own walks with the Lord; however, for those who don't know Jesus as your Lord, I hope this book inspires you to see how very real and amazing God is. I've learned that God truly wants a deep and intimate relationship with everyone on this earth because He created each of us. Over the years of walking with Jesus, I have found that God speaks to everyone in several different ways, and it is so wonderful to watch. There will be many instances where God has spoken to me that I share throughout this book. I pray that you begin to experience God in new and exciting ways for yourself. As this started happening to me, it radically changed my life and my walk with God. All I knew for several years of my life was a distant God. However, now I know him as my dear Friend, Father, and Husband, just as the Bible tells us.

I named this book *22 Keys to Freedom* because, on one particular night in 2014, God spoke to me through the sky. When I was in the most desperate places of needing him, I began to hear from Him in the most new and unusual ways. Something happened to me when I was in Federal prison back in 2014, and I find it extremely significant to share now. He wrote the number 22 across the clouds for me with the most beautiful and perfect calligraphy. As clear as you see something being written before your eyes on paper, this was how He wrote to me in the sky. I looked up at the sky while worshipping God during my prayer time. It was a clear night. I could see the stars and only one small cloud right above me. I then closed my eyes to begin praying again. That's when I heard Him say in my spirit, "Look up my child." As I looked up, now for the second time, He began writing the number 22 for me out of that one small cloud in the sky.

At the time, I had no idea what this number meant; however, after much studying and seeing this number repeatedly for eleven years, I believe this vision is upon us today. The number 22 biblically represents deliverance out of chaos and disorder, and also means wisdom. This brings spiritual awakening and divine revelation. Spiritual awakening brings insight and awareness, providing clarity into God's purposes and His plans. It is time to awaken the church! God is sifting the wheat from the tares right now and is bringing divine order into the body of Christ along with His divine wisdom as we have never seen before.

God will pour out His Spirit upon all flesh in the near days to come, and people will come to know how very real Jesus Christ of Nazareth is. He was not just a man or a prophet of old, but He is the one true God, and He is bringing an awakening upon the earth right now. In 2020, God woke me up with an audible voice telling me that I come from the bloodline of David. Holy Spirit reminded me about another vision of keys that I had back in 2017 during deep worship, when I was caught up into the throne room of heaven. The Words of Isaiah 22:22 came into my spirit. This verse says, *"I will place upon his shoulder the keys to the house of David, what he opens no one can shut, and what he shuts no one can open."*

We are in significant times right now and must be paying attention to the signs God is showing all of creation. Romans 8:18-22 from the Passion Translation says, "*I am convinced that any suffering we endure is less than nothing compared to the magnitude of glory that is about to be unveiled within us. The entire universe is standing on tiptoe, yearning to see the unveiling of God's glorious sons and daughters! For against its will the universe itself has had to endure the empty futility resulting from the consequences of human sin. But now, with eager expectation, all creation longs for freedom from its slavery to decay and to experience with us the wonderful freedom coming to God's children. To this day we are aware of the universal agony and groaning of creation, as if it were in the contractions of labor for childbirth.*"

We are in this time. God gave me another powerful vision in November of 2020 that is a huge key for the body of Christ to give birth to what God wants us to release upon the earth. I will share these visions in greater detail through the chapters of this book. I saw the name of this book in my mind in the beginning of 2021 and the Lord said, you will write this for my Bride. This book is a manual that I believe God will use to bring freedom to both the body of Christ and the new believer. I have written this manuscript to be read over 9 weeks because there is a lot of information to digest in each chapter. At the end of each day, there is homework and keys to begin implementing into your life. This will help bring you deeper intimacy with Jesus by learning to rewire brain patterns, creating new habits, and healing your heart. Once you know how to master these keys, you will be amazed by the doors of destiny that will begin opening in your life.

These logical yet straightforward keys will unlock deep places within the hearts of individuals who feel like there is more to this life but haven't been able to get there yet. These keys have broken me free from many strongholds and idols in my life. It is my hope and desire to share with you some stories of my life to inspire your heart and cause it to beat for the deep longings that you have been made for! You were created for a time such as this! There is a powerful reason why you are living in this exact time and season.

I am here to help propel you into your purpose by breaking free from any lies you have believed about yourself or about God. Keep in mind that this takes discipline, consistency, and time. You may find that one day's reading and homework for this book might take 2-3 days or even a week, because of how deep I challenge your heart to go. This is Ok! I encourage you to take your time and give yourself grace. Our hearts have many layers, and our brains take time to rewire. I pray that you remain patient, stay steadfast, and persevere to finish this journey strong.

WEEK 1

What Are You Partnering With?

1 Choose Wisely

Going through life, we have the choice to partner our thoughts with many things, even though most of us are not even aware of the spiritual entities we can partner with. Negative thoughts are one of the most dangerous things we can agree with. However, no one thinks at a young age, "Wait a second, is this thought good for me?" Half the time, we are trying to find ourselves, searching for true identity in validation through others or in the things of this world to feel fulfilled. For example, gossip is a destructive habit that creeps into our lives at a very young age.

We usually engage because this seems like the cool thing to do; not knowing that we are partnering with such negative and condemning thoughts towards others which in turn hurts our own hearts. We actually come into spiritual agreement with the spirit of gossip. This agreement can build into pride and create walls within our hearts, clouding our judgment. I will discuss the crucial importance of spiritual agreements later in this book.

But this is why God tells us to capture every negative thought by bringing it into the obedience of Christ and then to think of things that are true, lovely, pure, worthy of praise, and of good report. We must be aware of what we put into our minds because whatever comes into our minds can get into our hearts. This can create bad habits and poor cycles that you never wanted for your life. God warns us in Proverbs 4:23 to guard our hearts above all else.

At the end of this chapter, let's take a few moments to analyze your thoughts over this past week. Are most of those thoughts negative or positive? Think about little instances that threw you off or irritated you. How did you act or respond? The first step we must take is recognizing our wrong thought patterns. Most of the time, people feel so exhausted by the stressors of life that they are just surviving. I have met very few people along my journey through life who are thriving in all they have been created for. I am not saying I thrive in every area, but this is my goal. We should make this a goal of our everyday life until we leave this Earth.

Most people have no clue what their destiny is nor really believe that there is a purpose in their life besides working a job, providing for their families, and just trying to do their best to stay afloat. I say this not out of judgment in any way, but it has inspired me to write this book because I believe everyone was brought into this Earth for a reason. Think about it; no other person carries the same DNA as you. No one can do what you can do! There may be similarities, but we all need each other because we carry special gifts that others do not. God made you for a specific purpose! I want to challenge you to start focusing on the positive things about yourself because this is one of the most indispensable strategies that can give you immense breakthroughs.

From the moment your brain awakes in the morning, you must begin to recognize negative thoughts, take them captive, and replace them with God's Truth immediately. *2 Corinthians 10:5* clearly tells us how to get on the path of correct thinking. It tells us that we must take captive every thought to the obedience of Christ, which means every thought and every demonic entity putting negativity or deception into your ear has to bow to the power of Christ within you! You are the only one who can begin this process in your life because you are the one who chooses to partner with your thoughts. And you are the one who has to get into a habit of crucifying your flesh. We will talk about this in a later chapter. I know negative thoughts will come in. They can try to infiltrate all day long, but it is your choice to partner with that particular thought.

Start to take hold of any wrong thought, which is anything that rises up against the holiness of Christ within you. This could include perversion, anger, bitterness, unhealthy judgments, etc. Throw them out when they come, and replace them with God's Truth. Here are some examples of thoughts I have had to learn how to take dominion over through the years. One of the things I have battled with most in my life is fully believing in myself. This is one area that many, if not all, people struggle with because we have an enemy that never wants us to believe in all that we've been created for.

This was the first scheme the adversary used against Adam and Eve in the Garden. He got them to question their identity and the goodness of God. They were in complete union as Spirit beings, one with Father God until eternity, yet they didn't truly know it. It was their lack of faith in who they were in Christ, so they questioned the goodness of God after they were tempted by the devil. Our thoughts are the main doorways that tempt us into slavery. This is why we must be aware of them!

One of the main reasons I struggled with believing in myself is because I went through years of sexual molestation that started at the age of 3 and lasted until the age of 12. Then, I allowed people to use and abuse me for the next eleven years of my life because I did not know my worth. I believed the lies that I was only worth the hand that was dealt to me. It wasn't until I was genuinely captivated by the love of Jesus Christ that I finally began to believe in all the beauty that was within me by choosing to partner with Him. This has taken me years due to all the trauma in my childhood. For all of you who have gone through trauma, be patient with yourself, knowing that several layers within your soul may need to be peeled back. As you allow the Holy Spirit to reveal and heal, He will lead you into freedom.

You see, many people have "come to Jesus moments," meaning they feel the presence of God powerfully in a service or at a specific time in their life. However, they aren't willing to take the next step, which is choosing to partner with His Word and no longer living for themselves. To truly walk in freedom, we must decide to make Jesus Lord in every area of our lives. We as humans are extremely prideful due to being born into a fallen world and must learn how to walk out the definition of humility and obedience. If we believe we felt a deep encounter when we got saved, and Jesus is real, then what is the block? If He is our creator, then ask yourself, why would I not allow myself to learn from the all-knowing mighty one who created me and knows me better than anyone?

The takeaway here is that many people operate from a place of fear, rather than truly out of love. I have met many people who have looked at Jesus and the Bible through the lens of religion and not with the Holy Spirit to see a heart relationship with Jesus. We must learn how to fellowship with Jesus, Father God, and the Holy Spirit, so we can genuinely walk out this life in their love! God is love; when we encounter His love, we can love-love ourselves and then love others.

Religion never allows you to truly love. It tells you that you will never measure up, while a relationship is an incredible journey that continues to build and never ends. In a later chapter, I will touch base on this primary key of intimacy, but I have met many Christians who are not living in the power they should be. Please don't get me wrong; this didn't happen to me overnight, and I am still learning daily. However, Christians who operate in fear and religion, as opposed to love and intimacy, are a huge reason why

Christians are looked upon as both hypocrites and powerless. This may seem harsh, but we are living in times when Jesus is coming back for a Bride who is ready. I don't know about you, but I want to be prepared! With this being said, I have become accustomed to asking myself this question all day long.

What are you partnering with? You must ask yourself this question in every area of your life. This has radically changed the way I live. I no longer allow myself to feel defeated for long because I choose to grieve and process when hard things happen. Then, I cry out to my King Jesus to raise me back up in His power and strength instead of my own, which is built upon His foundation. His foundation is always unshakable!

This has been a work in progress for about nine years, but it doesn't have to take you nine years. I am writing this book because, through the horrific trials of my life, God has downloaded wisdom and revelation to me for the body of Christ in this time! He is doing a quick work like never before in the times in which we are living and anointing the ones who are becoming His willing vessels. Willing is the keyword here.

I encourage you to diligently do the workbook at the end of each day. This will help you begin to rewire your brain and start getting you into healthy habits for your life. The workbook parts of this book will help you go deeper into the areas of what you should and should not be partnering with. Once you begin applying the keys of these chapters into your life, you will be amazed at how God begins to mold you in incredible new ways! None of this work should come out of religious acts in any way. It should help you grow into a deeper relationship with Jesus by learning to listen to His spirit.

I am a true walking testament that the keys in this book work. As you begin to ask yourself, "What am I partnering with?" The Holy Spirit will guide you and show you what is healthy for you to put into your mind and heart. This will help you recognize God's voice in a new way. In these times, knowing which voice is speaking and to whom we should be listening is imperative.

APPLYING WISDOM TO YOUR DAILY LIFE

Prayer for the day:

Jesus,

I repent for not allowing you to be Lord over every area of my life. Holy Spirit, I ask you to come into my heart and mind. I give you full access to make me aware of every negative thought & action that I no longer need to partner with. Lord, help me humble myself and see things from your perspective and not my own. Show me my worth in you, Lord Jesus. I give you all the days of my life. Help me walk through this nine week journey and finish strong. Thank you for revealing all that needs to be revealed to me during this time. I trust you, Father God. In Jesus Name, I pray, amen!

Scriptures to meditate on:

2 Corinthians 10:5: *"We destroy arguments and every lofty opinion raised against the knowledge of God, and take every thought captive to obey Christ."* (You have the authority to do this because Jesus Christ lives on the inside of you! Start practicing this daily and do not stop).

Philippians 4:8: *"Finally, brothers and sisters, whatever is true, whatever is noble, whatever is right, whatever is pure, whatever is lovely, whatever is admirable—if anything is excellent or praiseworthy—think about such things."* (This is one of my life scriptures that I have engrained so deeply in my mind and heart that I am constantly asking myself, why am I thinking this if it doesn't line up with this Scripture)?

Colossians 3:23: *"Whatever you do, work at it with all your heart, as working for the Lord, not for human masters."* (When we begin working on our relationship with Jesus and begin to feel His love, you will start to do things for Him and not man. This is so incredibly freeing and will be a process, but keep this scripture in your mind at all times. This will help you).

Philemon 1:6: *"I pray that your participation in the faith may become effective through knowing every good thing that is in us for the glory of Christ."*

These next 4 steps are great tools to use throughout the entire journey through this book. You will be given more tasks each day, but remember to use precept upon precept to keep your consistency in this journey to freedom. I highly recommend reading the prayer, scriptures, and declaration out loud daily. There is power when we speak life!

Key #1: Replace All Negativity With God's Truth

Reflection:

1. I want you to begin paying attention to every negative thought that comes in throughout your day. From the time you wake up until you go to bed. This includes thoughts about yourself, others, and even the slightest of irritations. Take time to write these down in your journal throughout your day. This will help you learn how to have victory over every lie where the enemy has tried to keep you bound.

____

____

____

____

____

____

____

____

____

____

2. Then, at the end of your day, reflect on your thoughts with the Holy Spirit. Ask Him to show you where these negative thought patterns come from:

____

____

____

____

____

____

____

____

____

____

This is important because God usually wants to reveal deep roots in our hearts so He can heal them.

3. A good strategy to help you expose any roots that have created these negative thought patterns is something I call, The "Why" System. Once you recognize a negative pattern, whether it is thoughts or actions, ask yourself "why" you are feeling that way or why you do that. Then, ask yourself "why" to that answer. Once you get to an answer where you can't ask why anymore, you have found the root that has allowed some sort of tie to demonic attacks. An example of this "WHY" exercise is listed below to help guide you.

4. Once you find this root, you can then go even further to ask "what" caused this or "who" did this. This will allow you to recognize people who come up in your mind and who you probably need to forgive. Allow the "whys" to bring you deeper into your thought life. Continue doing this exercise until God brings you back to the exact instance or memory of why you continue to act or feel a particular way. Then ask the Holy Spirit to help you release, forgive, and then repent if you have to, and begin replacing the lies with God's Truth.

Here is an example of the "why" exercise:

<u>It is extremely important to be as honest and vulnerable as possible; This will help you find the roots that keep holding you back:</u>

1st Question to ask yourself: What is something that I struggle with? Find the answers and write them down, then begin asking why to every answer you come up with. Keep asking why until you come to an answer where you cannot ask why any more.

Example: fear

Q: Why do you feel fearful?
A: Because I don't know what's going to happen.
Q: Why do you feel this way?
A: Because I want to know what is going to happen (Take a biblical principle)~Is it your job to know the future? No.
Q: So why do you feel fearful when the Bible tells us not to fear and to trust God?
A: Because I feel the need to control.
Q: Why do you feel the need to control?
A: Because I grew up never knowing what would happen and it wasn't peaceful, I learned at an early age that I had to take control.

It would be here where you find the root. This root of fear is linked to this person to get them to partner with spirits of manipulation and control. This usually comes from a fear that someone will hurt or try to control them, so they have been in control and not allowing God to lead them. This spirit of fear came in through this person's childhood because they grew up in a very chaotic world. They didn't have parents who nurtured this area of teaching them how to live with God nor how to trust God. This person would then take time to sit with the lord and ask where they need to repent. Repentance is key to bringing change into your life! For this instance, the first place to start would be to repent from pride because we are not God and we are not in control. The only person we are in control of is ourselves and then they would repent for not trusting God because they allowed fear to come in, even though it wasn't their fault. The key to this exercise is to be as humble as possible and to not justify but to be truly honest with how you feel and why you act the way you do. This is a very powerful exercise if you can be honest with yourself and with God.

BEGIN WRITING YOUR WHY EXERCISE HERE:

____

____

____

____

____

____

____

____

____

Declaration:

Father God, I thank you that I am your beloved child, and you are gracious towards me, which means I will be gracious towards myself as I am working through these things to break free. I know this may not happen overnight, but I will endure until the end because I am a good work of you, Lord Jesus, and I am sure of this; he who began a good work in me will bring it to completion at the day of Jesus Christ (Phil 1:6). The radiant glory of God and the exact imprint of His nature, upholding the universe by the Word of His power lives in me! Jesus is the only way to purify and take away my sins, and He is at the right hand of God, forever interceding for me! (Hebrews 1:3 ; Romans 8:34)

2 Winning the War

You see, God gives us access to choose and have free will, just like He gave Adam and Eve in the Garden. He gave them access to the tree of knowledge of good and evil but told them that they should not eat from it. It is up to us what we are choosing to feast upon. Meaning, what are we feasting most of our time and energy on? Jesus tells us we have the victory in Him, but are we truly walking that out? Jesus tells us specific actions to take in order to win this war of life here on planet Earth. One of the main things He tells us to do is to take every negative thought, every argument that rises up against His Truth, and every offense within our heart to Him, and we should not even entertain these things.

He also tells us that the battles we fight here on Earth are not against flesh and blood but against spiritual powers and rulers of darkness. What does Jesus mean when He says we do not battle against flesh and blood? He means that we are in a war, but this war must be won in the spiritual before it can manifest in the flesh. Everything originates in the spirit realm, and then it can be manifested into existence. Look at the beginning in Genesis chapter 1: God spoke, and things came into existence; the Spirit hovered/brooded over the waters, and then life manifested; God breathed into Adam from which he was dust, and then life came, etc. God has given us the keys to win these battles every time. I want to provide you with some essential steps to win this spiritual war because it all starts in your mind.

When I state the question, "What am I partnering with," it is not just some cliche saying. This has become my life anthem because the spiritual realm is all about legal agreements with God or Satan. We have a choice, and God gives us divine direction all throughout his Scriptures. I could write an entire book on this topic, but I'll cut this to a quick, digestible chapter here. I believe that every time you partner with a negative thought or a bad report, you give legal access to an enemy of God, which is some demonic spirit. I am not telling you to live in fear or be demon-conscious by any means, but we must wake up to the enemy's tactics. There are several Scriptures that prove this to be true, but there are two that I want to bring to your attention.

The first one is in Proverbs 18:21, reading out of the amplified version: Death and Life are in the power of the tongue, and those who love it and indulge it will eat its fruit and bear the consequences of their words. In the last chapter, we read about our thoughts, but today, I want you to actively think about your thoughts and spoken words. We must learn how to guard our tongues because God clearly tells us whatever we say can indeed manifest. This is why the new age practices work so well and deceive many. They understand this Scripture and the law of attraction. We must get this.

This will be a process for you to start doing, so please remember to be patient with yourself. Just as you learn what thoughts to partner with, you must also start paying attention to what you speak. Every time you speak a word from here on out, I want you to ask yourself, is this glorifying God? Am I edifying myself or others by how I am speaking right now? This will begin helping you to break free quicker than anything. We all go through healing processes, so I am not saying that you cannot speak of your feelings.

I believe that it is ok to verbally process at first but be quick to repent if you need to and figure out what words you just spoke that brought life or brought death.

Have you ever noticed that if you're having a bad morning and then start complaining throughout your whole day, bad things continue to happen? Like hitting every red light, spilling your coffee, getting frustrated with co-workers, and then with your spouse when you come home, etc. You get the point. It may be because we first partnered with negative thoughts and then began speaking irritating negative things, which then started to attract more of those things that tried to bring death to our joy, peace, and love. What happened? We just partnered with demonic spirits, who the Bible tells us are literally waiting to devour us in any way they can. When we choose to partner with such negativity, we give the demonic ammunition by creating the perfect spiritual atmosphere for them to gain legal access.

I've got good news, though! Just as this can happen in a negative way, it can also happen in a positive way. And let me tell you that light and life will always overpower darkness and death!! How do I know this? Because Jesus conquered death! So, don't you think we should get on board with partnering our thoughts and words with all God says instead of what we think or feel? I do, and I have learned how to put this into practice. It has radically changed my life for the better, and I know it will for you, too, when you begin putting this into your daily life.

Another powerful point on winning the war is from the book of Job. This one is significant because it says in Job that God allowed Satan and his minions to sift Job. We must remember that God is sovereign and hold onto the Truth that God is a good God and He is a good Father! Scripture tells us in Isaiah 46:10 that God knows the end from the beginning and allows things only for our good and His purpose to come forth through us in this lifetime. There are 74 scriptures throughout the Bible that refer to God as a judge. Now, this could be a coincidence, but there is significance here, and there are legalities when it comes to the spiritual realm. We must keep in mind the position that God has given to us as believers in Christ.

I'll be paraphrasing the scriptures in this paragraph, but I highly recommend you read them on your own! In 1 Peter 2:9, God calls us royalty. In Romans 8:15, He says we are adopted into the kingdom of God. In Proverbs 25:2, He tells us that we are kings and that it is up to us to seek out the answers in God's Word; this is for everything in life. Ephesians 1:20 & 2:6 say that God raised us up with Christ and seated us with him in the heavenly realms in Christ Jesus! Then, in Romans 8:16-17, God tells us that His Spirit bears witness with our spirit, that we are children of God, and that this makes us heirs of God and joint heirs with Christ glorified together. We must realize how to fight each battle we face correctly. God tells us that these battles are indeed spiritual and that we can overcome them!

The Book of Job gives excellent insight into this legal access I am referring to. In Job 1, God tells us about "the sons of God," who are angels, and how Satan approached God. This was, in a very legalistic way, something we would see in a courtroom today. God is the Judge, and Satan seems to be somewhat like a prosecuting attorney. This gives us great insight into how things happen in the heavenlies and why things come about within this Earth. God gave us authority through Jesus Christ, but we can get off balance if we do not know how to operate in a Godly order and authority.

In Genesis 1, when God is speaking in the very beginning, who is He talking to? I believe He is talking to a whole counsel of Angels; again, this seems to be in some court setting, where God is establishing laws in the heavenlies and in all of the Earth. This is my opinion, but it makes sense to me. Another thing to look at is when Job states in chapter 3:25-26 that he has greatly feared all that has come upon him. This tells me that he could have opened the door to allow the enemy to torment him by getting into an agreement with the spirit of fear instead of trusting God fully.

I will say that God had lessons for Job to learn, and the trials he went through brought him closer to God than ever before. There are always lessons that we can take away from our trials and tribulations. These are and will always be to help strengthen us in our identity in Christ, help us be a witness to others around us, and/or equip us for the next battle that comes against us. We are not exempt from trials and must keep this in the forefront of our minds; God is the redeemer of all things! God restored more than Job could think or even imagine in the end!

The trials were gut-wrenching, but God did turn it all around for Job's good. There are laws in the heavenlies and laws within the Earth. God put laws in place to protect us and to keep everything in perfect harmony. God is a God of Order and Justice. Take a moment to think about the laws of science, like the law of gravity, for instance. When you dig into researching these things, scientists cannot even prove or explain some of them. God's design is vast, and some are unexplainable, yet everything works together harmoniously for God's perfect purpose. Someway and somehow, God always shows off.

Please do not get off balance by getting into fear and looking for any and all doors you may have opened or get into condemnation every time you sin. We must remember the power of the blood and everything that Jesus did on that cross! We are redeemed, not exempt from trials, but when we know who and whose we are, we will triumph and overcome mightily. We are seated in Heavenly places; it is up to us to be in the right standing with Jesus to access that place. Jesus is King, and when we make Him Lord in every area of our lives, He begins to deliver us. It is important to constantly run to Jesus, asking Him to bring us into a place of holiness by allowing His Spirit to convict our hearts; yearning for His ways will always bring us into purity and love.

APPLYING WISDOM TO YOUR DAILY LIFE

Father God,

I repent for any and all rebellious ways within me. Please help me to stay sensitive to your Holy Spirit and your leadings. I want my words and my ways to be pleasing to you. I give you full permission to access every area of my heart that may be hardened. Show me your ways, Lord, and guide me in your Truth so that I may walk out your plans and purposes upon my life here on earth. I am your vessel, God. Guide me and put a guard upon my mouth. In Jesus' Name, I pray.

Scriptures to meditate on:

2 Corinthians 10:5: *"We demolish arguments and every pretension that sets itself up against the knowledge of God, and we take captive every thought to make it obedient to Christ."*

Ephesians 6:12: *"For we do not wrestle against flesh and blood, but against principalities, against powers, against the rulers of the darkness of this age, against spiritual hosts of wickedness in the heavenly places."*

Luke 10:19: *"I have given you authority to trample on snakes and scorpions and to overcome all the power of the enemy; nothing will harm you."*

Proverbs 18:21: *"The Tongue has the power of life and death, and those who love it will eat of its fruit."*

Romans 8:34: *"Who is the one who condemns us? Christ Jesus is the One who died [to pay our penalty], and more than that, who was raised [from the dead], and who is at the right hand of God interceding [with the Father] for us."* (This means that Jesus is not the one who condemns us, but it is the enemy. The Holy Spirit will convict us but never condemn us. Jesus is for us and is constantly fighting for us)!

Reflection:

1. Please take time today to reflect on all of your situations and thoughts from yesterday and today. You will continue to do this each day from here on out. At first, I do want you to physically write these things down in your journal; this will get you into a habit of doing so, and then you will become more aware of the thoughts you have allowed to come in and/or are choosing to partner with. When you do this, your brain will automatically start choosing from the right tree. You will start to become very aware of anything opposite from the word of God as long as you keep a humble heart, read your word every day, and allow the Holy Spirit to convict your heart.

2. Every night from here on out, before you go to sleep, I encourage you to reflect on your day as you did earlier in the above exercise. Allow the Holy Spirit to convict you on any thoughts, spoken words or

actions that were not of Him. This will become a healthy habit to start thinking about what you are partnering your thoughts, words, and actions with. Simply repent if you have to and forgive anyone if you need to. It is important to keep our hearts soft towards the Lord and others to allow conviction at any time, if needed. This also helps you close any spiritual doors that may have created an opening for the demonic that day.

Let me give you a couple of examples so you know what to look for:

- If you gossip about someone to another person or even just slip by saying something negative about them to yourself. Quickly repent. Tell the Lord you are sorry and then be very aware of that thing so you can begin to turn away from gossip. If you feel this is a massive issue in your life, you may have to repent and then renounce all agreement with the spirit of gossip. So, in this case, you would say: "I renounce all agreement with the spirit of gossip, and God, I ask you to forgive me. I repent for this sin and ask the Holy Spirit to quicken me so I am aware of this spirit and learn how to speak life over myself and others. In Jesus' name."

- You can do this exact thing for any spirit that rises up against you throughout your day. This may include perversion, profanity, fear, anxiety, lust, lethargy or laziness, confusion, etc. Anything that you feel has a grip over you, could be a demonic spirit that you are fighting and the quickest way to defeat that is by renouncing agreement, repenting, and crucifying your flesh. I have found that most of the time, it is about crucifying our flesh. The key is to keep your heart sensitive to the Holy Spirit, read your Bible every day, and listen for His still, small voice to correct you along your journey in this life.

Declaration:

I decree and declare that I am a child of the most high God and an heir to His throne. God has chosen me, and I will allow the Holy Spirit to convict and guide me every second of every day. God has given me the mind of Christ, and I will thrive in every area of my life! Jesus Christ lives within me; therefore, I give Him access to work in and through me. Have your way in my life, Lord.

3 God Redeems All Things

I am going to share a couple parts of my testimony that I believe will give you hope that you will be able to enjoy the same freedom that I now walk in. There is power when we choose to go through tests in life with Jesus because it truly becomes a powerful testimony of what ONLY GOD can do. I have shared my testimony with several people, and most cannot believe I am the person I am today with all the hardships I have experienced. This is a true testimony of God's redeeming love!

As I mentioned before, I went through years of molestation, and one may think that was bad enough. However, when I finally surrendered my life to Jesus, He allowed me to have flashbacks of past traumas that I never knew had happened to me. These traumatic memories and having to walk through them again were way worse than just the molestation. You see, our brain has a powerful self-defense mechanism that blocks out trauma. I believe that God will allow you to face the traumas you need to face in order to completely heal and then have authority over the exact areas where the enemy held you back in bondage for so many years.

I remember opening my heart in a way that I never allowed it to be open before. When I decided to fully surrender these memories to Jesus, I began to have even more flashbacks of the horrible things that were done to me from the young ages of 3-6 years old. It was a powerful thing that began happening. I started crying like never before, facing my past, and finally, the deep wounds started to heal. I began having dreams that were so intricate in every way that there was no denying these dreams were from God. A huge battle was going on in the spirit for my life between good and evil.

The flashbacks were extremely cloudy and that actually made me doubt if I ever truly went through these horrible things. Then, when I went to university to get my Bachelor's in Psychology, I found this to be a very normal way for people to begin to process old memories from trauma and pain. In these flashbacks, I could sense the smell and the feeling of a wet, cold, and moldy basement. I remembered being undressed, then being tied to a cold, damp wooden chair, and forced to watch horror movies while sexual things were being done to me by three men. It is no wonder I blocked something like this out for 20 years! I believe God allowed it to come to my remembrance for several reasons.

The first reason is that when trauma happens to us, especially early in life, there is a part of us that actually stops growing and stops maturing. It was here where the Lord had to bring me back and allow me to begin healing properly with Him. Second, I have been tormented by night terrors since my childhood into my early adult life with extreme demonic activity. God needed to show me the exact areas where I now carry authority to kick the devil and his demons out of my life as well as other people's lives.

God will turn all things that the enemy intended for evil around for our good if we allow Him to (Romans 8:28). God also revealed to me that it was here at this moment where the door opened for the demonic to gain legal access into my life besides a generational curse that I also broke free from. Lastly, I believe it was to show me that I needed to trust God. Going back and walking through the harsh seasons of my life helped me to face my fears and allowed God to refine me through His process. I tried to heal on my own for years, but there is power when we finally trust King Jesus.

This is one of the hardest lessons to learn as we fully surrender our lives to Jesus. The areas we don't want to face the most are the exact areas of bondage that we must press through so the enemy cannot keep us bound any longer. You see, I could have partnered with the fact that this was a horrible thing to have to go through as an innocent child, and why would God allow such terrible things to happen. Granted, I went through a long season of not completely trusting God because I did initially partner with these exact thoughts. However, as I continued my walk with Jesus, I grew in the wisdom of God by digging deep into His word and worshiping Him. With time, I began to trust Him. Even though we go through trials, God will always turn it around if we allow Him to. We must completely surrender it all to Him trusting that He is a good Father and He wants the absolute best for His children..

At this time, God started my journey toward learning my true identity in Him. It was not what my past dictated. He began having me do exercises every day that helped me trust Him more. You will find these exercises at the end of this chapter. I encourage you to take time with God. Ask the Holy Spirit to reveal any areas where your growth in life was hindered, then begin applying the exercises in this workbook to your daily routine.

I have so many stories I could share with you that line up perfectly, revealing how I overcame partnering with the wrong thoughts. Still, I'll share one more in this chapter, specifically on how to overcome strongholds in the area of bondage. I was unjustly imprisoned for a crime that was basically done behind my back at the young, naive age of 21. I didn't do any prison time until I was the age of 30. This is a long story, so bear with me because it shows how to trust God through impossible situations.

When I was 21, I met an older gentleman who took me under his wing as a business mentor and friend, or at least I thought. I was extremely broken at this time in my life, craving attention from older men and looking into opportunities to become "successful." This was a huge motivation in my life at this time because I cared so deeply what the world thought of me. The reality is that I was in the wrong moment at the right time and completely naive. This man ended up being a con artist who got me and my entire family involved with real estate investments that went terribly wrong. They forged my name and falsified information on over 50 documents for loans to go through. This was in 2006-2007, during the time when stated income loans were allowed. I had no idea anything fraudulent had happened until 2011, when I was interrogated by the FBI for almost 7 hours!

Now, mind you, I had never been in trouble with the law before, and even during this interrogation, the FBI led me to believe that I was a little fish in this massive scheme, and they would let me know if charges were to come against me. At this time, in 2011, I'm thankful that I had already been diligently walking with Jesus for 2 years. I ended up being indicted for Mortgage Fraud one year later, and I was facing 31 years in prison. You talk about some real fear beginning to manifest in my mind? This was it. I only had $10,000 in my name, and it would cost me $250,000 to retain a federal lawyer to take on my case. This was when my intense training grounds began for what I would partner with.

The facts were that I was facing 31 years in Federal Prison, and the evidence they had against me was strong enough because ignorance would not hold up a defense in a Federal Court of law. The truth that I had to begin to partner with and hold onto was that I serve a big God. He is a God that turns all things around for my good. I decided to trust Him for a miracle. I meditated on and began speaking about every scripture on freedom and how powerful my God is. I battled the courts with continuation after continuation for two long years, facing 31 years of prison that lingered over my head. Can you imagine the faith that I and my husband had to keep during this time? I share this with you because I have walked through the refining fires of faith. These nuggets of wisdom I am sharing in this book come with personal experience of how God works when we partner with His Truth!

The outcome of this story is that an attorney took me on for $10,000 (a miracle, by the way) and shared my naivety in this case in great detail with the prosecuting attorney. The prosecuting attorney actually took time to read my several letters of character references and looked into the life I was living at this time, as well as when the crime had been committed. I was offered a plea agreement stating that if I signed that I was guilty, I would only serve a five to seven-year sentence. I signed the plea because I was not willing to give my life away to 31 years of prison. However, this was a massive leap of faith because everything in me did not intend to defraud anyone, which is what I had to confess to when I signed this plea. I did realize the severity of all I was facing, though, and was willing to take full responsibility for my negligence to further research the legalities of all I was involved with back in 2007. Let's just say, I learned several lessons throughout this trial.

I'll never forget when I read my last words to the Judge on my sentencing day. It was here that I got to pour my heart out with true sincerity of repentance, taking full responsibility for my ignorance yet giving all the glory to God and willing to face whatever sentence was given. The Holy Spirit helped me write every word, and there was such conviction through my words that even the prosecuting attorneys had tears running down their cheeks. I had one of the hardest Judges in all of Chicago and He was known for giving people the maximum sentence, which would've been anywhere from 7-31 years in my case.

I went into that courtroom with complete faith that my God would show up mightily for me; all the while, my knees were shaking like crazy! To my shock, the prosecuting attorney began fighting for me harder than my own attorney. He told the Judge that I was a grown, changed woman and that it would basically be a dishonor to punish me this many years later when I was a good, abiding citizen. This argument between the judge and the prosecuting attorney went on for twenty minutes, and finally, the judge made his decision. He settled on giving me only three years, which was extremely difficult to swallow at the time but I was thankful it wasn't any more than that! After I had been sentenced, the prosecuting attorney came directly up to me and apologized to me, stating that I shouldn't even have to do one day in prison because He did not believe me to be a threat to society. He apologized again, saying, "I've done all I can."

Now, it was not easy for me to comprehend that the next three years of my life were basically going to be gone, but I chose to trust God again! I decided to partner with faith and not all the fear that wanted to swallow me whole! I had six months to surrender to federal prison to get all my affairs in order, as well as finally having a wedding ceremony before saying goodbye to my precious husband for the next three years. This was hard! Probably one of the hardest things I've had to walk through in my life, but with God, we truly can get through anything. After walking through a debilitating car accident, years of sexual abuse, overcoming cancer, and now this, I realized that I was being trained for so much more in this life. I chose to partner with this fact instead of constantly feeling sorry for myself. All of this propelled me into becoming the loving powerhouse I am today through God.

<u>APPLYING WISDOM TO YOUR DAILY LIFE</u>

Prayer for the day:

Father God,
Forgive me for not always partnering with your Truth. I want to know You and Your ways, Lord. Help me to understand Your Word. I humbly ask You to open both my eyes and heart to receive revelation knowledge and the power that comes from knowing my identity in You. I know that Your ways are so much higher than my own. Holy Spirit, lead me when I go astray and help soften my heart so I can accept the rebukes that need to come. Help me to stay strong as I am learning to walk in obedience. In Jesus' Name I pray, Amen.

Scriptures to meditate on:

Philippians 4:8: *"Finally, brethren, whatever things are true, whatever things are noble, whatever things are just, whatever things are pure, whatever things are lovely, whatever things are of good report, if there is any virtue and if there is anything praiseworthy—meditate on these things."*

Isaiah 44:22: *"I have swept away your offenses like a cloud, your sins like the morning mist. Return to me, for I have redeemed you."*

Psalm 46:1-3: *"God is our refuge and strength, an ever-present help in trouble. Therefore we will not fear, though the earth give way and the mountains fall into the heart of the sea, though its waters roar and foam and the mountains quake with their surging."*

Reflection:

1. Now that you are becoming more aware of negative thoughts, I want you to replace those with positive ones in your journal. Make sure that your positive thoughts align with God's Word. Take the things you've written down over the past couple of days and try to see where you could have been in alignment with God's Word instead of choosing to be negative or rebellious. Most people never take the time to analyze their thoughts and ask why I am even thinking this or acting this way. It becomes a habit without thinking intentionally, and most times, we've been conditioned from early on in life. This will help you start being intentional with your thoughts and learning how to control them, which will then help guide your actions.

____

____

____

____

____

____

2. Begin writing out examples that come about daily in your journal; you will soon get into the habit of crucifying bad behavior and looking up Scriptures to align with.

____

3. Is there a difficult situation you are facing at this moment? If so, I want you to repent if you have partnered with fear in any way and begin writing out scriptures over your situations. Speak them out over yourself and your situation daily. This will help your mind to come into the obedience of Christ as well as help build your faith. Write these here:

____

This may sound silly and almost too simple to do but it is quite the contrary. You will begin to recognize how incredibly negative your thoughts can be and how this derails your life. As you do this repeatedly, it will become clear that this process is a great way to change wrong mindsets and thought patterns, which can then change our actions. I can now recognize if it is my own thoughts, God's, or someone else's because of the power of persuasion or if it is the enemy's. This helps you begin to step into your true identity in Christ. Holy Spirit will start to lead you to His thoughts and help you begin to believe His truths about Him, you, and others.

Declaration:

I decree and declare that I am a child of God and that God is for me! He knows my exact situation, and He will fight for me! I can do all things through Christ, who gives me strength. I am rewiring my brain with God's Truth, and He is setting me free from every stronghold within my mind. Thank You, Lord; I trust you! I am becoming more and more free every day that I walk with You!

4 Make Jesus Lord

Once I got to prison, this question, "What am I partnering with," became my life anthem! What would I choose to partner with for the next 3 years of my life? The first 6 months were extremely tough to try and adjust mentally, physically, and spiritually. I was no longer a free human being. I was a prisoner who was now called not by my name but by a number, who had an 8X8 cell to share with a complete stranger, had to shower and use the bathroom on shared facilities, and only had 2 sets of men's clothing to wear. First, I had to face the reality that this would be my new life for a while and learn to be ok with that. Learning to be ok in a place where complete chaos and disorder ran rampant, all the while being controlled by power-hungry guards, was not an easy task. I also had to hold onto my true identity in Christ because the abuse of what you go through mentally blew off triggers from my childhood.

If I could explain the prison system briefly, I would call it chaos with manipulating control. Guards who patrol the prisoners expect to see different results in them by giving them absolutely no rehabilitation techniques. Everything that I experienced while I was there seemed to be a ploy to try and keep prisoners there longer. In my opinion, the B.O.P. does not stand for the Bureau of Prisons; it feels like "backward on purpose." I wish I had better things to say about the United States prison system, but I cannot. What I experienced firsthand made me extremely sad that our government is using taxpayers' dollars to poorly babysit and brainwash broken individuals, all the while making it seem like prisons are there for rehabilitation.

If anything, one day, I will be able to go into prisons and speak to prisoners about having a choice and encourage each one of them that there is a chance for redemption. They must understand that it would be their choice, but it is possible. Everyone needs encouragement and love. All that I saw being offered in prison was manipulation and control. So, I partnered early on that God had chosen me to be a missionary in that place and that I would be sensitive to all that My Lord and Savior wanted me to do while I was there. This is when Jesus truly became Lord in every area of my life. God gave me Isaiah 61:1 three times directly after my sentencing day through three different sources. I knew God had chosen me for a time such as this. This was a key Scripture that I had to partner with because it got me through some of my toughest days.

~Isaiah 61:1~

The Spirit of the Sovereign Lord is on me, because the Lord has anointed me to proclaim good news to the poor. He has sent me to bind up the brokenhearted, to proclaim freedom for the captives and release from darkness for the prisoners

I had to make myself a strict schedule outside of my work assignments to keep my sanity. This included several hours of praying in tongues and reading my Bible to hold onto the promises of God. My work assignment was a G.E.D Tutor, where I taught ladies of all ages basic Elementary-High School subjects and equipped ones with potential who could actually pass the test to receive their G.E.D. I was supposed to be a tutor, which meant I was to assist a government teacher who taught classes for the G.E.D program. This never happened, not once. I was the only one who ever taught these ladies, and the best tools they gave me to teach from were out of a 1990's G.E.D book! I share this with you because this is part of the chaos I am talking about.

It was extremely frustrating for me to take my job seriously and want to help these women but not have the right, up-to-date tools to do so. However, with God, I was able to help a few women receive their GED. Most importantly, I was given the chance to help these women see the beautiful gifts inside each of them and stir some belief to help conquer their fears.

Most people don't know that prisoners have to work on the compound and that we only get paid a tiny percent of what the outside world makes. I would teach 25-30 hours a week and only received $14 monthly. Talk about humbling! Also, everything that we had to buy at the commissary was marked up by 20-30%! I also had restitution, so if my husband put more money than $200/month on my books, I would get penalized, and they would take $100 from me a month. It was crazy! Please think about this for a minute.

I'm sharing all of these things with you because I had to learn to stay positive and keep my heart soft. I had to learn to truly trust God. I had to learn how to partner with His Truth and not what I saw every day. I had to choose to walk in love with some of the most hardened, broken people I've ever come in contact with, including extremely controlling guards. I had to be intentionally aware of what I would allow myself to partner with daily.

If I didn't, I could have ended up in a downward spiral of depression very quickly just because of my surroundings. Not to mention, I also could easily drown in a pit of self-pity from missing my husband and my free life immensely. Unfortunately, I learned that prisons are made to break you down more and institutionalize you instead of rehabilitating you. I could go on and on about life in prison. I sometimes joke with Christians, saying that every Christian should go for a short time in their life because it helped me live out what complete surrender and trusting God truly looks like. It also helped me to be crushed daily, allowing pure oils to come with sweet aromas from the fruits of the Holy Spirit.

There isn't one day that goes by now where I don't thank God for my freedom, the comforts of my home, and the precious people around me. Perspective is key in this life, so I am challenging you to start implementing the keys in this book into your daily thought process. No matter what situation we find ourselves in, we can always choose to see the good, knowing that we are free in Christ. The choice is up to you. This book has several activities to start you on your powerful journey to complete freedom. Know that I am praying for every person who reads this book and that you will be supernaturally transformed.

This supernatural transformation comes when we truly make Jesus Lord over our lives. When we accept Jesus as Lord, we automatically come into right standing with God by the blood of Jesus. Do we know what this means, though? I won't go into depth about this, but I encourage you to research the definition of Lordship and all that it entails within a kingdom on your own. We can learn some powerful takeaways when it comes to making Jesus Lord over every area of our lives.

When we make Jesus Lord of our life, we make Him Master. He becomes the boss and the ruler over our lives and all things. We are no longer in the driver's seat! This can sound intimidating, but it is one of the most exhilarating things we can do as Christians. Here, we can then allow Him to move on our behalf. This is where we trust Him; we follow His precepts and His leadings so He can move powerfully in our lives. Here is where the miraculous happens because it is no longer me who lives but Christ within me who lives! This is where we align our thoughts with His, our tongues with His Word, and our wills for His will.

This is such an essential piece of our identity in Christ. We must realize that we are seated in heavenly places and can do all things through Christ. Jesus tells us that He has given us the keys to have authority here on this earth through Him! It is only when we partner with Him, with His Word, and allow Him to flow through us that we can overcome all things! Remember to continue reading this book with an open heart and diligently apply the keys within it to your everyday life. You will begin seeing powerful changes in you and those around you. The time is now to close the doors of your past and open your doors of destiny! Trust God to walk you through this process of recalibrating your mind.

It is imperative that Christians come back into alignment with the Word of God. Over my many years of walking with Christ, it is shocking to me how many people I have met who call themselves Christians, yet they do not read the Word. We must remember how John poetically introduces Jesus Christ in John 1:1. John tells us that *in the beginning was the Word, and the Word was with God, and the Word was God.* We cannot separate our Christianity from the Word of God, which is the Bible, who is Jesus Christ. This is precisely how so many Christians will be deceived in these end times by the anti-Christ spirit. With this being said, this is what this book will help you do. It is going to help you to get into His Word daily, learn to hear the voice of God, as well as begin to rewire your mind and sharpen your discernment.

The very first place we must start is within our minds. I am giving you Scriptures to meditate upon each day so you get into the habit of reading your Word and begin learning how to sit with God. I encourage you to meditate with the Holy Spirit on these scriptures. When you do this, as well as being diligent with choosing your thoughts, you will train your soul to partner with your spirit! The soul realm is within our minds, so it is here where we have to make a change first. 1 Peter, chapter 22 tells us how important it is to be obedient to the truth! God's Word is the Truth, which is the Bible. The Bible is a blueprint of directions for us throughout this life here on Earth. It is truly incredible how much wisdom we can learn to walk in when we get this truth deep down inside of us. We must begin aligning our thoughts and words with God's Word.

When you begin putting these keys into action, remember to ensure that your positive thoughts align with God's Word. The Word is powerful! Angels respond to the Word of God, and Jesus used the Word to make the devil flee from him in Matthew 4:4. Jesus said after forty days of fasting when Satan came to test Him, *"for it is written, Man shall not live on bread alone, but on every word that comes from the mouth of God!"* We must remember that the Bible is the inspired Word of God. This means that people who wrote the Bible heard directly from God to write it! The Word is powerful!

And lastly, you must remember to take every negative thought captive. This means declaring over that plaguing thought that it has to bow to the mighty Name of Jesus and then replace it with God's empowering Word over your life and your situation. We must keep in mind to truly have successful breakthroughs, we have to implement consistency, doing this every day. Studies have shown it takes 21 days to break and create new habits, but you must do your homework daily. The choice is yours.

APPLYING WISDOM TO YOUR DAILY LIFE

Prayer for the day:

Holy Spirit,

Thank you for revealing to me the areas within me that need to be purified. I ask You to help me face the negativity and trauma from my past. Thank You for bringing me comfort and peace in my times of frustration when I want to rebel and run from the difficult things that I know You want me to face. Help me to be patient and learn to sit with You. Open my ears to hear Your voice alone, Lord! Give me the push I need to finish this journey strong. I trust You Jesus! I give you full access to my mind and my heart! Help me Jesus! I know that I can do all things in Your precious Name, I pray! Amen.

Scriptures to meditate on:

Philippians 4:13: *"I can do all things through Christ who strengthens me."*

Romans 10:9-13: *"If with your mouth you confess Jesus is Lord and believe in your heart that God raised Him from the dead, you will be saved. . . . For whosoever shall call on the name of the Lord shall be saved."*

Ephesians 5:26: *"To make her holy, cleanse her by the washing with water through the word."*

2 Corinthians 10:5: *"We demolish arguments and every pretension that sets itself up against the knowledge of God, and we take captive every thought to make it obedient to Christ."*

Psalm 46:10: *"Be Still and know that I am God."*

1 Samuel 3:9: *"Therefore Eli said to Samuel, "Go, lie down; and it shall be, if He calls you, that you must say, 'Speak, Lord, for Your servant hears.' So Samuel went and lay down in his place."*

Reflection:

1. Keep journaling all your steps from day 1-3

2. Put a 5-minute timer on and learn how to lay in silence, asking the Holy Spirit if there is anything that He wants to share with you. Say outloud, "Speak Lord, Your servant is listening." Journal what you hear. If you can do longer than 5 minutes, I encourage you to do so. Be intentional about doing this every day from here on out.

3. It is of the utmost importance to follow these steps consistently. They will help you rewire your thought processes, form good Godly habits, and learn to hear God's voice.

Declaration:

I Decree and declare today that Jesus Christ is Lord over my life. I give Jesus full access into every area of my life. Have your way, Lord, I give you: (As an act of faith, list all things and/or people you've been holding on to too tightly and release them to Him now). I trust my Lord Jesus, and I know that His ways are higher than mine. I release all and any control now. I am being led into God's Truth, peace, and freedom daily! My brain is being washed from every traumatic situation and every wrong thought pattern that rises up against the Truth of God's Word. I have the mind of Christ, and I am walking out His Truth precept upon precept.

5 God Loves You

Matthew 22:36-38 says, *"Teacher, which is the greatest commandment in the law?" Jesus said to him, "You shall love the Lord your God with all your heart, with all your soul, and with all your mind." This is the first and greatest commandment. And the second is like it: "You shall love your neighbor as yourself."* This is a fantastic verse to live by but it is tough to walk out in life if you do not love yourself, nor know the love of the Father.

You see, when I first came back to surrender my life to Jesus, I had to learn how to do this, and I'm not going to lie to you; this was a process. I had no idea how to love God with all my heart, because, honestly, my heart was utterly broken, let alone know how to truly love others, because I didn't truly love myself. I also had huge trust issues, so this was another massive barrier that I had to work through. However, it wasn't until I had my first encounters with Jesus that I finally came to realize this. I thought I knew what love was, and I thought I loved others well, but my definition of love had been so skewed growing up that God had to show me where my ways of "loving" were total counterfeits.

God began to reveal to me how manipulative I was. He began exposing many ugly roots within my heart that needed to be plucked out. He had to show me these things so I would bring myself into a place of humility, crying out for His lead on how to heal me. When I did this, He showed me this Scripture in Matthew 22. Then, I began on a journey with Him, getting to know His character and allowing Him to crush me through horrific circumstances in my life. He allowed this crushing to happen only so He could rebuild me upon His foundation, His Truth, and His Love! Without embracing the crushing, I wouldn't be who I am today.

Our Christian walk must grow from this place in Scripture. Do we truly love God with all of our hearts and all of our minds? This means that God has access to every area of our life because we trust His character and know His love. We trust and love who He is. This may be challenging for some of you, but look at this as a good thing because it purges stuff out of you that no longer needs to be there. This challenges me daily at times. However, it keeps me in a constant state of humility wanting to know God more and understand His vast love. When we constantly pursue Him, this helps us stay in a place of walking out His character, which includes patience, compassion, grace, justice, righteousness, meekness, humility, and abounding in love.

We humans are far from perfect but this is why Jesus left us with His Spirit. If you have been born again through Jesus Christ, then you know that His Holy Spirit is living inside you. He will help guide you in how to live out all His beautiful attributes. He will convict you, but it is up to you to listen to the conviction, repent, and obey. This is how you begin to walk out God's love towards yourself and others. We must allow ourselves to get saturated in His love. I encourage you to spend intimate time with Him daily. Worship Him and learn how to SIT in silence with him, which was your exercise from yesterday. Ask him what He thinks of you, and listen for the Holy Spirit to respond. If you have a hard time hearing

His voice, look up Scriptures on what He says about his children because if you are a believer, you are a son or a daughter of the most high God.

In the beginning stages of surrendering my life to Jesus, He had me do most of the exercises I am giving you. I want you to have grace for yourself and be patient because it took me almost 3 years to start to truly love myself. One assignment the Holy Spirit told me to do was to begin looking into the mirror daily and speak life. It was as if Jesus inside me was telling me who He created me to be. I felt deep love and compassion through His eyes going deep into my soul. This was extremely difficult for me to do, and some people may even find this vain, but God knew what He was doing in and through me.

He was healing deep wounds of intimacy inside of me that I did not want to face. This was an act of obedience to allow God into the deep places of my heart that I was always afraid of. We hit wounds of self-hatred, suicide, poor self-esteem, pride issues, vanity, and self-rejection. It is amazing what happens when we are obedient to the leading of His Holy Spirit. This may seem silly, but God used it to help make me whole. I encourage you to do anything the Holy Spirit leads you to do while on this journey to freedom. It may look different for you, but that is ok! Remember, God has a specific way He speaks to each of us, so I encourage you to embrace all He is telling you or showing you.

<u>APPLYING WISDOM TO YOUR DAILY LIFE</u>

Prayer for the day:

Jesus,

I ask that You fill me with Your love and Your strength to follow through with these small action steps to fully believe in all that You have created me for. Holy Spirit, I give You full permission to access the areas of my heart that still need healing where I do not believe in Your love for me. Help any unbelief that may be inside of me, Lord. I know these have created stumbling blocks in my life and I ask for You to clear the path and make my ways straight. As I trust in You, I know You will make my paths straight as it says in Proverbs 3:5-6.

Scriptures to meditate on:

John 3:16: *"For God so loved the world, that he gave his only begotten Son, that whosoever believeth in him should not perish, but have everlasting life."*

Philippians 2:1-8: *"Therefore if you have any encouragement from being united with Christ, if any comfort from his love, if any common sharing in the Spirit, if any tenderness and compassion, then make my joy complete by being like-minded, having the same love, being one in spirit and of one mind. Do nothing out of selfish ambition or vain conceit. Rather, in humility value others above yourselves, not looking to your own interests but each of you to the interests of the others. In your relationships with one another, have the same mindset as Christ Jesus: Who, being in very nature God, did not consider equality with God something to be used to his own advantage; rather, he made himself nothing by taking the very nature of a servant, being made in human likeness, And being found in appearance as a man, he humbled himself by becoming obedient to death—even death on a cross!"* **(Once we become like-minded with Christ, we can share in all the Holy Spirit wants us to walk in. These processes that you have been walking out this past week will put you on a path to holiness).**

Jeremiah 9:23-24: The Lord Says, *"Let not the wise man glory in his wisdom, Let not the mighty man glory in his might, nor let the rich man glory in his riches; But let him who glories glory in this, that he understands and knows Me, That I am the Lord, exercising loving kindness, judgment, and righteousness in the earth. For in these I delight,"* says the Lord. **(This is a great scripture! Let us not glory in how we love but in the fact that the only reason we can love is because God first loved us and once we get this revelation, allowing Him access into every area of our hearts and our lives, we can then walk out His love in action).**

Key #2: Embrace & Accept God's Love For You!

This is where everything changes. . . It is only from this place of truly embracing how much God loves us where freedom truly begins. Every good thing flows from this place.

Reflection:

1. You must learn how to be nice to yourself and truly love yourself before you can give love to others or be fully thriving in life. Take some time to make a list of every negative thought you believe about yourself:

____

____

____

____

____

____

____

____

____

____

Now, make a list of positive things replacing those negative things you believe about yourself. For example, having the thought, "I do not like my body." Bring that thought captive and be kind to yourself, telling yourself that you are beautifully and wonderfully made inside and out. Another great relatable example is "I feel alone or unwanted." Replace this lie with God's Truth by saying, "I am not alone; I have the greatest comforter in the world, and I invite you, Holy Spirit, to come into my life and be my Lord and comforter. Thank you for filling me up with your love and your truth!"

____

____

____

____

____

____

____

____

____

____

2. Now, make a list of everything you see within yourself but can't quite believe yet, as well as anything you truly desire to become. For example, maybe you're an eloquent speaker but have terrible stage fright, yet deep down, you wish you could speak publicly one day. In contrast, write down that you are an amazing speaker who will speak powerfully to thousands one day being able to share all that God has put on the inside of you! Then, take small steps into action. Begin sharing in front of close friends, doing lives/reels, or joining a public speaking course or a community like Toastmasters. (Making a list like this may be difficult for some of you. I encourage you, if you cannot find enough positive beliefs about yourself, ask your closest person to make you a list, and then I want you to ask God to tell you what He thinks about you). If you are new to seeking God in this way, sit with him and say Jesus, I invite you into my mind and my heart right now, and Holy Spirit, show me what our Father in Heaven says about me. You will begin to have thoughts that will come in ever so gently. It may be anyone of these: beautiful, wonderful, unique, creative, fiery, strong, bold, gentle, kindhearted. I encourage you to then google Bible verses to back these words of affirmation. Then take time as you read each verse to allow the Holy Spirit to highlight which verse speaks to your heart the most. These specific Bible verses will get you through the days when you want to quit.

____

____

____

____

____

____

____

____

____

____

____

____

____

____

____

____

____

3. Now, we must put action behind our words of affirmation. Examples of action steps: If you want to get healthier, start exercising and eating healthier foods. It could be a 10 min walk a day and healthy meal prepping as you speak health and love over yourself. If you feel lonely, get into your Word and remind yourself that God is with you. You could also join a group at your church to surround yourself with like-minded believers, etc. Make a plan to put on worship music and get into the presence of God every day so you can feel His tangible love. We must implement what we want to see in our physical and spiritual lives. Write down some action steps that you can start doing today and apply these steps/goals into your daily life. (If you need accountability partners, get some! It's ok to ask for help).

____
____
____
____
____
____
____
____
____
____
____
____
____
____
____
____
____
____

Declaration:

I Decree and declare that I am loved by my Heavenly Father even on the days when I may not feel it. I am not led by my feelings or emotions. I am led by God's Holy Spirit, who is steadfast, true, and everlasting. I am a (Daughter or Son) of the most high God, and I am amazed daily by how much He loves me. I am overflowing with His love, and I allow that love to pour out through me. I am His vessel to do whatever He wants in and through me!

Enjoy Your Weekend and keep paying attention to all the steps you have been given this week.

Remember precept upon precept. You can do this and you are breaking free!

WEEK 2

His Ways Are Higher

1 Time To Refocus

Over several years, I have learned to look at life through a lens of God's perspective. Have you ever noticed that if you hold something so close to your face that you cannot see it, but as soon as you begin to bring it out from your eyes to focus, you can finally see it? I know this is a simple analogy, but this is how we must look through the lenses of our lives. When trials come, when the pain seems too overwhelming to breathe, this is when we have to take some steps back. It is essential to allow yourself to go through the grieving process when needed for the severity of the trial. However, we must pull ourselves out of self-pity and honestly look at our situation clearly by trusting God through the process.

When you properly walk through pain, allowing yourself to feel and heal along the way with Jesus, you will finally see things more clearly. Sometimes, we have to take a step back and inspect ourselves. What I mean by this is that you must look at your behavior and ask yourself why. It is about learning what we've been going through since last week. Ask yourself what thoughts I am partnering with. Are you constantly partnering with fear and negativity? Or are you choosing to partner with the strength that is inside of you, who is Jesus, knowing that you will overcome? (1 John 4:4). I believe God has put immense strength in every single person on earth, and we have free will to choose whether or not we want to tap into that strength.

I'm going to share with you a prime example of where I was, both mentally and physically, back in 2008-2011. I was in a car accident in April of 2008 that gave me complete body whiplash, which affected my entire spine. I was 23 years old at this time and what felt like overnight, I lost my young adult years. I could no longer do the simplest tasks, like tying my shoe, bending over to grab the laundry, let alone dance or work out, which were huge passions of mine. My life, in an instant, completely changed. I had good and bad days, which made me indecisive, so I went into a downward spiral for about three years.

I want to share with you all the negativity I began to partner with first so you can be aware of some of what I was facing. Within one year, I had over $70,000 of medical debt that I allowed to eat away at me month after month. I began to lose friends because the only thing I could do was talk about my pain, how angry I was that I was in pain, and how corrupt the insurance system was. Mind you, it was extremely difficult for me to talk about anything else because I was always in physical pain. The disc damage caused weird nerve defects in my body that would cause me at any moment to go into convulsions with muscle spasms all throughout my body.

I could not sit or stand for longer than an hour without my body going haywire. It was extremely difficult to get comfortable. I had many sleepless nights which made me feel crazy. Overall, I never knew how I was going to feel, and every doctor visit seemed to get worse and worse because they couldn't figure out the exact diagnosis to give me. They told me I had fibromyalgia, that I was depressed, and gave me just about every narcotic and nerve drug known to man. I was basically an experiment.

I finally hit my breaking point near the end of 2009 and decided I would end the pain once and for all. During this time, I was in the early stages of my walk with Jesus, and ultimately, the utter pain and distress from this car accident is what made me finally surrender my life. I knew God had a call upon my life and I also knew it was time to surrender my life fully to Him and allow Him to heal my heart. However, this was also during the time when I was enduring horrible flashbacks from my childhood, as well as several night terrors.

I remember this moment like it was yesterday. I had hit rock bottom, doing everything I knew to do in my power to try and keep my sanity and believe that I would heal one day, but it was all too much. I slipped back into my old ways within one weekend. I went to a house party with old friends where they fed me illegal drugs, and I drowned in my sorrows after the illusion of "fun" wore off. I came home around 6 AM and began to cut myself, which was a habit from my past. As I watched the blood run down my legs, I decided I was done with my life.

I then took half of a bottle of sleeping pills and pain pills to end my pain once and for all. I remember writing a letter to myself telling me how much I hated myself and all that was done to me from my childhood until then. It was basically a letter of complete surrender. It was incredibly selfish, but it was everything I truly believed and felt at that time. I had lived 20 years at this point and never told anyone about the sick and twisted molestation that I went through as a child.

I had allowed the shame from my past to put me in a prison within my mind. I was allowing the physical pain from this car accident to kill the very depths of my being. I chose the word allow because I have been through several trials since these and I now know that we have the power to choose life in every situation if we want to. This next part of what I will share is my testament to how real God became to me. I think every born-again believer starts out in this place of brokenness where you finally realize you need a Savior and that you cannot do this life anymore on your own. Perhaps you were raised in the culture of Christianity, but there finally comes an authentic experience that one cannot explain. It happens to be that moment when you finally BELIEVE that you actually feel the real tangible presence of God.

This was my first experience of many that I will share with you. I woke up that next morning feeling completely fine—no headache, no hangover, no sickness from all the drugs I had taken. On the floor next to my bed were two books lying open face down. One of them was a book called *The Shack*, and the other was my *Bible.* What I'm about to share next was not coincidental with where these two books had fallen open.

The shack was open to a place where the Holy Spirit showed the young man in his brokenness, a torn-up, messy garden that he was living in. When we allow God to come in, our mess becomes beautiful, and He truly turns everything around for our good. This book gives you a visual of this garden beginning to grow with the most gorgeous flowers and trees. At this exact time, in my bedroom, I could smell the most real and potent aroma that carried the sweetness of flowers and fruit. It was so incredibly strong that it made me sick to my stomach, but I felt God's presence like never before. I couldn't move; I felt like I was a thousand pounds because God chose to show me His glory at this exact moment. I was crushed by His love for the first time in my life and could not stop weeping.

I was overwhelmed with compassion and joy that God would come to me in such a way after I just tried to take the most sacred thing He gave us, life. Through my tears of joy, I began to read the page that my Bible was open to, and the Scripture highlighted to me by the eyes of the Holy Spirit was Philippians 4:13. It says, *I can do all things through Christ who gives me strength.* God began to provide me with a download of revelation for what this verse means. Too many people use this verse flippantly, but God showed me the true power of this verse at that very moment.

I heard the Lord say to me inside my mind, "Kristin, if you will trust Me to walk out this journey with you, I will show you the true strength that lives within you!" Jesus has strength that empowers you to overcome all things in this life, and He will give you the ability to call out that strength in others, bringing people into their true destiny as you walk out yours.

Then, later that day, I received a text message from a dear friend, who is now my mamma in love, sending me that exact same Scripture, saying that God had placed me upon her heart to pray for me, and this was the verse He wanted to give me along with Jeremiah 29:11. It was right there and then that I began to surrender my will and trust God's will. I found Scriptures to hold onto and read daily for my emotional and physical healing. Even though it was painful, I pushed myself to join water aerobics and began working out the best I could five days a week.

I began eating healthier, juicing, and partnering with every good thing in my life. I went back to school to get my psychology degree, and I started looking at my condition from God's perspective instead of my victim mentality. I was reminding myself it could be so much worse, and I began thanking God for both my good days and my bad, asking Him to speak to my heart on the bad days so I could learn through my suffering.

APPLYING WISDOM TO YOUR DAILY LIFE

Prayer for the day:

Lord,

I give You full permission to expose any and all offenses within me. Show me if there is any unforgiveness in my heart, and help me fully release it and give it all to You. I know this is a process, but thank you for softening my heart and helping me do this. Lead me in Your Truth and Your righteousness. I humbly ask You to give me Your eyes to see situations and people the way that You see them. Help me to walk in love with others and have grace for myself; in Jesus' name, I pray.

Scriptures to meditate on:

Isaiah 58:8-9: *"For My thoughts are not your thoughts, nor are your ways My ways," says the LORD. For as the heavens are higher than the earth, So are My ways higher than your ways, And My thoughts than your thoughts.*

Romans 12:2: *"And do not be conformed to this world, but be transformed by the renewing of your mind, that you may prove what is that good and acceptable and perfect will of God."*

Key #3: Choose God's Perspective

We all have the freedom to choose our thoughts and our actions. God created us with free will, but we must use it wisely! I challenge you to begin implementing this key into every area of your life. So many times, we will grab hold of negative thoughts and partner with the fact that life is unfair, letting the spirit of offense grip us, but I'm here to tell you, you have the power to rise above!

Now that you have just gone through one whole week of partnering with the right thoughts, I want you to begin partnering with God's perspective in your life and for others. Ask God to show you His perspective on the issue in every situation that arises from irritation, anger, bitterness, sadness, and offenses to unforgiveness. This is an immensely humbling process, but trust me, you will begin to grow supernaturally. This will help you start to partner with the mind of Christ and how He sees the problematic situations that we cannot comprehend or fix in our own strength. I believe God will give each person strategies to power through intense situations in life and be able to walk in victory.

Reflection:

1. Continue from week one, asking yourself all day long: What am I choosing to partner with? But this time, ask: Am I going to choose God's perspective and His Truth on this matter or my own feelings?

2. Take time to journal throughout your day or in the evening to reflect on your thoughts and situations that arose from your day. Write these down and analyze your thoughts to see if you have partnered with your feelings instead of God's Word. If this is the case, simply repent and then replace those feelings

with God's truth about you, the other person, and your situation. For example, if you find yourself partnering with gossip, look up Scriptures to see what God says about gossip. If you are partnering with fear, look up Scriptures on fear. If you are offended by anyone, look up what God says about holding offense. Begin writing out and speaking out the promises of God over yourself, your situations, and others, then abide in what His Word tells you to do. If you slip, simply repent and start again! Journal some things here from today, then begin journaling in your other journal daily.

____

____

____

____

____

____

____

____

____

____

3. This will help rewire your brain to begin partnering with God's Truth instead of your feelings. We must remember that the flesh and the soul will always lie to us and want us to fall into the temptation of offense and bitterness, but the Spirit brings freedom! Choose freedom today!

Declaration:

I decree and declare that I have the mind of Christ. I am learning daily how to see things from God's perspective by meditating on His Word and allowing Him to transform my mind. I am allowing God to sharpen my discernment by listening to His voice and obeying His leadings. I am humbling myself, allowing God to show me things through His eyes, not my own. I am a work in progress. I have grace for myself and for others. I am patient, and I endure all trials until the end. I declare this by faith in Jesus' name.

2 Let Jesus Encounter you

What I will share with you next is another unforgettable encounter with God three months after this first encounter. I share this with you to bring you encouragement! It was truly as if God came running after me to show me how incredibly real He was, and He knew exactly where I was and all that I was facing at that time in my life. I went to a Wednesday night service at a new church, which is an amazing story of how we even stumbled upon this church, but I'll get to the best part. It was a service that was hosting a man by the name of Mario Murillo. I had no idea who this person was, and mind you, I'm still in the beginning of my walk with Jesus, so I wasn't mature enough to receive a message like the one he preached that night.

I remember being extremely turned off and offended by his message, but God used it mightily that night! We must not forget that the Word of God will offend the flesh and the soul because it is meant to build up our spirit and help us crucify our worldly desires. As Mario was closing the service in prayer, he said aloud that God was interrupting him because there was someone there who needed healing. At that moment every hair on my body stood up. It was as if I knew he was speaking directly about me. Mind you, there are probably 250 people in this service, but sure enough, he points to me and says, "You there, the beautiful lady who is definitely not height-challenged!"

This was quite funny because he is on the shorter side; keep in mind that I am 5'11", and I was wearing heels. But then He got earnest as he began to prophesy over me. He said, "I see Jesus healing you." He called out the exact discs that were bulging in my spine, and then he began to see in the spirit that I was cramping and that my nerves were very off balance. He said the enemy had tried to twist my spine but to not be afraid because he had no power over me and that God was doing a miracle. Mind you, I hadn't told anyone what the doctors had just told me, which was that my spine looked as if it was going into an S-curve to cause Scoliosis.

I was too afraid to even speak that report about myself to anyone! Then Mario went on to say that the enemy has tried to destroy me since birth and he brought up two significant times in my life, when I was three years old as well as eleven years old. Then he told me that God wants to do a miracle in my life and that he is going to use me in a powerful way to heal others. Here is a man I've never met before nor ever heard of, who just saw into my life with such intimacy that I couldn't explain it.

He knew the exact ailments that were going on in my body as well as very intimate details that no one knew from my childhood. At the age of three, my innocence was stolen due to sexual molestation, and at the age of eleven, I tried to hang myself. Only God would have known these things. It was as if God was telling me again to trust Him because He holds no wrongs against me and wants me free from all shame and bondage from my past, including the pain I was in at that time.

I wish I could tell you that I was instantly healed on that day, but I wasn't. I am actually still walking this out in faith, 16 years later, that my spine will be completely healed. However, God did heal me of extreme nerve imbalances over time, as well as all the shame and pain from all the years of abuse I went through. You see, good things will begin happening when we partner with hope from the Word of God and choose to trust that His ways are higher and that He knows best. We must start to look at every situation from God's perspective.

APPLYING WISDOM TO YOUR DAILY LIFE

Prayer for the day:

Father God,

Help me recognize every time You have shown up for me in my life. Show me where You have always protected and helped guide me when I couldn't see clearly. Thank You for Your love and protection even when I don't feel like I can see or feel it. Help me to sense and feel Your love and protection, Lord. I know You love me and that You are for me. God, I ask for deeper encounters with You. I invite your Holy Spirit to have His way inside of me. Help me cleanse this vessel in every way I need to be cleansed. Amen.

Scriptures to meditate on:

Ephesians 1:11-12: *"In him we were also chosen, having been predestined according to the plan of him who works out everything in conformity with the purpose of his will, in order that we, who were the first to put our hope in Christ, might be for the praise of his glory."*

John 4:42: *"They said to the woman, "It is no longer because of what you said that we believe, for we have heard for ourselves, and we know that this is indeed the Savior of the world."*

Reflection:

1. If you have had encounters with Jesus, I want you to take some time to write those down in your journal. If you have already written these down in the past, I want you to pull that journal out and read them out loud. This is a powerful thing to do through every season of your life because it will remind you of the goodness of God and how He showed up for you every time! It may not have been the way we had planned or thought, but He showed up! So we know He will show up again in His timing and His way! It is our job to trust and have faith until the breakthrough comes.

____

____

____

____

____

____

____

____

____

____

2. If some of you feel like you haven't ever had "encounters" with Jesus, I want you to spend some intimate alone time with Holy Spirit and ask Him to show you every time He has shown up for you. Humble your heart here knowing it may not be in the way you thought, but has God ever protected you? And with this, even though your situation may be horrible, it could always be worse, right? This is a time to keep humbling yourself, get out of any victim mindset, and allow God to show you His mercy. Other simple encounters with Jesus could be those you didn't even recognize, but it was God actually wooing you. For example, did you ever have a gut feeling like you shouldn't do something or be somewhere or be with someone? This was God trying to intervene. Have you ever felt deep love and compassion for someone else? We can love only because God is love. God is always trying to encounter us. However, it is up to us to embrace His love and wisdom. Journal some of your encounters here to remind you that God is for you:

____

____

____

____

____

____

____

____

____

____

____

____

I think we as Christians can get too caught up with comparisons; meaning you may want to compare my encounters with your own and mine might look more spiritual than yours, so you think you didn't have an encounter. But I am here to tell you that God encounters all of us in different ways, and I want you to recognize these special encounters so you know that He speaks to all of His children and wants to encounter each of us in His own way. One of the main ways He speaks, though, is through His Word, so reading your Bible every day is imperative.

Declaration:

I declare that I am an open vessel for God to work in and through me. I am humble, and I allow the Holy Spirit to enter every place of my heart and mind that needs healing. I am sensitive to hearing His voice and following His lead. God is good, and I am in constant awe of His wonderful ways! His ways are higher than mine, so I surrender my will for His will!

3 Ask what instead of why

This life hasn't been an easy ride for me. However, God has used it all, and it is all for his glory! It was shortly after this encounter when I was interrogated by the FBI for seven long hours as well as diagnosed with melanoma, but God! I have become a true believer that everything happens for a reason, even when it is challenging to understand. It sometimes takes years for our hearts to heal, but there will come a moment when we realize, "Wow, maybe this is why I had to walk through that trial." It took me years to finally understand the reasons behind my innocence being stolen at such a young age. However, now I can stand here with confidence, fully healed, and a walking testimony of God's goodness by helping others to walk into their freedom.

As I have walked through this life, I have realized that our individual circumstances are seldom just about us. What I mean is when we go through something really difficult, we can choose to make it all about us and stay in a place of self-pity, or we can choose to surrender and allow God to use us to help others heal from the exact thing we suffered from or are possibly still suffering from. God will always bring us through the fire of the trials unscorched when we invite him to walk through the process with us. This is why the Scripture from Matthew 7:13-14 speaks about only a few choosing the narrow path. Jesus never said we wouldn't suffer, but He did say He would be with us as we walk through it!

I now choose to look at life from God's perspective. When something terrible happens, I allow myself to grieve because this is important, but I then choose to look deeper into my circumstance. I no longer ask why this is happening to me. I ask what I can learn and what this is doing to bring me closer to God and into my divine purpose in this life. This is a great perspective that you should begin trying out for yourself. When we get out of the 'why me' category thinking, we no longer stay in a place of victimization. When we ask ourselves "what" we can do with this, it gives us a sense of empowerment, knowing we will get through this, giving us strategies to grow through even more difficult situations that may come along in our future.

Now, I want to challenge you to apply God's perspective not only in your life but in the lives of others as well. This has been a wonderful learning curve in my life and helps me daily to be able to walk in love with others. I am going to give you a couple examples. Have you ever met someone that gets on your nerves? How about working with someone who rubs you the wrong way? What about someone even at your church that possibly irritates you? I'm sure you have because you are human, but when you begin applying this key to your life, I guarantee your perspective will begin to change about that individual.

You see, asking God for His perspective on the lives of others will help us know what He sees. He will probably show you possible insecurities or hurts on the inside of them and will give you powerful ways to pray for them, and you'll be amazed at how much your irritations begin to fade away. God usually shows you things within yourself as well during this time that you need to be working on because we all should be able to walk in love with others. We should continuously decrease so Christ within us can increase and shine brighter than our judgments or insecurities.

Another great area to apply this key in your life is within your relationships, especially if you are married, but this pertains to any relationship. God's perspective will always give us insight to forgive, be patient, stay humble, and walk in love. I always say that God is way better at convicting others than I will ever be, so I give my husband to Him when I have an issue and ask God how I need to pray for him. When we put God first in our relationships, we begin to gain His perspective, and He will always show you the best way to love another one of his kids because He knows them.

He knows exactly what is going on in their hearts, He knows their past, and He knows how to use you to help heal them if you are willing to listen to His leadings. God's ways are so much higher than ours. Isaiah 55:8 clearly states, *"For my thoughts are not your thoughts, and my ways are far beyond what you can imagine,"* this is why it is essential to begin implementing His perspective in life rather than our own.

There is power when we choose God's perspective over our own. We become a willing vessel for God to use us. He sees the end from the beginning. He knows every situation and He has the keys to open the doors to set us and others free. We must learn to hear His voice and draw wisdom from His word and communion with Him daily. We are in a time right now where this is imperative. There will be more rumors of wars arising as well as even more false prophets leading people astray.

We must know the voice of our Father and be obedient to His leadings and open our hearts to receive His perspective on every situation in our lives. How do you do this? Be in a constant state of humility, asking God what He thinks about that particular situation or person who happens to be irritating you. Watch how He gives you insight. It is up to you, to humble yourself, to listen and then abide. As believers in Christ, we are living in some of the most exciting times right now. I encourage you to begin spending more intimate time with Jesus. He is speaking and showing His heart for people more than ever because He is preparing the Bride of Christ. He wants His children to grasp His heart and perspective this time!

APPLYING WISDOM TO YOUR DAILY LIFE

Prayer for the day:

Forgive me Lord for questioning your ways. Who am I to think that I know better than You! I lay down my own understanding and I choose to trust You! I may not understand Your ways but I choose to trust You. I trust that You truly love me and that You know the best paths that I need to take in order to learn and grow into the person You created me to be before I was in my mother's womb. Thank You, Lord, for leading me and guiding me through this healing journey. Help me to fully trust where my heart is still wounded. I choose to trust You, in Jesus' Name I pray.

Scriptures to meditate on:

James 1:12: *"Blessed is the man who remains steadfast under trial, for when he has stood the test he will receive the crown of life, which God has promised to those who love him."*

James 1:2-4: *"Count it all joy, my brothers, when you meet trials of various kinds, for you know that the testing of your faith produces steadfastness. And let steadfastness have its full effect, that you may be perfect and complete, lacking in nothing."*

Philippians 3:13: *"Brothers, I do not consider that I have made it my own, but one thing I do: forgetting what lies behind and pressing forward to what lies ahead, I press toward the goal for the prize of the upward call of God in Jesus Christ."*

Philippians 1:6: *"And I am sure of this, that he who began a good work in you will bring it to completion at the day of Jesus Christ."*

Genesis 50:20: *"You intended to harm me, but God intended it for good to accomplish what is not being done, the saving of many lives."*

Key #4: Stop Asking God Why

Reflection:

If you can begin grasping this concept, it can set you free in many areas. We must remember who God is and that we are not Him. He is sovereign and He knows the end from the beginning. He allows things for reasons we cannot fathom, and sometimes we may not understand until we get to Heaven, but we must trust in God's goodness. He has a plan when trials arise. He knows how to help you break free from generational curses and every hex or vex that comes your way from the enemy and his minions.

He knows exactly where we are, and for some reason, He has allowed it, so it is best to ask, "Lord, what can I be learning, and how do You want me to move forward in this difficult season?" In this, we can begin partnering with God's perspective. He will show you glimpses, and you must humble yourself completely in this area. It can be a dangerous place when we get angry and stay in self-pity because pride wants to rise up, and we can begin to act like we are God, which leads us down a path of destruction.

The quicker you begin applying this key to your life, the more freedom you will begin to walk in. This has helped me grow immensely; you will finally begin seeing things through God's eyes. Trust that God is good and that He is for you! He will bring you through it if He brings you to it! Our job is to pray, speak His Word out, and be patient, trusting Him through the process until we see victory! Have grace for yourself to be able to feel all the emotions and grieve if grieving is necessary but be aware of the enemies lies during this time. Lastly, be encouraged through your trials! God wants the absolute best for you! However, sometimes He uses the trials that rise up against us in order for us to rise into our best to be able to steward our next season well.

This key gives you power over the lies of the enemy that wants to bombard your mind with the self-pity "why's" and how unfair everything is. When we learn to trust that God loves us and that he has us. We can then begin to trust that he will bring us through whatever may come! Somehow, this empowers us to walk through every trial triumphantly. Yes, it may get messy along the way but know that out of every mess, it can become your message if you allow God to move in and through you.

1. Think about any hardships you may be facing right now or that you have had in the past. Write these down and be honest if you are asking God why this is happening? Or why did you allow that to happen? I want you to take time with the Lord and be very honest about where your heart is in this area. Dig deep because it is usually in this place where we feel defeated and allow the lie to come in, saying that God is against us in some way and that He doesn't want the best for us. This puts up walls in our hearts and makes us distrust God. It is in these places of asking why when the enemy can gain legal access to plant seeds that then can get watered into harmful belief systems.

2. Ask God to show you his goodness and to help heal your heart from wrong belief systems within this area. It is okay to be upset with God, as this shows you that you have a real and true relationship with him. However, it is important to humble ourselves, remembering that He is God and knows what is best. We must lay down our will for His will. It is about getting to a place of true humility and vulnerability, saying I don't like it, but I trust You, God!

____

____

____

____

____

____

____

____

____

____

____

Declaration:

I am no longer a victim! I am a victor and I overcome every obstacle through the blood of the lamb and by the word of my testimony! My Father in Heaven loves me, and He is for me! I will not fail because my God never fails! He will bring me through whatever trial comes against me. If he brings me to it, He will bring me through it in Jesus Name! I am a mighty vessel for Jesus Christ to work through me. Thank you Lord, that I am a conqueror through You!

4 The Dividing Line

I need to touch base on this topic because it seems more than half of the church struggles in this area. However, our new identity in Christ should be the first thing we begin to work on as soon as we accept Jesus into our hearts. This topic is extremely heavy upon my heart, so please know there is no condemnation for what I am about to say. Allow the Holy Spirit to show you and confirm what He has shown me. We as Christians need to know where our identity lies because we have an extremely broken church right now that is being led astray, and it is up to the remnant of the Bride of Christ to help lead people into the truth. Jesus says He is coming back for a Bride who is ready. I want to be prepared, and I want to help the church get in touch with her true Identity in Christ because it is here where Jesus' love and power can flow.

Please bear with me in these following paragraphs; they may seem intense, but I know 'God' showed this to me for a reason. I want to share a very disheartening word that the Lord shared with me about His church early in 2021. He allowed me to feel His heart for the Church, and there was such sadness and despair that I thought it was literally going to crush me from the weight he was allowing me to feel. At this moment, he told me that a high percentage of professing Christians would not make it into heaven if they passed away right now. They think they would, but the truth is that they are far from me.

Let me elaborate here for a moment because I'm sure some religious demons are going to try and have a heyday here. I also do not want you to get into condemnation, but allow the Lord to search your heart here. I am also not telling you that you must work for your salvation because it is all about a relationship. Once we are in a loving relationship with Jesus, we then begin obeying Him because we want to please Him. It is no different than Him coming here to earth to please His Father in heaven, doing His Father's will rather than His own. It's about our hearts being close to the Lord. We will fail daily but must keep our hearts close to Jesus.

I want to talk about what I was taught since I was young, and you may have been taught this too. I was told that once you accept Jesus into your heart, then you are always saved. However, as I have grown in my relationship with Father God, Jesus, and the Holy Spirit, this is not the whole truth. People can get saved when they are younger but then choose to turn their hearts away from him fully later. Through several scriptures, Jesus clearly states in the Bible that the "once saved, always saved" motto is not true. I will list a few but there are several more that I encourage you to seek out for yourselves. We have to be careful of the slippery grace messages as well as the "I can work my way into heaven "mentality." It is imperative to take the time to seek out what the Word truly says about being saved by Jesus Christ.

Jesus tells us in John 3:15-21 *that whoever believes in Him should not perish but have eternal life. For God so loved the world that He gave His only begotten Son, that whoever believes in Him should not perish but have everlasting life. For God did not send His Son into the world to condemn the world, but that the world through Him might be saved. He who believes in Him is not condemned; but he who does not believe is condemned already, because he has not believed in the name of the only begotten Son of*

God. And this is the condemnation, that the light has come into the world, and men loved darkness rather than light, because their deeds were evil. For everyone practicing evil hates the light and does not come to the light, lest his deeds should be exposed. But he who does the truth comes to the light, that his deeds may be clearly seen, that they have been done in God.

Jesus is telling us that once we believe in Him, we shall not perish but have eternal life with Him. However, when we come to Him, we will no longer live in evil's darkness. Once we truly encounter His love, we then come into his light and His truth. Our deeds begin to be done unto God and no longer for the evil ways of our old desires or this world. God sets guidelines for us like a good father should to lead his children well. Jesus may find us in the filthiest places, but He loves us too much to leave us there. However, it is up to us as Christians to obey God's leading.

Another scripture is in Matthew 5:7 It says, *"Blessed are the merciful, for they will be shown mercy."* Again, are we walking out our lives as Jesus commands us to? Matthew 5:14-16 says, *"if you forgive those who sin against you, your heavenly Father will forgive you. But if you refuse to forgive others, your Father will not forgive your sins. And when you fast, don't make it obvious, as the hypocrites do, for they try to look miserable and disheveled so people will admire them for their fasting. I tell you the truth, that is the only reward they will ever get."* Do you see the harsh stipulations here? We are called to do as the Father tells us to do. We are called to be Christ-like. Jesus said He only did what the Father did. Will we fail? Yes, but we can quickly repent and start over. We must be in a continuous state of humbling ourselves to do His will instead of our own. And I want to encourage you that when you do this, you will begin to fall more in love with God because you will begin to see His goodness in every situation.

Matthew 15:8-9 says, *"These people honor me with their lips, but their hearts are far from me. They worship me in vain; their teachings are merely human rules."* Here, Jesus is talking about the fact that we should walk out the example of His loving life, genuinely wanting to follow Him. We will want to do things His way for His glory because we are in a close, intimate relationship with Him. But some are just using Him to get attention and/or to gain control somehow. Matthew 7:21-23 says, *"Not everyone who says to me, 'Lord, Lord,' will enter the kingdom of heaven, but only the one who does the will of my Father who is in heaven. Many will say to me on that day, 'Lord, Lord, did we not prophesy in your name and in your name drive out demons and in your name perform many miracles?' Then I will tell them plainly, "I never knew you. Away from me, you evildoers!"*

Woah! This is scary and dangerous! I have seen many people using the gifts of the Holy Spirit but do not truly have His fruits. This is because the gifts are given without repentance, as it tells us in Romans 11:29. We must be highly aware of this and why Jesus tells us to be aware of wolves in sheep's clothing. It is right here in this Scripture that even though the person may look like a Christian operating in the gifts of the Spirit and may be very anointed, underneath it all, they are wolves looking to deceive and devour the sheep. This is why a close relationship with Jesus is imperative. He will lead us, and we will know His voice.

These Scriptures can seem pretty intense, but they are all written by Jesus himself in Matthew, and the context in which these Scriptures were written is all about having a pure and genuine relationship with God through Jesus Christ. Being a Christian means walking out a heavenly relationship with Christ here on earth, which means reading His word, knowing the voice of God, and abiding in it. People should be drawn to us by Jesus' light inside of us! We should look different from the world because it says clearly in the word of God that He has set us apart. Romans 12:2 clearly states this. Only from this place will you reap the rewards of this heavenly relationship.

I am not telling you this to get you into any condemnation, but if you feel like you have not been truly seeking Jesus to get to know Him intimately, repent. Once we get to know Him and His love, we will want to be obedient to however He leads us. Repentance is such a powerful key to keeping our hearts right when seeking the Lord. When we repent, it humbles us to see that God's ways are higher and His word has the final say. The Word of God should cut us so deep that we begin to look different from the person we were before we met Jesus. If we allow it to, it will keep us diligent in cutting off the desires of our flesh, and it will help align our souls to match up with God's Spirit. We need this! A genuine relationship with Jesus will guide us into all truth throughout this life. A believer in Christ's first mission is to work on building an intimate relationship with God. Everything beautiful flows from this place. It is all about a relationship.

APPLYING WISDOM TO YOUR DAILY LIFE

Prayer for the day:

Father God, Jesus, & Holy Spirit,

Please forgive me if my heart has been far from You. Show me any areas where I need to repent for not walking in obedience to You. Show me any wicked ways that are within me that I may be blinded to. Help me to understand what it looks like to walk in a loving relationship with You instead of trying to earn my way into a relationship with You. Lord, protect me from all antichrist spirits including the spirit of religion. Reveal to me if I have partnered with these in any way and teach me how to break free. Thank You for giving me Your wisdom to lead me out of any traps that the enemy has tried to keep me bound in. In Jesus' name I pray.

Scriptures to meditate on:

Matthew 7:21-23: *"Not everyone who says to Me, 'Lord, Lord,' shall enter the kingdom of heaven, but he who does the will of My Father in heaven. Many will say to Me in that day, 'Lord, Lord, have we not prophesied in Your name, cast out demons in Your name, and done many wonders in Your name?' And then I will declare to them, 'I never knew you; depart from Me, you who practice lawlessness!"*

Matthew 10:34-36: *"Not Peace, but a Sword: "Do not think that I have come to bring peace to the earth. I have not come to bring peace, but a sword. For I have come to set a man against his father, and a daughter against her mother, and a daughter-in-law against her mother-in-law and a person's enemies will be those of his own household."*

Romans 1:1: *"Paul, a servant of Christ Jesus, called to be an apostle and set apart for the gospel of God."*

First and foremost, you must partner with the truth that God is love! However, with this, we must understand that love corrects, and perfect love will not intermix with evil. God is a God of Love and Justice. He is perfect in all His ways and knows what is best for us and others.

The first scripture in Matthew chapter 7 talks about all the people who operate out of the spirit of religion, doing works for Jesus but wanting the glory. They are not allowing Jesus to be Lord over their life and giving Jesus all the glory. They do not have a relationship with Him, and the whole reason Jesus came to do what He did here on earth was so that we could have a relationship with God through His blood and enter into the kingdom of heaven. It is all about having a love relationship with God!

The second scripture in Matthew chapter 10 may seem contradictory about wanting loving relationships. Still, Jesus warns us that division will come once we make Him Lord over our lives. God loves us too much to leave us where we are. He will promote us beyond our destructive living where we were before we met him. Jesus had to come to earth and go to hell to overcome evil and defeat the devil. It is now up to us, His Bride, to get as close to Jesus as possible so He can purify us and bring us into our destiny for Him in these end times.

As we do this, we will begin to look more like Jesus. This will begin to offend the way others want to live their lives and this is even when we walk in love with them! Why? Because we begin to choose Jesus over anything or anyone else. When we do this, Jesus begins to purify and sanctify us. We begin to fully live for Jesus and no longer for the world. This will unfortunately cause some division because the people closest to us will not want to choose Jesus. Now, even when this division happens, it is important to keep our hearts right towards the ones we divide from because we must continue praying for their salvation.

The third scripture in Romans is so powerful because not just Paul but all Christians are called to be bondservants. Once we say yes to Jesus, we should become His bondservants. This word here in the Greek is Doulos, which means bond slave, one who is the entire property of another (Dake Bible). This is convicting! Are you living as a bond slave to Jesus Christ? This is how we are called to live as Christians!

Reflection:

1. I want you to take time today with the Holy Spirit. Allow Him to reveal deeper revelation to these Scriptures I have discussed today. I also want you to ask Him about the Scriptures of His grace and see if you have ever taken advantage of His grace on purpose. Do not get into condemnation. This is about allowing God to expose any lies that we have believed that allow us to continue in our sin. Be open and vulnerable here to see if He convicts you of anything, then repent when you are ready. Remember, this is between you and the Lord, but this is an area where the Body of Christ is rebelling, and it is time to come into a place of humility and maturity to get freedom. Make a list of any area where you have taken advantage of His grace so you can be aware of this in the future:

____

____

____

____

____

____

____

____

____

____

2. On the other hand, I want you to take time to see if you are trying to work for God's love or approval, work your way into Heaven, work your way into your identity in Christ, or work your way into ministry, etc. A relationship with God through Jesus Christ and being led by His Holy Spirit is the only way we

begin stepping into our true identity. God created you; He knows everything you have been through, so let Him guide you! He is the only answer to your true identity. It is not your family, your job, how many friends you have, or how successful the world deems you to be. It is all through our relationship with God through Jesus Christ. Do not beat yourself up here; allow God to show you areas where you are still working for love and acceptance. Then ask him to lead you into His truth about all the deception that is trying to keep you from His plans and purposes upon your life:

____

____

____

____

____

____

____

____

____

____

____

____

Declaration:

I declare that God is for me and I am firmly planted on the foundation of Jesus Christ. My foundation is being built on the Word of God and I hear His voice as he leads me because I am one of His sheep. I am a bond slave to Jesus. I give my life fully to Him. For it is no longer I who lives but Christ within me who lives.

5 Embrace the Shaking

I have learned over my last 16 years of walking with Christ that being a Christian is no joke, and calling yourself a Christian should not be used flippantly. I have learned there is a high price to pay when you fully surrender your life to Christ, but there is even a higher price if you do not. Hell is a very real place, and if you do not know this intimate relationship that I am speaking about, I encourage you to ask the Holy Spirit to show you and give Jesus access to every place in your heart. Humble yourself to repentance, and He will lead you into all truth! He loves you, and He is for you, but you must seek him out as He tells us to do in Proverbs 25:2. Seek Jesus and allow him to show you. Please know that I am saying this out of love. If you feel condemned in any way, reject all condemnation and try to hear this from the love of a Father's heart who does not want any of His children to perish.

I know this may seem like I am on a rant, but I have to be bold because some people need to hear this. We must stop professing that we are Christians if we do not have a genuine relationship with Christ because it is giving Christianity a bad name and leading many astray. We are not perfect by any means, but knowing Jesus intimately means we will be set apart from the world and its ways. Our lives and actions should look different from the world. If we are representing Jesus poorly, it makes people want to run from Him instead of to Him.

God showed me how the enemy influences the Church, which all has to do with the Body of Christ not knowing their true identity. If you simply profess that you're a Christian but have no actual relationship with Jesus, you won't see the truth that God wants you to have in your life. Nor will you see the true power of God working through you or have the fruit of the Spirit. This is a colossal issue why people do not want to have anything to do with Jesus or the Church because so many Christians are living without love and have become total hypocrites. Love is the first fruit that people should see in us as followers of Christ.

God has shown me that it is time for the Bride to come into her identity! If you are a Believer in Christ, and I presume you are because you are reading this book, then I want you to ask yourself this question. Would you still be happy if you were stripped of everything in this life? I want you to sit in your thoughts for a few moments here. Think about all the comforts in your life: your home, your health, your clothes, your significant other, your children, your entire family, your closest friends, your career, and even your physical freedom. If all of that was stripped from you, could you still live your life for Jesus and be fulfilled?

I am asking you this question because where our world is going, we need to have this strong conviction that no matter what, I am content because I have Jesus! If everything was stripped from me, it would be okay because I know Jesus is with me, and He has a plan for me, and that plan is good! I have had this conversation with many Christians, and most stay quiet, saying that's heavy or look at me with a deer in the headlights kind of look, and this is not okay! Are you hearing my heart here? For a lot of you, I'm sure you are, but for some of you, you need to listen to this. Why? Because God told me so and I have learned over the years that when He tells me to do something, I do it! It is a deep desire from my heart that you hear this in love with conviction and not any condemnation. Know that I love you and am praying for all of you reading this book, but more importantly, God loves you!

If we truly live for Jesus, we should do so as the Bible says. This means that once we truly make Jesus Lord over our lives, we will become CHRIST-ians. From this place, we will know love, joy, patience, and kindness and exude self-control, generosity, faithfulness, and gentleness. We will exude His power even during our suffering, as it says we can in 2 Corinthians 12:10. We, as Christians, should be exuding the gifts of the spirit! Why? Because we should be filled with His Spirit and feeding His Spirit more than our fleshly desires and souls! When we succumb to the desires of our flesh, we are in dangerous territory. God warns us that the flesh is always in enmity with the Holy Spirit, as it says in Galatians 5:17-25.

Let me share a few stories throughout my life that have gotten me to where I am today. Again, I am learning and may fail daily, but I can boldly say that Jesus is my everything. I know I would be okay if I lost everything around me because I truly know Jesus is for me. As you know, I was in Federal Prison but while I was in there, I had every single thing stripped from me except my Jesus. I'll never forget walking into that facility on August 14, 2014. I hugged my precious husband goodbye with tears pouring down my face that I never thought would stop. The pit in my stomach ran so deep from fear that it took my all not to run away or fall back into my old ways of thinking into hopelessness and suicidal thoughts.

God had given me Isaiah 61:1 before I was sentenced, "The Spirit of the Lord is upon me, for the Lord has anointed me to bring good news to the poor. He has sent me to comfort the brokenhearted and to proclaim freedom to the prisoners." I knew that I had to hold onto this every step of the way while I was in prison. This helped me die to myself, knowing that this sentence wasn't just about me but about helping others and that God had anointed me to help save. I held onto His promises no matter what I had to face.

I walked into prison that day, having to be stripped down naked, humiliated, handed an outfit to change into, got my picture taken and was given a new ID. The guards told me, "Welcome to your new life 4417442!" This was my inmate number. It seemed I no longer had a name, they were so adamant that I memorized this number and never lost that ID. I thank God for this difficult time in my life, though, because it made me dig deeper into Him.

I was faced with 31 years in prison, and God made it happen that I only received 36 months with 2 years probation. I only served 31 months and was released early from my probation within 6 months. God is good! If we choose to trust Him and lean on Him for everything, He will make ways you never thought possible! Incredible power comes when a genuine love relationship with Jesus happens. I could share so many stories where I have been stripped but how I consider them all pure joy now because with every stripping, it brought me deeper into my identity in Christ.

If you google my maiden name, it looks like I am the ringleader of a huge scheme to defraud the federal government, and it will show my bankruptcy, too. I am sharing this with you because God has worked on my identity. There are some facts that people will find, but people who truly know me, especially God, know my story and the truth. This is one of the hardest things Christians will face in this life and it is the fact that the enemy will try to use every tactic to destroy your identity. The devil starts at the very beginning of your life, so it is imperative that we begin to learn who we are in Christ as soon as possible! It is also essential to help our children have love encounters with Jesus at a young age, so if they are ever misled, they will return to Jesus, knowing His love is real.

There have been times in my life when I have been stripped of my health, my finances, my husband, my friends, my home, my credit, my name, my family, my babies, and my freedom, but I wouldn't change any of it because it made me dig deep to see what was truly inside of me. You see, God allows the stripping to happen only because He knows what we are destined for and a lot of times let's just be honest; we like comfort! The flesh is always in enmity with the Holy Spirit, so God has to allow our spirits to be quickened and strengthened through the trials of this life. He also has to work with free will and this fallen world system but somehow He always makes a way! It is incredible to watch.

We will go over this in more depth later on but I am here to challenge you to ask yourself, where does my identity lie? Everyday we should be aware of what we are running to for our identity in order to feel loved and fulfilled. Is my identity truly in Christ? Or is it in my children? My spouse? My finances? My success? My home? My health & fitness? My material things? Social Media likes? TV? Drugs? Alcohol? The list can go on and on but truly humble yourself and be honest. Pay attention to what you may still run to when things get hard. Just because we go over something one week does not mean we are fully healed, so keep in mind some of this may seem repetitive, but believe me, we need it!

God has chosen you and we as Christians to live an exemplary life, just as the disciples did. We are far from perfect and we will probably miss the mark daily but when we know our identity in Christ, we can do all that God has called us to do. There is a massive identity crisis going on in the world right now, if you haven't noticed, and it is only going to get worse, according to what the Bible says. This is why I am pounding down on this topic. The next area I want to go into is why knowing our Identity in Christ is so crucial.

God has been giving me a more profound revelation into how the sheep will be led astray so easily by wolves in sheep's clothing that are already here. But we are coming into a time where this is going to be extremely prevalent so we need to be wise and aware. We must be so rooted in Christ, knowing His voice and knowing Him so intimately, that when things go haywire, we will be led only by Him! Knowing our identity in Christ also helps us to stop comparing ourselves. When you genuinely know who you are in Christ, the nagging comparisons in your mind stop. Why? Because you begin to truly love yourself, and as you get to know Jesus more, He shares your destiny with you.

Within this, you find out that you are the only one who can actually bring about your destiny. There are books written about each of us in Heaven and one day, when we get to Heaven, we will be judged based on what we have accomplished down here on Earth! Did you know that? Psalm 139:16 and Malachi 3:16 tell us so. I definitely did not realize this until about five years ago. That means I walked out my Christian life for almost ten years without knowing this. This makes me think that there are other believers out there who don't know this.

I am not telling you this so you get into fear and start working hard to fulfill your destiny, but I am trying to encourage you to draw so incredibly close to your Creator that you want to live out every single thing written in your book. When I get to Heaven, I want to hear, "Good job, my faithful servant! You stepped out boldly in faith as I led and you didn't give up!" When we build this intimate relationship with Jesus, we begin to hear His voice with precision. He literally cares about every single thing in our lives. He cares about the tiniest details of our lives. Sometimes, He even tells me to not put something in a particular space on the counter, knowing it could fall and make a mess. It can be the littlest of things where He will begin speaking to you in order to train you to hear Him for the bigger decisions we have to make in the future.

There is a vital key in this life to knowing our identity in Christ and living out our destiny. This key is the ability to hear God's voice clearly. This takes training and it only gets done through an intimate relationship with Jesus. When the outside world criticizes you, that won't matter because Jesus's voice will be louder, and you will have built a firm foundation on what He says about you. When everyone goes one way you know doesn't feel right in your spirit, you can stand firm, knowing boldly that Jesus told you not to go that way. For the times that lie ahead, we must know God's voice and we must be obedient because there is a call upon each of our lives! Mathew 22:14 says that we are chosen and called by God!

Figuring out who you are in Christ is vital to achieving your God-given calling because God will not reveal your calling until you know who you are in Him. This revelation of who you are in Him can only come FROM HIM!! You can use Scriptures that resonate with your spirit to tell you who you are in Him, but you will truly begin to know, that you know, that you KNOW who you are in Christ, when you get close to Him. He begins to reveal His promises to you and who He already knows you to be. Sometimes, we have to endure things for Him to show us that His power is already in us; we just need to go through it so it builds our trust and faith in Him.

It is absolutely imperative that we listen to God's leadings in our life. We were bought with a price and our life is not our own (1 Corinthians 6:20). We were predestined before we were in our mother's wombs and there is a reason you will feel unsatisfied until you are living out your destiny. It is all inside you and was put there before the beginning of time! Psalm 139:16, clearly says this: *"Your eyes have seen my unformed substance; And in Your book were all written the days that were ordained for me, when as yet there was not one of them."*

God created us to be carriers of His glory in this world. We must come into the loving companionship He offers us to do this. Amazingly, He lets us partner with him to bring Heaven's destiny upon this Earth! You and me! Let that sink in for a moment! God Almighty wants to partner with YOU to bring out His plans and purposes on Earth! Most Christians today do not fully understand this, nor are they being championed to do so. We live in a time where all of creation is groaning for you to arise into all that God has created you to be! Romans 8:19-23 is upon us now! God called us to be World Changers! So the question we must ask ourselves is, are we changing the world or are we allowing the world to change us?

There is another point that I want to share with you about why it is so important to love yourself. We touched base on this last week, but Matthew 22:36-40 clearly states that this is Jesus's most important command. First, we are to love God with everything in us, then we are to love our neighbors as we love ourselves. As mentioned before, we cannot give love to others if we do not know God's love nor truly love ourselves. Once we begin to surrender all to Him and draw near to God, getting to know Him through His word and Holy Spirit, we begin to experience His agape love.

This then brings us into love encounters with Him. From here, we are supposed to begin to love ourselves but many believers have an issue here because of roots that are still undealt with deep within our hearts. I know you have been working on some of these root issues, but continue digging because these deep wounds block us from loving others as we should. As we continue growing in our relationship with Jesus, He begins to reveal the roots that are still holding us back. They block the revealing of our true identity, which helps us enter into our destiny. If we don't deal with the roots in our hearts, we will continue to go around the same mountain. We must learn to deal with our heart's root issues by softening our hearts to the Lord daily. It is the only way to walk in the freedom that Christ died for us to have.

APPLYING WISDOM TO YOUR DAILY LIFE

Prayer for the day:

Father God,
I ask for You to shake out of me anything that I no longer need in my life. Anything that is a stumbling block to get closer to You and to do Your will in my life, I ask You to remove from me. I ask You for such a sensitivity to Your Holy Spirit that I can hear Your voice clearly whether to do something or not do something, whether to go somewhere or stay home. Help me to learn to discern the distinct difference in Your voice from the other voices that try to trap me. I am all Yours Lord! Forgive me for holding onto things I no longer need and for doing things my own way. Forgive me for following others when I should have been following You. Teach me to hear Your voice clearly. I want Your way and Your will for my life in Jesus Name I pray.

Scriptures to meditate on:

Galatians 2:20: *"I have been crucified with Christ. It is no longer I who live, but Christ who lives in me. And the life I now live in the flesh I live by faith in the Son of God, who loved me and gave himself for me."*

2 Corinthians 5:17: *"Therefore, if anyone is in Christ, he is a new creation. The old has passed away; behold, the new has come."*

Ephesians 2:10: *"For we are his workmanship, created in Christ Jesus for good works, which God prepared beforehand, that we should walk in them."*

2 Timothy 1:7: *"For God gave us a spirit not of fear but of power and love and self-control."*

Ephesians 1:5: *"He predestined us for adoption to sonship through Jesus Christ, in accordance with his pleasure and will."*

1 Peter 2:9: *"But you are a chosen people, a royal priesthood, a holy nation, God's special possession, that you may declare the praises of him who called you out of darkness into his wonderful light."*

Isaiah 43:1: *"But now, this is what the LORD says, He who is your Creator, Jacob, And He who formed you, Israel: "Do not fear, for I have redeemed you; I have called you by name; you are Mine!" (Put your name in the places where it says Jacob and Israel).*

Romans 8:19-23: *"For [even the whole] creation [all nature] waits eagerly for the children of God to be revealed. For the creation was subjected to frustration and futility, not willingly [because of some intentional fault on its part], but by the will of Him who subjected it, in hope that the creation itself will also be freed from its bondage to decay [and gain entrance] into the glorious freedom of the children of God. For we know that the whole creation has been moaning together as in the pains of childbirth until now. And not only this, but we too, who have the first fruits of the Spirit [a joyful indication of the blessings to come], even we groan inwardly, as we wait eagerly for [the sign of] our adoption as sons—the redemption and transformation of our body [at the resurrection]."*

Key # 5 Please God Instead Of Man!

Reflection:

1. Pleasing God instead of Man is very hard to start walking out, but I am telling you that if you train yourself to do this, it will be one of the most potent keys to breaking free in this life. The fear of man literally cripples people, and the enemy is going to use this tactic immensely in these end times. So, I encourage you to start putting this key into practice now if you haven't done so already.

2. Pay attention to certain situations that arise where you feel your people-pleasing alert going off and stop! Ask God what He wants you to do and wait for His instruction instead of what someone else wants you to do. This is where you will begin learning how to set healthy boundaries. Remember that you owe no one anything except to love them (Romans 13:8). It is imperative to start training in this area. I am still learning how to do this, but I am growing immensely, and it has been so freeing!

3. Take time to write down anyone you feel you have to please or any situation that comes to mind when you have been a people pleaser. Then, take time to ask the Holy Spirit how you could have handled that differently and how to handle situations that arise in the future differently. Once you begin doing this, it will help you rewire your brain and be very conscious of the boundaries you will have to begin setting.

____

____

____

____

____

____

____

____

____

____

____

____

Author's note:

Please know that God wants us to serve out of love, but sometimes, when we come from a past of trauma, we unfortunately learn how to please people and say yes to things that we were never called to. This can sometimes lead us to places where God never intended for us to go. But! We must remember as long as we keep our hearts right towards God, He will always teach us and help us grow through whatever situation we get ourselves into. He is that good and He will always lead us into our destiny when we keep trusting Him!!

Declaration:

I am chosen by God. He has predestined me to do His will; I walk that out in obedience daily. I lay down my life and my ways for His because He knows the very best plans He has for me. I am His workmanship created to do His good works here on Earth. I hear and know the voice of my Heavenly Father, and I walk in the ways He leads me. I am obedient to God over man. I renounce all agreements with being a people pleaser and I aim to please God from this day forth.

WEEK 3

Becoming One With Jesus

1 Thirst For Him

I had a powerful encounter with Jesus in 2022 through a vision where he brought me into an experience of becoming one with him. This occurred during my healing process through my 2nd miscarriage. I was broken beyond belief at this time, and I was so mad at God, but I learned how much power there is when we invite Jesus into our pain. He can take it from us and heal us completely if we let Him! It took me almost a year to heal my heart from my first miscarriage, and it only took me seven days to heal from the 2nd one because I invited Jesus in and chose to release. It was truly miraculous! I have had several more miscarriages since then, but I have learned to fully allow Jesus into my pain. This has radically shifted my life in a powerful way. I now choose to trust Him no matter what may come my way.

I will share this vision piece by piece throughout this week because there are so many powerful takeaways. I need to share it this way since it was so profound. This vision was incredibly intimate, with the most beautiful details and clarity I've ever experienced. This vision is highly significant because it is for the Body of Christ, His Bride, at this time. You will read about this encounter in the following few chapters. I encourage your heart to be open to receive profound revelation. I will touch on some things that the Lord wants me to share so that you can gain more freedom in your life and prepare yourself for what is coming.

There were several moments throughout this vision where Jesus kept asking me if I trusted Him. At each of these moments, He showed me the areas of my heart that I hadn't fully surrendered to Him and asked me to trust Him to finally heal those areas once and for all. As I did this in complete surrender, releasing all shame, He enveloped me, and we finally became one. This is where Jesus is longing to bring His Bride. The ability to give it all and fully submit will only come when we encounter His Love. Abundance and divine alignment will begin to flow from this place and this is where God is leading His Bride.

The vision began with me walking in a dark, cool forest just before sunrise. I could feel the crisp chill around me; every time I took a breath, I could hear it and see it. The silence around me was almost deafening. With every step, I could listen to the crunch echoing through the woods and every leaf falling from the trees. Then, I suddenly became very aware that I was not the only living thing in that forest and fear tried to creep in. However, at that exact moment, massive beams of sunlight began bursting through the treetops, making every one of my fears vanish instantly, bringing me warmth, peace, and a sudden burst of joy.

Authors note:

*This vision has so many powerful messages for the Bride of Christ in this time. In the very beginning you notice the stillness around me. God is asking His Bride right now: Are we able to sit & wait? Are we taking the time to hear Him? (**Lamentations 3:28**) To Be still? (psalm 46:10) Are we walking in pure obedience to His call upon our lives? (**Deut 8:6**). God is calling His Bride into this place of stillness to be able to hear Him clearly. We do not want to miss all that He is saying right now. This is for the end times.*

He is revealing to those who are seeking. Then the very next part of this vision talks about fear trying to come in. Real fear and persecution is coming to the Body of Christ but if we fear the Lord more than anything in this world, we will not be overcome. It is only by sitting with God, getting to know His character where we can learn the true fear of the Lord. (The Awe of God by John Bevere, is a great book explaining the fear of God). When we are so full of Jesus, we will not be moved by fear because we know who our God is and all that He can do. He is raising His Bride to come into this radical faith). We are going to need this type of faith for all that is coming. This is not to scare you but to warn you and to help you prepare.

In the next part of this vision, after the beams of light showed through, I felt a deep longing and a yearning, as if some force was drawing me forward with a fantastic sense of love and exuberance. As I took another step in obedience toward this intense yearning for His love, a beautiful path of liquid gold appeared before my feet. I heard a voice asking me, "Do you trust me?" I suddenly became overwhelmed by wonder and awe at all that I began to see before my very own eyes.

I began to take steps of faith, saying, "Yes, I trust you!" I was walking on liquid gold; every step I took had to be taken in faith. Then, the liquid beneath me changed into the most beautiful colors of blues, turquoise, reds, pinks, greens, and purples. It looked like copper when burned in a fire but with even more colors than the eye had ever seen. I don't quite have the words for the excitement I felt from within because it was so surreal yet so incredibly tangible at the same time. I then began running and skipping with elation like a child because more colors began to appear with every step I took.

Author's note:

*There is great significance in every part of this vision. I will break it down every couple paragraphs with scriptures and the message I believe God has for us in this time. When I felt that deep longing, it reminded me of **Psalm 42:1-2**, "As the deer pants for streams of water, so my soul pants for you, my God. My soul thirsts for God, for the living God. When can I go and meet with God?" We must come to this place of hunger and desperation. Are we thirsting to meet with God as if it were our last sip of water in the desert? This convicted me to my core because this life can be so distracting at times but we must chasten ourselves to seek Him first and get excited to meet with Him!*

Every part of this vision could be a blueprint of how to walk out our daily walk with Jesus until we leave this earth because we are His Bride. The next part of this vision, where I see this liquid gold path appear and He asks me to trust him to step out basically onto the water as Peter did, is such a beautiful depiction of our Jesus. He will never override our free will. We must choose to trust Him to lead us in everything we do. I also found it interesting that the gold was melted down for me to walk on. I know this represents purifying while trusting. The Bride of Christ is being invited into a purification process until our Bridegroom comes. There are several scriptures that come to mind that I will list below in the meditation & reflection part of today's workbook. But the main takeaway here is once we learn to fully trust God with everything in our lives, allowing him to refine us, He truly makes everything beautiful! In His timing of course, but we must trust Him because it is here where we can find joy, peace, love, excitement even while going through fearful situations.

APPLYING WISDOM TO YOUR DAILY LIFE

Jesus,

I repent for not putting You first and making You a priority in my life. I want to meet with You everyday and I want to invite You into every area of my life. Help me to be obedient to meet you in our secret place everyday. I want to get to know You in deeper ways. I give You my life, my time, my family, my burdens, all of it Lord. Help me and guide me. I trust you Lord, in Jesus Name, I pray!

Scriptures to meditate on:

Psalm 37:23-24: *"The Lord directs the steps of the godly. He delights in every detail of their lives. Though they stumble, they will never fall, for the Lord holds them by the hand."*

Proverbs 16:9: *"We can make our plans, but the Lord determines our steps."*

Psalm 31:14-15: *"But I trust in you, Lord; I say, 'You are my God. My times are in your hands."*

Proverbs 20:24: *"The Lord directs our steps, so why try to understand everything along the way?"*

Psalm 119:105: *"Your word is a lamp to guide my feet and a light for my path."*

Proverbs 19:21: *"Many are the plans in a person's heart, but it is the Lord's purpose that prevails."*

Isaiah 48:17: *"I am God, your God, who teaches you how to live right and well. I will show you what to do, where to go."*

Reflection:

I want you to be completely honest with yourself and with God. . .

1. Are you taking the time you need to get to know Jesus on a deeper level? ______Are you building your relationship with Him daily? ______Do you spend time listening to hear His voice, to sit quietly with Him? ______Are you seeking out answers for your life in His Word?______Then are you meditating on His Word and His promises?

If any of your answers are no, I do not want you to feel condemned, but I want you to get excited! Renounce all agreement with condemnation and defeat right now! Begin to stir your spirit-man by getting excited to study who Father God is, who Jesus is, and who the Holy Spirit is, and focus on getting closer to each of them! Yes, they are one, but they all have different functions. I want you to promise Jesus and yourself that you will make time every day to meet with him in your secret place from this day forward. What is a secret place? It is where you meet with Jesus intimately, just you and Him.

I want to encourage all the busy people right now who feel like they do not have time. God knows how much time you have, so if it is only 20 min or 60 min, do that! Be honest about the time you do have, and you may have to give something else up to do this, such as scrolling on social media or setting your alarm before anyone else in your home wakes up. He has had me give up some things, so I now give Him my first hour of the day and a couple of hours in the evening. My week goes so much better when I give him this time.

2. Write down a schedule that you will stick to everyday for you and your God time.

____

____

____

3. This time should be a time where you are finding out how you best hear from God and connect with Him. Pay attention to the ways God speaks to you throughout your day or in the times when you come to meet with him. Some people connect with God by sitting in silence, or listening to soaking instrumental music. Some like to be moving, this could include walking, working out, dancing, or even doing art work. For some it is speaking in tongues to be able to hear Him more clearly. We are all different and it is important to find out how you connect best with God. This should not be out of a religious act but out of a deep desire in your heart to want to connect with God and get to know Him more intimately in all the ways of the Triune God. Keep in mind that this can change throughout your walk with Him, so be careful not to put you or God in a box. He is steady but also always leading. His leading can change from time to time, especially as we grow in Him. Be intentional to take notes over this next week on how you best connect with God here:

____

____

____

____

____

____

____

____

____

____

Declaration:

I decree and declare that I am God's beloved! I am His beautiful bride who waits patiently for Him, and I thirst for Him like a deer pants for water. Jesus, I thirst for more of You! I want to get to know You so intimately that I allow You into my deepest, darkest parts. You shine light on every dark thing that has held me back, and I am healing! I trust You, Jesus, and will go where You lead me!

2 Trust Him

After walking and leaping along that liquid path of gold, I heard that voice again. Jesus asked me to begin picturing the most beautiful castle I could ever imagine. So, I stopped in my tracks, and I started to do this. As I did, it literally began appearing right before my eyes. I was now at the bottom of a massive concrete staircase to this immaculate, extravagant castle. Jesus appeared before me at the top of that staircase, and I knew He had been waiting for me for thousands of years. My heart was overcome with a longing I'd never felt before. It was like I could breathe for the very first time. He held out His hand for me to come up to Him, and I heard Him ask again, "Do you trust me?" As I took the first step to show Him that I do, I suddenly felt immense pressure holding me back. It felt like a strong anchor had been tied to me, keeping me from moving forward. I quickly looked backward out of fear to see what was gripping me, but immediately, I heard Jesus say, "Keep your eyes on me every step of the way; I've got you!"

Author's note:

Here is a great reminder. Are we taking time to stop and listen to what God is saying for the next steps in our lives? And then, are we trusting Him to obey what He tells us to do or step into? **Isaiah 26:3-4** *says, "You keep him in perfect peace whose mind stays on you because he trusts in you. Trust in the Lord forever, for the Lord God is an everlasting rock."* **Proverbs 3:5** *says, "Trust in the Lord with all your heart, and do not lean on your own understanding."* **Psalm 37:31** *says, "The law of his God is in his heart; his steps do not slip."*

So, as I kept my eyes locked on Jesus, I felt as if that anchor got cut from behind me, and it ended up slingshotting me up five sets of stairs. God will always accelerate us when the time is right. Nothing in life is wasted. He truly uses all of it to sharpen, stretch, grow, and then accelerate us even though we may feel like it is one step forward and two steps back. He can use every single thing in our life to catapult us into our destiny once we have humbled ourselves and grown with Him to step into the new He has for us.

Then, as I began walking up a new level of stairs, I had to battle new strong forces with every step that were trying to hold me back. However, I knew I needed to keep my eyes fixed on Jesus, trusting Him completely. As I continued to do this, I heard the sounds of heavy metals with glass shattering breaking loudly behind me on the concrete stairs. I continued to take steps and quickly realized the sounds I heard were giant contraptions falling off me down the stairs and breaking into pieces along their way. It was a struggle, but I trusted my King with every step I took, knowing He was allowing this for a reason. I could literally feel my spirit coming into new levels of strength and freedom even though my flesh was being beaten and torn apart.

With this newfound strength in my spirit, my body felt excessively worn down when I reached the top of those stairs. Jesus stood there smiling at me gently and then asked me if I would come dance with Him. I was overcome by His love and grace, but then, suddenly, I became very aware of my present state. I looked down to find that both my clothes and my skin were filthy and ripped, as if I had been torn apart by wild animals. I was bruised and bleeding as if I had just been through a war. Jesus then took my chin into His hand, reminding me how lovely I am. Within an instant, all my shame left, however, what was left was an immense amount of humility.

Author's note:

*Take time to pause and reflect again on the significance here. The enemy will always try to hold you back from your connection with Jesus, from the call that is upon your life, and from your freedom! It is the devil's ultimate job to keep you in bondage and try to destroy you! We must pay attention to the distractions that are happening right now! These distractions have a lot to do with wounds in our own hearts because we are getting entangled in things that God is not leading us into. We must humble ourselves to allow God to show us what is holding us back. There are things in your life that God asks you to let go of. **What are those things?***

*We must be keenly aware of the areas where we do not fully trust God. Be honest with yourself. We must allow God to show us these areas within our hearts and lives! This is not a time to mess around. If you want to be used mightily by God to do what He has put inside of you to do upon this earth, then I encourage you to seek Him in this area. **Psalms 139:23-24 (KJV)**, "Search me, O God, and know my heart: Try me, and know my thoughts: And see if there be any wicked way in me, And lead me in the way everlasting."*

*The next part of this vision is that, yes, this journey of laying down our life for Jesus is challenging and will be hard, but when we keep our eyes fixed on Him, trusting Him, He will bring us through mightily. We go through seasons of testing and hardships to produce good fruit. God will give us opportunities to kill the flesh daily. He allows difficult things to come into our lives to humble, stretch, and strengthen us so we can rise in Him! I love this last part when I get to the top, and I feel so ashamed, but God shows me such love that all the shame melts away! **1 Samuel 16:7**, But the Lord said to Samuel, "Do not look at his appearance or on the height of his stature, because I have rejected him. For the Lord sees not as man sees: man looks on the outward appearance, but the Lord looks on the heart."*

I was weeping through a lot of this vision so I encourage you to let the Holy Spirit prick certain places in your heart that may need to be softened. Jesus then invited me in to dance with Him once again, and the moment I said yes, these beautiful, massive, ornate doors burst open to the most magnificent ballroom in this foyer of the castle. He guided me in like a King welcoming his bride. However, within seconds, He picked me up, put me upon both of His feet and asked me again, "Do you trust me?" As I said yes, He began to twirl me around in a beautiful waltz. This brought me to a place within my mind and heart of being like a little girl dancing on her daddy's feet, trusting him with everything! With every swirl of this dance, he brought me through every season of my life, showing me that He had been with me every step of the way.

He began showing me that I had the power to defeat every lie that has ever tried to hold me back from past memories, including all my harmful belief systems. As I began doing this with him, my ragged, dirty, old, torn clothes began turning into the most magnificent garments I had ever seen, and my skin started healing and glistening as if I were no longer human but becoming some sort of heavenly being. This part of the vision took me almost 2 hours to get through due to so much trauma from my past, but I allowed Him to dance me through my entire life timeline.

APPLYING WISDOM TO YOUR DAILY LIFE

Jesus,

I pray for your protection as I begin to face the things in my past that may be difficult to fully conquer. I pray for your grace, mercy, faith, and your strength. Thank you Lord for loving me and guiding me through this process. I trust you and I give you my entire heart to search and show me any areas within me that need healing. Show me any walls that I need to take down in order to let you in. Forgive me for any fears I have toward you. I trust you Jesus, have your way in my heart, my mind, and in my life!

Scriptures to meditate on:

1 Corinthians 10:13: *"No temptation has overtaken you that is not common to man. God is faithful, and he will not let you be tempted beyond your ability, but with the temptation he will also provide the way of escape, that you may be able to endure it."*

Romans 8:28: *"And we know that for those who love God all things work together for good, for those who are called according to his purpose."*

Reflection:

1. I want you to sit and reflect upon your life but invite Jesus into this. You may be healed from many things; believe me, we are all in a process until we leave this earth; I am not saying this is a one-and-done. However, I encourage you to be raw and vulnerable with yourself and your Lord, Jesus, today and every time you come to a place where you need healing with Him. Write down any memories that come up for you in your journal, and ask the Holy Spirit to show you where God was in that situation. Then, write down what he shows you.

____

____

____

____

____

____

Take time to pray about this with Jesus, the Holy Spirit, and Father God. Allow Him to show you any area where you are still not allowing Him to access your life. Ask Him to show you any area of your life that still needs healing and any walls that need to come down. I encourage you to lie down, put on some instrumental soaking music, and allow the Holy Spirit to bring things up that need to be dealt with. One of my favorite soaking songs, and the one I was listening to when I had this encounter, is here:

https://www.youtube.com/watch?v=wNSsH5SVv7U&t=863s Jesus Is Holy/Violin/30 Min Instrumental

2. Write down any areas that still need healing in your heart and any victories you may have had today during your secret place time with Jesus. Please do this at least 2 times per week, at least on this particular subject, while you are on this healing journey. Remember that we should enter the secret place and hunger to encounter Jesus daily, though. This is what brings radical change to our lives.

____

____

____

____

____

____

____

____

____

____

____

____

____

Declaration:

Jesus, I am yours! I give You every part of me and I know You are working all things out within me and my life for my good! I trust You Jesus! Thank You Lord for all You took on that cross for my healing and for me to be free! I am healed only by Your blood! I am whole in You!

3 Calling You Higher

As our dance came to a close, Jesus danced me into a graceful finish to the bottom of the staircase, which was made out of glistening glass like diamonds. He asked me, "Are you ready to rise higher?" As soon as I said yes, our journey began up this breathtaking staircase, and with every step, the stairs glistened with colors beyond my wildest dreams. The atmosphere became exuberant with energy that I had never experienced before. I instantly knew that all of heaven rejoiced because I was finally returning to my rightful place. The very air around me was breathing and dancing with God's glory as we took our last steps to the top of those stairs.

As we reached the top, we were greeted by two massive doors of pure gold with hieroglyphics written all over them. As I stood there with complete wonder and total awe, Jesus told me through His mind that this is your book. Audible words were no longer needed because we could now read one another's minds. "Everything beyond these doors will show you all that you have been created for," and as He spoke this to me through His mind, I automatically knew He would ask that question again before taking me through these doors. "Do you trust me?" As I once again said, "Yes," He said, "Come, now it is the time to become one with me."

Author's note:

*A few things to reflect on here. When Jesus brings you out of a tumultuous season, there is always an upgrade in your life as long as you stay surrendered and obedient to Him through that season. (**John 15:4-5, 7-8**). Jesus danced me through some intense fearful things I had to face, and now we are ascending the staircase made of diamonds. What do diamonds represent? The absolute beauty that comes from imperfection and pressure! Hallelujah! Then, I went to a place where I could begin understanding what Jesus was thinking; there was no longer a need for spoken words. This represents a place of intimacy with Him. I like to say, "Into me, you see."*

I can now hear His voice clearly, and I am letting Him lead me in every way I think and act. Again, He is not ever overriding my will. He asks me again and again if I trust him. We must choose and then learn to fully walk out our trust in Jesus. Now, this next part gets truly intimate, and I want you to throw out any perversion that may try to intervene because this was a place of such purity, holiness, and love as I've never known before. It was all about releasing shame and getting to a place to be able to come back to the garden of Eden before Adam & Eve knew they were naked. . . This was when they were still ONE with God. . . Before the fall of man had happened.

As Jesus repeated those words to me, but now with His mind, "Do you trust me?" I said yes, and the golden doors burst open with divine power, and I could feel the exhilaration running through every fiber of my being. As I began to walk into the room, I became keenly aware that this was my Bridegroom's chambers. He had been waiting thousands of years for this very moment! Then Jesus said, "It is time. Are you ready?" As I said, "yes!" He asked me again, "Do you trust me?" I said, "Yes, Lord." He then supernaturally undressed the beautiful garments He had just clothed me in and asked me again, "Do you trust me?" Once again, I said, "Yes." He whisked me into His arms and gently laid me onto the most beautiful, Kingly bed full of Gold and jewels. This was a total supernatural experience, as if we were floating together. He then asked me to reveal anything I was still trying to cover up.

He could see the areas that I still needed to release in my heart to fully trust Him. However, He honored my free will, giving me time to fully release and give them up. I knew then that He wanted into every crevice of my body, soul, and spirit. As I released these final parts of me where I still felt shame, Jesus then came into me. It was like He floated over me and just came into me. As simple as that, we became one.

I began to fully transform from my sparkling and glowing flesh into a whole spirit being, finally becoming one with my one and only true love from before the beginning of time. The ceiling of the Bridegroom's chambers then began to completely open up to the heavens, and my eyes became open to the spiritual realm. There was no longer any distance or separation by the flesh; I finally saw and heard for the first time how I was created to be.

Authors note:

This part of the vision was of the utmost purity. There was absolutely no ounce of perversion during this undressing period like we have in this world. It wasn't about becoming one flesh like it is here on this earth between a husband and wife. It was something truly supernatural. A time of trusting to become one with Jesus in every way; mind, body, and spirit, but it was like I left the fleshly part of my body behind. This was a Hebrews 4:13 encounter. This Scripture says Nothing in all creation is hidden from God's sight. Everything is naked and laid bare before His eyes to whom we must give account.

Everything in that moment came to life. I could literally see light and sound. They had beautiful colors and movements that I cannot do justice to explaining. Everything was living; even the breath that I breathed had a lovely rhythm of sound, light, and color that was worship unto God. Then, all of a sudden, there was a massive burst of light that came out from the inner being of both me and Jesus when we came together as one. The next moment happened so fast that it was as if the Holy Spirit supernaturally zapped us into the Garden. Jesus brought me to the Garden of Eden!

I got to see how creation was before the fall of man had happened. The Lion was laying with the lamb, and Adam and Eve were talking with the animals, the flowers, and the trees. Adam and Eve did not appear to have human flesh on them like we have now. They were beautiful light beings in the form of a human body, but not bound by the decaying flesh that we have now. They were literally beaming with God's Glory. It was magnificent to witness. This is difficult to explain, but it is profound what God wanted to show me through this entire vision.

This might be difficult for some of you to take in, but we must remember that we are supernatural beings once we become Christians/born-again Believers in Christ. Everything in the Old and New Testaments shows that we serve a supernatural God. Once we allow Jesus to come in and fully reign in our lives, He can work through us miraculously by giving us His Holy Spirit. But the question we have to ask ourselves is this: Are we allowing God to flow through us? Do we trust God so much that we believe in every word He has said? Every word written in the Bible?

We are about to see the most significant revival and reformation that the earth has ever encountered, and God wants us to be prepared for these end times. He also wants us to prepare for His 2nd coming, just as the five virgins in Matthew chapter 25 were wise to prepare. This also represents the Bride getting herself ready, as talked about in Revelation 19. The last part of this vision was exactly that. We will be caught up in the blink of an eye! God is preparing His End Time, Bride! Are we preparing, and are we ready?

APPLYING WISDOM TO YOUR DAILY LIFE

Prayer for the day:

Jesus,

I pray for Your Holy Spirit to comfort me as I face more of the things that have been hidden deep within my soul for so many years. I give You permission to uproot any of the other areas that do not want to be revealed within me. I ask You to take all blinders off of my eyes and for You to soften my heart. Help me to be vulnerable and I ask for You to expose the enemy where he has been able to keep me bound. I surrender my will for Your will Lord. Help me to begin living with an eternal mindset instead of an earthly one, In Jesus' Name I pray. Amen.

Scriptures to meditate on:

Proverbs 3:5-6: *"Trust in the Lord with all thine heart; and lean not unto thine own understanding. In all thy ways acknowledge him, and he shall direct thy paths."*

John 11:25: *"Jesus said to her, "I am the resurrection and the life. Whoever believes in me, though he die, yet shall he live."*

John 17:22-23: *"I have given them the glory that you gave me, that they may be one as we are one— I in them and you in me—so that they may be brought to complete unity."*

Hebrews 4:13: *"Nothing in all creation is hidden from God's sight; everything is uncovered and exposed before the eyes of Him to whom we must give account."*

Revelation 19:7-9: *"Let us be glad and rejoice and give Him glory, for the marriage of the Lamb has come, and His wife has made herself ready." And to her it was granted to be arrayed in fine linen, clean and bright, for the fine linen is the righteous acts of the saints. Then he said to me, 'Blessed are those who are called to the marriage supper of the Lamb!' And he said to me, "These are the true sayings of God."*

Key #6: Intimacy With Jesus Daily

Becoming One with Jesus takes intimacy. This may sound simple, but this is a choice we must continue to make daily, maybe even minute by minute. This powerful revelation of focusing on keeping my intimacy with my King has helped me to rewire several wrong patterns within my brain and in my life. Becoming one with Jesus means inviting Him into every area of your life. You no longer try to keep things hidden from your King and recognize that this Life is no longer your own. It means inviting Him into every thought, everything you do, everything you plan, etc. It has a similar meaning as when we become one with our husbands or wives in marriage but with even more honor. We must remember that we are the Bride, and Jesus is our Bridegroom. There is genuinely something supernatural that happens when we begin having God encounters daily. Christians must get to this place so we can go out daily and help others have encounters with Jesus. Are we living this out daily?

1. The first thing you should do before you get out of bed is praise Jesus. Thank Him for your life, and invite Him into your day. Give Him free rein to lead you & speak to you. Tell Him that your heart and ears are open to listen to Him. Ask Him what He thinks about the things that concern you, what you have going on that day or week, etc. Once you begin doing this every morning, it will become a great habit you no longer have to think about. Suddenly, you will start to abide in Jesus, allowing His Holy Spirit to lead you. John 15:4-11 says, *"Abide in Me, and I in you. As the branch cannot bear fruit of itself, unless it abides in the vine, neither can you, unless you abide in Me. I am the vine, you are the branches. He who abides in Me, and I in him, bears much fruit; for without Me you can do nothing. If anyone does not abide in Me, he is cast out as a branch and is withered; and they gather them and throw them into the fire, and they are burned. If you abide in Me, and My words abide in you, you will ask what you desire, and it shall be done for you."*

2. I want you to continue journaling from yesterday's assignment this week. Keep asking the Holy Spirit to reveal any place in your life where you are still having trouble letting Him in to fully trust Him. Make sure you face any & all areas of shame and unworthiness. The enemy loves to hold us back in the areas of shame and condemnation, so be open. This is between you and Jesus. No one else, so let Him in. And always remember that healing is a process. This isn't about becoming free in seconds, which sometimes the Lord can do, but be gracious to yourself if it doesn't happen overnight and be open to how Jesus helps you heal along this journey.

____

____

____

____

____

____

____

____

I trust You, Jesus! I know You are more powerful than any demonic stronghold in my life, so I give You full access to my soul, body, and spirit. I give You the reins over my life to lead and guide me. I repent for being Lord over my life. Today, I fully dedicate my life to you, Lord Jesus. You are my Lord, and I want all of You! I am becoming one with You. I am sensitive to Your lead and Your voice. I hear Your voice clearly and I walk in obedience to Your instructions. I know that what You have for me is good! I trust you Lord!

4 Be On Guard

Let me break down some more parts of this latter part of this vision with scripture and the significance of what God asks of us in these End Times. Since I have had this vision, God has shown me the power of becoming one through intimacy with Jesus as one Spirit and not having to be bound by the flesh or the sins of this world. We must remember that the flesh never wants us to encounter God's love or His goodness over our lives because the flesh came from the fall. The flesh always wants to be in control. We see this in Genesis chapter 3. The Bible tells the story of Adam and Eve eating the forbidden fruit and then the fall of man happens.

There are a couple revelations I'd like for you to take hold of here. First, it's interesting that the fall had to do with food. It was mainly pride, but God used this example of being lured from the flesh or worldly/fleshly desires. We must be careful what we are feeding our flesh, which is a huge reason why Jesus tells us to fast! When we deny our flesh from the most essential thing the body wants, food, it helps us become more sensitive to our spirit! Fasting is a necessary component of living a successful Christian life. I recommend studying the importance of fasting if you do not do this regularly.

The second thing I'd like to point out is how we must be keenly aware of the voices that we are listening to. It says in Genesis 1:27 that God created man in his own image, in the image of God. Then, in Genesis 2:7, it says that God breathed His breath of life into Adam. These two verses prove that man was made just like God, created from His very own being, meaning they already had access to everything God had for them. They were one with God in Spirit and in Truth.

Then, when we fast-forward to Chapter 3, Eve allows herself to get entangled in a conversation with the enemy. A side note to pay attention to is that it says Eve was talking with the serpent. Remember my vision of the animals and nature being able to converse? It is interesting to think that perhaps it was normal to talk to animals and other living things that God created.

However, the vital thing to remember here is to be aware of getting into a conversation with the enemy. This is a trap that we must pay attention to. When you know a thought comes into your mind that does not align with your identity from the word of God, do not engage with it. This is why it is imperative that we read the word of God with revelation through the Holy Spirit. God longs for us to hear and know His voice, as it says in John 8:47 and 10:27.

Eve's first mistake was engaging in a conversation with the enemy. Her second mistake was that she doubted God's word over her identity and who she was in Christ. The serpent tested Eve by twisting the Word of God about the tree and who she already was. The enemy is a master at making things look like they are from God and even using the Word of God to twist you into deception. This is why we must ask Holy Spirit to give us revelation as we read our Bibles daily. We must know the Word so well by having intimacy with Jesus daily so we will not be deceived!

You see, God was honest about the tree from the start and that they were already made in God's image. He told Adam that he would surely die if he ate from that tree, which is precisely what happened. He became instantly cut off from his direct life source of being eternally one with God in the Spirit. They succumbed to the curse of the flesh and sin by eating the forbidden fruit, which resulted in death and the knowledge of sin, leading to this fallen world.

Another thing I want to point out here is to be aware of going after too much knowledge. What I mean by this is the more knowledge we go after, it can sometimes take us away from God. Why? It slowly entices us to think we are wiser than God and could lead us into fear instead of faith in these End Times. I believe the tree of knowledge of good and evil represents the things in this fallen world that make us stray away from the one and only true God. There is a difference between knowledge and wisdom. As we grow in God's Word, we become more wise. Gaining wisdom is far greater than just having knowledge. We can consume a lot of useless knowledge from the world that could lead us astray, so be aware of this.

There are a few more exciting revelations that I want to share with you here. The first is about becoming one with Jesus, just as we do as husband and wife. This takes a great deal of intimacy and effort on our part. Another one is that once we become born again, we can embrace this intimate oneness with Jesus, but are you making an effort to do this? Do you know that this is tangibly available for you? This revelation can take longer to grasp and fully live out, but it is imperative that we run after this.

When Christians are born again, they come alive to spiritual things and alive unto God. Not all Christians are Born Again, and this can be an issue because without having the Holy Spirit living on the inside of you, you will be dead to spiritual things. You will not be able to fully comprehend the revelations within His Word or the things of eternity, which we are called to as Believers in Christ. We are all born with a fallen sinful nature but once you get born again, your fallen spirit becomes alive in God! God now looks at you through the blood of Jesus, which covers your sins and gives you access to becoming One with Him.

When you get born again, you begin to hunger for the ways of God. Just like Adam & Eve were in the very beginning when God first created them. However, our souls and our bodies do not get born again; this is why God gives us clear direction throughout His Bible to crucify our flesh and to renew our minds with His Word daily. It is essential to have daily intimacy with Jesus, the Holy Spirit, and Father God. We must hunger to get to know His Character and build a relationship with Him once we get born again. This will help lead you and equip you for the mighty call upon your life. I want you to get this because this is a huge supporting factor that gives us direct access to God through Jesus for anything we need.

It says that it wasn't until after the fall of man that God had to make garments of flesh for Adam and Eve (Genesis 3:21). If we believe that Jesus is the Last Adam, as it says in 1 Corinthians 15:22, then we should consider this! We can be free from all the sin that comes with the flesh from the fall of man because Jesus went to hell (1 Peter 4:6, Ephesians 4:9) and took back the keys from the enemy and has given us the right to access those keys (Isaiah 22:22). This includes walking in obedience to Holy Spirit and crucifying our flesh daily to run after the things of eternity instead of this earthly fallen world.

We need to be reminded that once we are Born Again, we become supernatural beings, not just humans who have to walk in the restrictions of our fallen flesh. There is a process here, and we must humble ourselves to God's sovereignty, staying surrendered in faith and Truth. He will always bring you through miraculously for your good and for His ultimate plans upon this earth. He tells us in Romans 8:28 that as long as we continue to love Him, He is faithful to restore.

Another powerful revelation God shared with me is when Adam and Eve hid in the garden, and God asked them a fundamental question. Two things: The first thing to ponder is, what if God was giving Adam and Eve an opportunity to repent and come right back into their identity in Him by asking them the question, "Who told you you were naked?" As in, why do you believe that lie? God already knew where they were and all that had happened in the garden that day. He is God! So why ask them that question?

Can you imagine if they would have repented right then and there and believed what their almighty, loving Father God was asking them? Perhaps they could have come right back into divine standing with God, but instead, they decided to partner with the spirits that came in from eating off the tree of knowledge: shame, guilt, fear, and now the pride from the flesh. These all come from the body's flesh and this fallen world system. Adam and Eve partnered with that instead of what they were born into, which was God's pure love.

This is something to remember. Whenever the enemy comes in to tell us that we are not healed or delivered, we must choose not to partner with that lie but to partner with God and every bit of what God has said! We must continue to seek out what He is saying to us and how He is leading us through whatever journey we encounter. Jesus is the Last Adam, and He took every curse that came upon Adam, the first man, who fell in that garden when He did what he did on that cross!

The other part of my revelation to this question, "Who told you you were naked?" is to be very aware of what people are telling you. Again, what voices are you listening to? Throughout my Christian walk, I have listened to too many voices, even Christian mentors who have led me astray and away from my true calling by trying to keep me in a box. Learning how to hear and recognize the voice of our Heavenly Father, Jesus, and Holy Spirit is vital. When someone tells us something, whether it's a prophetic word or some other thing, we must always bring it before the Lord in prayer to ask Him what he says. The Holy Spirit will always lead us into all truth (John 16:13), and He will always confirm if it is from Him (2 Corinthians 13:1, Deuteronomy 19:15).

There was a time when I was struggling with all that I felt God was calling me into because I had a religious spirit over me telling me otherwise. God woke me up one night a year before I had this vision. I heard a loud voice inside my head asking me this exact question, "Kristin, who told you you were naked?" Meaning, God was asking me, did I tell you that? He lovingly reprimanded me and brought me into great truth for His plans for my life, not what man sees for me but what God has predestined for me (Ephesians 1:5,11,18).

APPLYING WISDOM TO YOUR DAILY LIFE

Holy Spirit,

I pray that you lead me and guide me into your truth! Open my eyes and ears to the wicked things you want me to stay away from and help me to follow things that bring me closer to you. I do not want to be naive any longer to the schemes of the devil. I pray for you to equip me Lord. I am ready to embrace all that you have for me. I am your vessel, Lord. Train me up as I seek you, Here I am Lord. In Jesus' name I pray.

Scriptures to meditate on:

Ephesians 1:3-14: *"Praise be to the God and Father of our Lord Jesus Christ, who has blessed us in the heavenly realms with every spiritual blessing in Christ. For he chose us in him before the creation of the world to be holy and blameless in his sight. In love he predestined us for adoption to sonship through Jesus Christ, in accordance with his pleasure and will—to the praise of his glorious grace, which he has freely given us in the One he loves. In him we have redemption through his blood, the forgiveness of sins, in accordance with the riches of God's grace that he lavished on us. With all wisdom and understanding, he made known to us the mystery of his will according to his good pleasure, which he purposed in Christ, to be put into effect when the times reach their fulfillment—to bring unity to all things in heaven and on earth under Christ. In him we were also chosen, having been predestined according to the plan of him who works out everything in conformity with the purpose of his will, in order that we, who were the first to put our hope in Christ, might be for the praise of his glory. And you also were included in Christ when you heard the message of truth, the gospel of your salvation. When you believed, you were marked in him with a seal, the promised Holy Spirit, who is a deposit guaranteeing our inheritance until the redemption of those who are God's possession—to the praise of his glory."*

Matthew 6:19-24: *"Do not lay up for yourselves treasures on earth, where moth and rust destroy and where thieves break in and steal, but lay up for yourselves treasures in heaven, where neither moth nor rust destroys and where thieves do not break in and steal. For where your treasure is, there your heart will be also. The eye is the lamp of the body. So, if your eye is healthy, your whole body will be full of light, but if your eye is bad, your whole body will be full of darkness. If then the light in you is darkness, how great is the darkness! No one can serve two masters, for either he will hate the one and love the other, or he will be devoted to the one and despise the other. You cannot serve God and money."*

Reflection:

1. I want you to begin reading a proverb a day. The book of Proverbs carries a ton of wisdom on how to successfully live out our lives here on this earth. There are 31 proverbs, so you can read one each day of the month. For example, if today was the 5th of the month, you would read Proverbs 5.

2. After reading my vision, please take some time to write down any lies you have believed about yourself lately or even lies that may be trying to plague you. I know you have been doing this already since the first week, but I want you to pay attention to any lies that always seem to attack your mind, specifically coming against your identity in Christ and God's plan for you. Write down those attacking lies here:

____

____

____

____

____

____

____

____

____

3. Once you begin recognizing these lies, I want you to remind the devil and yourself that God has not told you those things, so you will no longer be partnering with those lies! Write down the words that offset those lies over your life here and declare this out loud by faith in Jesus Name:

____

____

____

____

____

____

____

____

____

Declaration:

I am a (daughter or son) of the most high God. I am loved dearly by my heavenly Father, my beloved Jesus Christ, and my confidant Holy Spirit! I am the head and not the tail. I am above and not beneath. I trust what the Word of God says about me and the plans that God has upon my life. I am wise about seeing the schemes of the devil because I am led by Jesus' precious and powerful Holy Spirit and I am obedient to my King Jesus! Amen!

5 Nothing but Jesus

Intimacy with Jesus is essential to living your life to the fullest and walking in freedom here on this earth. We must spend time with Jesus daily and habitually get into our secret place with Him. This means getting alone with God without distractions and learning about who He is through revelation with the Holy Spirit through His Word. Throughout my walk as a Christian, I have been very misled, thinking that God was against me, as well as not fully believing who I was in Christ. I share this because as I look at the body of Christ right now, I see this very thing. There is probably a small percentage of Christians actually living out their destiny knowing who they are in Christ Jesus, solely depending upon their intimacy with him daily.

This is not to throw out judgments but to point out that life is busy, and people have become extremely distracted. I have seasons of this very thing, and God convicts me of this constantly, but we must be obedient when this conviction comes. Now is the time to get intimate with our King Jesus! He is giving strategic plans right now and pouring out His love upon those who are seeking His face and His ways.

God showed me the significance of this vision and told me that I have a mandate to help raise the Bride of Christ in these times. This is what the Bride of Christ needs. We need this intimate connection with Jesus and His Word. Remember that Jesus is the Word! We cannot separate the two. I needed to allow this intimacy to happen by spending time with Jesus and in His Word to help lead others into this powerful relationship that was destined before time.

We must have this intimate relationship with Jesus. This is the number one key to breakthroughs in our lives as Christians, especially now and in the future. We live in dire times, and it will only get darker so we, as the Bride, can shine brighter. We must know our identity in Christ and what our role should be as His beloved Bride.

Take a few minutes to allow the Holy Spirit to show you anything else He may want to show you. Trust Him to take you deeper if there is more that He wants to reveal to you. I recommend that you read through this vision again and take some time to write down any new revelations that God may show you. I encourage you to do this repeatedly until you get the powerful revelation that we no longer need to be tied down to any area of our flesh or this world! Once we are entirely in Christ, we can die to our flesh and our worldly desires!

This is not about working your way into intimacy but about hungering for intimate time with Jesus every day. We must choose this! At first, yes, it is about being obedient to spend time in the Word, worship, and prayer. Why? Because this is where we begin crucifying our flesh and coming into truth, which sets us free. It will become a natural hunger because you have learned how to feed your spirit instead of your flesh! It is a choice to crucify your flesh daily, but we have the power to overcome it because Jesus did, and He now lives inside of us. He will guide you if you let Him!

However, I must point out that this is all done with balance and the timing of God's sovereign will for our lives. The attacks over our flesh come from the fall of this evil world and our enemy. God only allows things to come upon our flesh to train us to get through it and overcome it. Study out the life of Job. Either way, we win. God promises restoration, and if we die here suffering on this earth, let it be a testimonial before you take your last dying breath. Do not allow the defeat of the flesh to take over your mind, but rise above it and consider it all joy as the Bible tells us to do. Suffering is a privilege because it brings us to the deepest place of trust and a deeper relationship with Jesus. Until one goes through such suffering, it is hard to understand it this way.

I want to share another recent vision with Jesus during a very dark time. I was going through a time when it looked like I had no way out, and I felt incredibly defeated. All the familiar spirits were trying to creep back in and torment me from my childhood and past, but then Jesus intervened. I was being haunted by wicked night terrors. I could literally feel demons in my room again at night, just as I used to suffer through fifteen years before this when I was first saved. I share this because the enemy likes to use patterns and old tricks to spiral us down into unbelief. He will always try to bring us back into the bondage where he once had us.

Over the years, I have grown, and I can now spot the devil's wicked schemes and not allow myself to fall into the temptations of being overthrown by defeat anymore. During this time, I decided to fast and pray for three days. I drank only water. There is divine power when we fast because it makes our flesh bow to the Spirit, and God shows up every time I do this. I will never forget this particular vision's impact and hope it inspires some of you who have gone through intense suffering.

This vision began with a King's chair before me, and I saw Jesus appear. He was bruised and bloody and almost unrecognizable, but He then allowed me to see even more suffering that He was going to have to endure. It was interesting because I could see his face, which I had never seen in a vision before. Looking upon the face of Jesus represents coming into His presence. I found this significant because this must happen for the Bride to arise in this time. It is all about being in the presence of Jesus. This is where deep wounds get healed, and freedom starts happening.

Jesus began limping over to this Kingly chair, and I then saw the crown of thorns beaten into His skull and the blood running down His face. He wanted me to see this in action to remind me that the battle is truly in our minds. If the enemy can get you to partner with evil thoughts, they can manifest. I knew Jesus told me to get my mind right and stop allowing the enemy in. Then, He did something that deeply impacted me. He barely got the words out, but He asked for me to come and sit on His lap. I remember thinking, no way, I will hurt you, but He insisted. Right before I got into his lap, I became a little girl, probably three or four years old. This was such a beautiful encounter of me sitting on my Papa's lap, fully trusting Him as a good Father, and He just held me and wept with me.

This vision was so incredibly real that I could literally feel His cold, wet, torn flesh against my hot skin! It was the saddest yet most beautiful place, which is difficult to explain, but what came next made sense as to why I felt the beauty in it all. He told me this, and I will never forget it. He said, "Kristin, very few people will ever get this close to me because they are unwilling to suffer for my sake even though I told them they would. I am proud of you, my beloved; I will never leave nor forsake you. Stay this close to Me always."

I was highly emotional after this encounter, and it hit me deeper than anything else. Deeper than my last vision of becoming one with Jesus. I know God allowed me to have this encounter because I needed encouragement for how much suffering I have been through. I wanted to give up on my Christian walk during this time. In sharing this, I hope it will encourage those of you who have suffered so much that, at times, it feels too difficult to go on. If you are suffering from physical ailments, or it feels like all hell has broken loose against you, be encouraged!

Having this mindset will bring you closer to Jesus than ever before. However, it is our free will to look at suffering as a privilege and not through the lens of a victim mentality. I have suffered, and I am even suffering through health conditions right now as I am writing this, but I am learning a great deal through my pain. I am also learning that every time I suffer, I desperately run to deeper intimacy with Jesus because He has the answers and will guide me through every time. Know that God is good, and know that Jesus is for you! This will get you through the darkest times here on this earth and will guide you powerfully home to be with your King for eternity.

APPLYING WISDOM TO YOUR DAILY LIFE

Prayer for the day:

Jesus,

Thank You for all You did on that cross so I can have eternal life with You. Help me to remember that this is the primary reason You suffered for me. It is difficult for me to fathom the degree of suffering that You had to endure. Remind me when I go through suffering that You know exactly what it is like and help me to realize that it is always for a greater purpose. I know this life is not my own, so I surrender it again to You. I trust you Lord. Help me get a deep revelation that it is an honor to suffer for You for I know that when I do suffer, it always draws me closer to you.

Scriptures to meditate on:

Galatians 5:24-26: *"And those who are Christ's have crucified the flesh with its passions and desires. If we live in the Spirit, let us also walk in the Spirit. Let us not become conceited, provoking one another, envying one another."*

Philippians 1:29: *"For you have been given not only the privilege of trusting in Christ but also the privilege of suffering for him."*

Psalm 105:1-4: *"Give praise to the Lord, proclaim his name; make known among the nations what he has done. Sing to him, sing praise to him; tell of all his wonderful acts. Glory in his holy name; let the hearts of those who seek the Lord rejoice. Look to the Lord and his strength; seek his face always."*

Acts 13:3: *"Then after fasting and praying they laid their hands on them and sent them off."*

Luke 2:37: *"And then as a widow until she was eighty-four. She did not depart from the temple, worshiping with fasting and prayer night and day."*

Reflection:

1. Write out any deep, dark secrets that you may still have. Get them into the light by writing them down. Write out any deep insecurities or even any anger that you may be harboring towards the Lord because of things that you have had to suffer through. (Be vulnerable and honest here. This is between you and God):

____

____

____

____

____

____

____

____

____

____

____

2. Write down any idols you know you are putting before the Lord. These could be family members, TV, books, social media, or whatever the Lord convicts you of. This is important to do because all of these things can be stumbling blocks in our spiritual and physical lives. Be honest with yourself and Jesus. He already knows them, but He longs for you to invite Him into these with you because He will not override your will but wants to set you free.

____

____

____

____

____

____

____

____

____

____

____

3. Now I want you to re-write all of the things from question 1 & 2 on a separate piece of paper. Take time with Jesus, Father God, and Holy Spirit. When you feel that you are fully ready to release everything you have written down, I want you to burn them in a fire. Set a special time aside to do this. This is between you and God. You are prophetically declaring that you trust Jesus and are making him Lord to lead you, guide you, and keep you in every way, shape, and form. That you are no longer bound by these things of your past. It is time to release them!

4. Lastly, if you do not fast regularly, I want you to begin implementing fasting. You should start small. It could be skipping one meal a day in the beginning or only drinking smoothies or soup for a day, and then you can work your way up to not eating for an entire day. Remember that the whole point of fasting food is to feast on God and His word. So fasting should be intentional. Jesus told us that some deliverances only happen by fasting, which is essential. Fasting helps us crucify our flesh and teaches us how to feed our Born Again Spirit more. Pray into this for God's leading.

Key #7: Fast Regularly

It is obviously good to be obedient whenever the Lord calls you into a fast. However, I have found that fasting regularly helps me to be incredibly sensitive to the Holy Spirit's leading at all times. It has been during my times of fasting and in complete despair that I have also had the most powerful encounters with Jesus. I'd like you to begin fasting one day every week or at least a few days a month. This will help you crucify your flesh and train your soul and body to align with the Holy Spirit's leadership. This will increase your intimacy with Jesus like nothing else can because you begin to deny your soul and your flesh of its desires. You will begin to hear God and discern His voice more clearly. He will reveal intimate secrets during this time.

Be aware, though, that it can take up to the last minute of your fast when you feel the breakthrough, and sometimes you may not get anything the first few times you fast. At least, this is how it usually happens to me. I share this not because God is the same with everyone but just in case it does happen like this. I don't want you to get discouraged. Fasting is a process because you are learning to die to yourself. It is challenging but rewarding once you begin doing this regularly. You are teaching yourself how to overcome your flesh and soul by submitting to the ways of the Holy Spirit. If Jesus had to fast, then we should fast.

I highly recommend fasting food when you fast, and you can always start off slow. It may be skipping dinner one night to spend time with Jesus or breakfast or lunch. Then you work up to an entire day and two to three days. This has radically changed my life and is the quickest way to your deliverance. If you are ever in a place where you have to make a serious decision or cannot get a breakthrough in your life, I highly recommend fasting. Fasting will always bring clarity and peace. I speak this from experience.

Another way to fast, in addition to fasting food, is to fast your time. Maybe you give up watching Netflix or scrolling on social media for one week. Every time you get bored, you begin reading God's Word, praying, and worshiping instead of running to the things that your mind (soul) is hungering for. This will help you develop healthy habits for your Christian walk.

Fasting has been challenging for me to do, and I find myself still battling at times, which is normal until we leave this earth. However, I know there is power when we truly get into the practice of dying to our flesh and the desires of this world. This has an incredible impact on your life! It will help you grow in discernment and how to love people like Jesus. You will begin to see things through the eyes and heart of Jesus instead of your own, and you will start to lean on His understanding. This is life-changing!

When we crucify our flesh, we help ourselves stand up against the spirits that have to do with the flesh, which come from the fall of man! This becomes a potent tool! Fasting has given me great insight and profound revelation into the spirits trying to come against me and stop the God-given call upon my life! This is available for you to tap into as well if you haven't been doing so already. Fasting will change your life.

Declaration:

I declare that Jesus Christ is Lord over every area of my life. I crucify my flesh today, and I know the Holy Spirit will help me do this from this day forward! I have released the strongholds from my past, and I have victory over every area of my life because I have Jesus Christ inside me! I remind every demonic entity that they have no legal right because I have confessed everything before my Lord and Savior. You cannot stay when I have repented and where the blood of Jesus resides. I am bought and paid for by the blood of the Lamb! I am letting go of any and all unforgiveness and bitterness within my heart daily, and I am releasing everything my Lord leads me to release daily. I command any spirit that rises against the Blood of Jesus Christ to leave me now in Jesus' name! I am delivered and set free!

WEEK 4

Jesus Holds Every Key That We Need

1 Know the Word

I know I started the 1st chapter of this book with "What are you partnering with?" and the following few chapters about the importance of getting to know God. But we must remember first things first! You must believe that Jesus is the primary key to breaking you free and unlocking every door to your destiny in this life. We can not have victory or true deliverance without Jesus. He is the only true living God and the only way to reach Heaven. None of the keys I give you in this book will fully work without Jesus. I say "fully work" because the spirit realm is very real, and we can manifest things on our own by speaking and partnering with demonic spirits. This is why the new age works so well and is very deceiving.

Without truly knowing Jesus, we will only experience a small measure of all that God freely gives. We cannot pervert the Gospel or the Word of Jesus Christ by watering it down or bringing a mixture into it. The mixture I am talking about is by deliberately adding our selfish justifications to it or taking away from the Bible to fit our desires. Unfortunately, this is what the Bride of Christ has done. This may be tough for some of you to hear, but the Bride has become a prostitute, and God is calling his Bride back into a place of purity and sanctification right now. I know this may sound harsh, but we, as the Church, are called to have one Bridegroom only, and His name is Jesus!

In this chapter, I want to focus on the importance of knowing the Word of God. I believe Christians are not appropriately aligned because they are not reading the Bible daily or studying it. We cannot have a relationship with Jesus without knowing His word! John 1:1 clearly tells us that In the beginning, there was the Word. The word was with God, and the word was God. Jesus is the Word; you cannot claim to be a Christian and not read the Word of God, which is the Bible. You cannot claim to love Jesus or even know Him without reading and studying His Word. Please understand that I am not saying this to make you feel condemned but I am saying this to convict your heart. Studying His Word daily will bring us close to Jesus, help us grow, and walk in discernment.

We are living in the end times. We are literally in the 11th hour right now! How will we, as Christians, stay strong to lead the way? How can we stay in peace and be the vessel God needs us to be in these times if we are not rooted in the foundation of His word and are being led by Him? How can we truly know Him or His promises? How can we understand prophecy or recognize the times or the seasons? I'm telling you, we better wake up as Christians and start maturing. The chaos will only worsen, and we must be prepared for all that is coming!

I have had to train myself to be obedient in reading my Bible daily. Yes, it was difficult initially, but it finally became a hunger to want to know and understand God more. I can honestly say that I find something new every time I read the Bible. I have been reading my Bible diligently daily for almost 10 years and still get blown away. It confounds my mind most of the time and is exciting! So, I encourage you to get a new attitude about this if you struggle to read the Word of God.

I have heard and still hear too many Christians say that they don't read their Bible because they don't understand it. This is an excuse and a huge tactic of the enemy. This will draw you away from God and you will be deceived in these end times. If this seems harsh to you, I implore you to fast and pray and read God's Word to see what He shows you about this. I trust God on this and know He will lead you to the truth. I don't mean to sound rude, but again, God has told me I have a mandate to help raise His Bride in these End Times. We should not apologize for being obedient to God's Word. Ever. The Bride of Christ must purify herself and begin training. It is time to put on her military boots because we are in a war against the devil and his kingdom.

Being in God's Word daily and around other strong, mature followers of Christ will help us grow in the Word, and our Christian walks overall. This also allows us to produce fruit from the Holy Spirit because this is how we gain nutrients from the Vine. Jesus is our Vine, and when we stay connected to Him, we step into our destiny. How? Because once you start believing the Word of God, you start trusting God and everything in His Word. You start believing in all that He has put on the inside of you. The Word of God starts coming alive with the power of the Holy Spirit every time you read it!

Being in God's Word daily and getting to know God is one of the most powerful things we can do as Christians. Getting to read the Bible is a true honor! There is coming a time when America will not be able to have a Bible, so we better get to know His Word now and cherish it daily. I aim to get it so deep in my heart that I become His walking Word. This means I will live out a life that exemplifies the love of Jesus. Getting so much of God's Word into our minds is imperative because it begins to sear itself upon our hearts and lives. From this place, we can start walking out the true gospel.

The Word of God is the final say. What do I mean by this? We cannot go off our feelings or our own "truth." I have seen a lot of so-called Christians do this. We cannot say, "Well, I do not agree that abortion is murder." Abortion is killing a living being; this is murder. I want you to pray and look up what one of the Ten Commandments says. Thou shall not kill. Studies have shown, and God's word says that life begins at conception, which means God intended for that life to come about and live. God is Sovereign, and He will turn all things around for our good if we love Him.

Using this motto and choosing to live by it fully has saved my life on many occasions. When my husband and I went through a separation, I had to hold onto the Word of God and choose to humble myself and fight for my marriage and for my husband. Why? Because that is what God told me to do and confirmed it in His Word. When I was facing 31 years in Prison, I had to choose to trust in God's plan for my life. I spoke the promises of His Word over my life daily, and He showed up mightily. God will always confirm things by His Word, and He will always bless according to His Word. We must choose to live our lives according to what His Word says. If we say that Jesus is Lord, then we should all be doing this.

Again, we may fail daily, but we can quickly repent and start again. Reading and abiding in God's Word will cut off the selfishness of our flesh like nothing else can. If we keep our hearts soft towards God when we read His Word, it will convict us. It will sharpen us and help us to live a victorious Christian life. This is why it is imperative that we believe God's Word above all else. This has helped me gain victory in situations that I never thought I would get through. All by partnering with God's Word being true, and He has the ultimate and final say, I choose to trust Him. Amen.

APPLYING WISDOM TO YOUR DAILY LIFE

Prayer for the day:

Jesus,

Forgive me when I have not sought after Your Word first. I ask You to put a deep hunger within me to want to read Your Word first thing in the morning and then meditate on it all day long. I ask you Holy Spirit to open my eyes and my heart to receive the mysteries and powerful revelations that are in your Word. Help me to understand more in the areas where I doubt your goodness. Holy Spirit, help me to see the Father's love and goodness every time I read your Scripture. Thank you for your grace and your mercy upon my life. I love You Lord and I want to know You more intimately. I ask for a deeper relationship with You. As I seek you, I am humbly asking you to meet with me Lord. Show me your ways, In Jesus' name I pray.

Scriptures to meditate on:

John 17:17: *"Sanctify them by Your Truth. Your word is Truth."*

Hebrews 4:12: *"For the word of God is living and active, sharper than any two-edged sword, piercing to the division of soul and of spirit, of joints and of marrow, and discerning the thoughts and intentions of the heart."*

John 6:63: *"It is the Spirit who gives life; the flesh profits nothing. The words that I speak to you are spirit and they are life."*

2 Samuel 7:28: *"And now, O Lord God, You are God, and your words are true, and You have promised this goodness to your servant."*

Proverbs 30:5: *"Every word of God is pure; He is a shield to those who put their trust in Him."*

Psalm 119:160: *"The entirety of Your word is Truth, and every one of Your righteous judgments endures forever."*

Ephesians 1:13: *"In Him, you also trusted, after you heard the word of truth, the gospel of your salvation; in whom also having believed, you were sealed with the Holy Spirit of promise."*

Joshua 1:8: *"Keep this Book of the Law always on your lips; meditate on it day and night, so that you may be careful to do everything written in it. Then you will be prosperous and successful."*

Key #7 Trust God's Word; He Has The Final Say

Reflection:

1.1 Thessalonians 5:21 tells us to *"test all things; hold fast to what is good!"* I want to challenge you in this. Take time to look at some difficult situations in your life that you are facing right now. This could be something that you are specifically dealing with or perhaps you are praying for someone close to you:

____

____

____

____

____

____

____

____

Spend time with Holy Spirit and ask Him to show you what His word says about those situations. Then, ask Him what scriptures you should begin praying over those situations. This is important to be led by Holy Spirit and not out of any selfish desires. His spirit will always bring clarity, peace, and freedom. Then, I want you to write those Scriptures down and declare them out loud every day until you see that situation changed. Speak them out loud every morning and night if you have to, especially when any attacks start coming in to thwart your faith. Some situations may take weeks, others may take years. When you get the breakthrough, journal it, so you can always reflect on God's faithfulness. I'm telling you, this will build your faith in ways I cannot explain. You have to experience it for yourself. God is faithful, and He tells us in Isaiah 55:11 that His word will not return void. Write down the scriptures that He gives you over each situation:

____

____

____

____

____

____

____

____

____

____

2. If you are unsure how you should live your Christian life, look up what the Bible says about how Followers of Christ are supposed to live. Study the Gospels: Matthew, Mark, Luke, and John. Study the book of Acts. For example, if you are confused about abortion, look up what God says about killing a life in the Bible and ask Holy Spirit to give you a more profound revelation so you can then teach others. If you are having sex outside of marriage, look up what God says about fornication and make sure you ask God to show you His Heart on why He says these things. His Word is always for our protection. It is not to lord over you in a controlling or manipulative way. Another one is if you are unsure how to be a good friend, wife, or husband, look this up in the Bible and see what God says! My main point is that we must bring everything to the Word of God. The Word of God will offend our flesh. It will humble us if we allow it to help sharpen us and grow our faith more than anything in this world. God's Word has the final say! It is not about our opinion or what we may think or feel. Take time to write down whatever areas you need to be sharpened:

____

____

____

____

____

____

____

____

____

____

3. I want you to begin memorizing one Scripture per week. I am currently doing this and it is helping me immensely. If you have trouble remembering where the exact scripture is, this will benefit you. Starting today:

____

____

____

____

If you have trouble understanding the Bible, ask the Holy Spirit to give you revelation and understanding of His Word. If you are obedient in this every time you go to read it, I promise you, God will show up. We must take the first step and then be obedient. Then just watch all that God will do for you. I am walking proof. It also helps to join group Bible study groups if you can, to help sharpen one another along your walk with the Lord.

Declaration:

I Declare that I am a lover of God and His Word. His Word is true and has the final say in my life. I receive profound revelations weekly from my Heavenly Father. I set time aside to read and understand my Bible every day. I am growing in the Lord as I read His Word and spend time with my Triune God. His Word is a lamp unto my feet, guiding me down the right pathways. I trust Him and His Word above all else in my life.

2 Beware of Distractions

We must beware of distractions, especially when it comes to reading our Word because reading the Bible daily helps us stay connected to the Vine, guiding us in every situation we face. I still battle distractions when I have my bible time, so I have to be diligent and fierce about staying on track to read daily. Again, this is about training your flesh and soul (mind, will, and emotions) to align with your Spirit, which is the Holy Spirit's dwelling place. If you have made Jesus Lord over your life, then you have the Holy Spirit living on the inside of you.

In John chapter 15, Jesus talks explicitly about us being the branches and Him being the Vine. When we stay close to Him, we will bear much fruit. But when we do things without Him, we do nothing fruitful. In John 15:6, Jesus clearly says, *"If anyone does not abide in Me, he is cast out as a branch and is withered; and they gather them and throw them into the fire and they are burned."* It sounds harsh, but Jesus is expressing how important it is to stay connected to Him and that when we detach from Him, we can be cast out, withered away, and thrown into the fire because we are like dead branches without Him.

This happens when Christians fall away from God's Word and daily intimacy with King Jesus. It is a slow fade, but death to their spirit will eventually come. Their old man, which Jesus tells us to crucify daily, will begin to come alive again. Jesus says when we come to Him, we must be born again to become born of the Spirit. This means we must feed our spirit man more than our old fleshly man so we can be led by His Spirit instead of our flesh and soul (mind, will, & emotions).

John 3:3-8 says, *Jesus answered him, "Truly, truly, I say to you, unless one is born again he cannot see the kingdom of God." Nicodemus said to him, "How can a man be born when he is old? Can he enter a second time into his mother's womb and be born?" Jesus answered, "Truly, truly, I say to you, unless one is born of water and the Spirit, he cannot enter the kingdom of God. That which is born of the flesh is flesh, and that which is born of the Spirit is spirit. Do not marvel that I said to you, 'You must be born again. The wind blows where it wishes, and you hear its sound, but you do not know where it comes from or where it goes. So it is with everyone who is born of the Spirit."*

This Scripture is very powerful, and I encourage you to camp out here for a bit to truly grasp how real our spiritual life is! We must get this concept deep into our hearts; to do this, we must read our Bibles. We will see that we serve a supernatural God and that His Spirit lives in us once we are born again. I also encourage you to get water baptized if you have not done so already. It is a mighty act of faith when we do this. Something happens both in the flesh and in the spirit.

I have even witnessed several people who got delivered from demons once they received their water baptism. The water baptism is between you and the Lord, but it is an outward public declaration that you are giving your life over to live for Christ. It is no longer you who lives, but you are allowing Jesus and His spirit to take over. This becomes a loud statement that your old man is dead, buried under the water, and then arising, you become a new creation in Christ, identifying with his death and resurrection.

We must remember that Jesus was water baptized, and the most powerful thing happened when He did this. Scripture tells us that the heavens opened up, the Spirit of God came down, ascending like a dove, shining light upon him, and God spoke audibly that this was His beloved Son, in whom He is well pleased! Come on! If Jesus did it, then we need to do it!

Romans 6:6-16 says, "*Knowing this, that our old man was crucified with Him, that the body of sin might be done away with, that we should no longer be slaves of sin. For he who has died has been freed from sin. Now if we died with Christ, we believe that we shall also live with Him, knowing that Christ, having been raised from the dead, dies no more. Death no longer has dominion over Him. For the death that He died, He died to sin once for all; but the life that He lives, He lives to God. Likewise you also, reckon yourselves to be dead indeed to sin, but alive to God in Christ Jesus our Lord. Therefore do not let sin reign in your mortal body, that you should obey it in its lusts. And do not present your members as instruments of unrighteousness to sin, but present yourselves to God as being alive from the dead, and your members as instruments of righteousness to God. For sin shall not have dominion over you, for you are not under law but under grace. What then? Shall we sin because we are not under law but under grace? Certainly not! Do you not know that to whom you present yourselves slaves to obey, you are that one's slaves whom you obey, whether of sin leading to death, or of obedience leading to righteousness?"*

This Scripture is powerful because it says that we become cleansed in righteousness and born again in Christ once we let Him into our hearts and start living for Him. However, Scripture then clearly tells us that we must continue to be diligent in putting away the lusts of our flesh and presenting ourselves as holy instruments for God to use us here on this earth. How do we do this? By staying close to Jesus. By being in His Word daily, praying to Him and talking with Him, worshiping Him, and allowing Him to speak and lead us.

The Bible warns us about being diligent. 1 Peter 5:8 tells us to be sober-minded, watchful, and vigilant because your adversary, the devil, prowls around like a roaring lion, seeking someone to devour. If we do not know the Word and find out how to defeat the devil and all the tactics that he will throw at us, how will we get victory? The victory is Jesus, and Jesus is the Word of God! Jesus is present throughout every book of the Bible, including the Old Testament, which most people do not know. He is there. He has been there since the beginning of time with God and Holy Spirit.

The entire Old Testament reveals Jesus in types and foreshadows. This is a fantastic study that you may want to pursue! The Word is one of the most powerful things that we have here on this earth besides the Holy Spirit. When you invite Holy Spirit to help you read His Word, being diligent in this every day, you will begin to see amazing changes happen in your life.

<u>APPLYING WISDOM TO YOUR DAILY LIFE</u>

Prayer for the day:

Father God,
I ask your Holy Spirit to lead and guide me in this area of my life. Help me to become highly aware of any distractions that try to get between me and my time with You. Help me be vigilant as Your Word says to be, and give me the strength to follow through with this commitment to read Your Word daily. Please forgive me for not being diligent in this area of my life. And Lord, help me have a better understanding and deeper revelation as I read Your Word this season. Thank you, Lord, I trust You. In Jesus' name, I pray.

Scriptures to meditate on:

Ephesians 4:27: *"Give no opportunity to the devil."*

1 Corinthians 2:11: *"For who knows a person's thoughts except the spirit of that person, which is in him? So also no one comprehends the thoughts of God except the Spirit of God."*

Colossians 3:2: *"Set your mind on things above, not on earthly things."*

1 Corinthians 7:35: *"I am saying this for your own good, not to restrict you, but that you may live in a right way in undivided devotion to the Lord."*

Romans 12:2: *"Do not conform to the pattern of this world, but be transformed by the renewing of your mind. Then you will be able to test and approve what God's will is–his good, pleasing and perfect will."*

Psalm 86:11: *"Teach me your way, LORD, that I may rely on your faithfulness; give me an undivided heart, that I may fear your name."*

James 4:8: *"Come near to God and he will come near to you. Wash your hands, you sinners, and purify your hearts, you double-minded."*

1 Corinthians 10:13: *"No temptation has overtaken you except what is common to mankind. And God is faithful; he will not let you be tempted beyond what you can bear. But when you are tempted, he will also provide a way out so that you can endure it."*

Reflection:

1. I want you to have a set daily time dedicated to reading your Word and stick to this! I like to have my Bible time with Jesus first thing in the morning to set my mind right for my day and right before I sleep. I highly recommend you do this because it has significantly impacted my life. I like to read one Proverb first thing in the morning to help give me wisdom and set my mind on the ways of God for my day. I also choose a Book of the Bible to camp in for a week or month, depending on how long it is. I pray and journal what I read. This helps it sink into my mind and heart. I then like to read the Bible leisurely

at night before I go to bed to allow my mind to rest, getting His Word into my soul and feeding my spirit before I sleep. Write down your specific time here and stick to this daily:

____

____

2. You must set up guardrails around this time and not allow excuses to come in. If your time is first thing in the morning, set your alarm to get out of bed earlier than anyone else. Ensure you put a minimum time limit of 20 or 60 minutes. Whatever time you are dedicating, put up guardrails. This will help you get into a good habit of doing this and to become diligent. Put your phone away and make this a special time with you and the Lord to get to know Him through His Word. I highly recommend journaling as you meet with Him daily to remember and comprehend what the Lord showed you that day. How much time will you dedicate to reading His Word? Write this here and commit to it:

____

____

____

____

____

____

____

____

____

____

____

Declaration:

I diligently read my Bible every day and stay vigilant against all distractions. I am committed to getting to know my Heavenly Father, Jesus, and Holy Spirit more intimately. I love the Word of God and receive deeper revelation and understanding every week. As I read my Word, I am growing in every area of my Christian walk. Thank you, Lord Jesus, for guiding me and never leaving me or forsaking me.

3 The word produces Good Fruit

If you are a Christian, you should be producing good fruit. You should grow consistently in your walk with the Lord and see that you are getting pruned regularly and producing fruit little by little. The fruit I am talking about is the Fruit of the Holy Spirit. Galatians 5:22-23 says, *"But the fruit of the Spirit is love, joy, peace, patience, kindness, goodness, faithfulness, gentleness and self-control. Against such things, there is no law."*

I want you to be completely honest with yourself and humble yourself here to see if there are any areas that you know you need to work on. Do you find yourself losing your patience easily? Blowing up on people? Yelling in your car due to road rage? How about getting offended? Do you find yourself controlling or manipulating a situation? After reading today's chapter, please sit back for a few minutes to recognize these areas you may still struggle in. We all have areas that we struggle in. Know that we are in a process until the day we leave this earth, but it is good to keep an open heart here, allowing God to expose those areas. Here, we can dig in to find some possible strongholds and idols holding us back.

If you haven't seen much of this Fruit in Galatians 5:22-23 being produced in your life, I highly suggest you spend some time with God to find out where any blocks could be hiding. Wounds from our past create idols in our lives to hide behind. The main idols I tend to see the most when counseling and discipling people are "idols of self." These can be self-defense, self-reliance, or self-preservation. In addition, I have seen survival instincts and rebellion or defiance manifested. This is dangerous as a Christian because Jesus says we are to die to ourselves and follow Him.

However, most do not even know they are hiding behind these idols because, with time, the wounds sear their hearts, and they become blind to them. When we experience any type of trauma from our past and have had to fight for ourselves, this creates self-defense mechanisms to protect us from ever getting hurt again. Unfortunately, the idols we tend to hide behind reveal a hardened heart of pride.

There are differences between idols and strongholds. The Lord has shown me throughout my years of healing that idols are actually created from the strongholds that were built in our minds, usually from a young age. These strongholds become walls around our hearts due to past trauma, which creates extremely unhealthy thought patterns and belief systems.

We create idols unknowingly because we are usually running from the exact thing that God wants us to face. This is how the enemy works. When we aren't dealing with the exact root issues, the enemy will lure us to fend for ourselves and/or to exalt other things to run to instead of God. This is a dangerous place to live in because we end up living in pride and trying to control our lives. Pride can lead us further away from God.

Another example I want to share is this because I want you to recognize idols, strongholds, and roots. Think about this scenario: Someone grows up in an impoverished childhood, then as a way to escape the fear of never wanting to live in poverty again, they run to money and worldly success. The idol they run to is money, the spirit behind it is mammon, and the stronghold is fear of lack. The root is then fear, which actually stems from pride. Therefore, until this is broken, they will operate from a place of fear instead of love, staying bound, without even knowing that they are in bondage.

Once you begin reading and studying God's word, idols will start to crumble long before you realize you even have them. Idols do their best work when they are kept secret, but the crumbling starts when you start immersing yourself in Truth. Holy Spirit begins challenging you to start working on the production of His Fruit. All other unclean things in your life start to get exposed. Once you begin shining light on any idols through the Word of God, tiny cracks appear, and little pieces start breaking off. You begin humbling yourself to the will of God by reading His Word, and His Word becomes real. This is when idols get exposed, and strongholds start to tremble. The Word of God is sharper than any two-edged sword, and it begins to tear down the strongholds where your idols were first created due to the lack of ability to deal with poisonous roots.

I want to share a testimony from a close, precious friend of almost 30 years. She was a fully functioning alcoholic by the time she reached the age of 24, being able to put down 2 bottles of wine every night with no problem. She wasn't delivered from this until the age of 34. She dealt with this demon tormenting her for 10 years, but really, it came long before that. This was due to a generational curse and father wounds. I want to share this because it is compelling to hear about her journey, as it completely adheres to what I am sharing. This is her story about overcoming her addiction.

In 2012, my idols started crumbling as I read the Word and listened to sermons. Once I became more educated on His Word and had a more profound revelation about how it could be applied to my life, that's what caused my idols to start shaking. It wasn't until the Spring of 2017, though, that one of my most powerful idols of alcohol addiction took its most forceful blow.

I remember sitting in my living room, watching an episode of Joyce Meyer where she said, "I don't know who needs to hear this, but you're already healed; you just need to receive your healing." I felt the Spirit of the Lord whisper to me that this Word was for me. I had been praying for the Lord to set me free from alcohol for years!! YEARS. Ever since I became pregnant with my second daughter in 2011, I had earnestly prayed with intention about my drinking, but even before that, I prayed that I would stop. Years of prayer. Years of pleading. Years of, "God, I hate that I drink. I know it's terrible for me. I hate the way it controls me. Please, God. Set me free."

Years of, "God, why is it that in the morning I am motivated to never drink again, but then at 5 pm, all I want to do is pour myself a glass of wine? God, please help me. I don't understand!" And years of "God. Why do I do the things I don't want to do and don't do the things I DO want to do?" But that afternoon, I sat on my couch and felt the Lord whisper, "You're already healed. Just receive it." I didn't even know what that meant. I had no clue.

But from that moment forward, my prayers changed. I went from, please, God help me, to Thank you, God, for your healing! My prayers changed from "How God? How could I ever live my life without alcohol when it's all I have known for so long?" to "I don't know how you're going to do it, but I know you're going to do it." I finally began taking God at His Word, which means I began trusting what the Word of God said!

Three months (MONTHS - not years - months) of praying like that, and the day finally came when the Lord told me it was time. He told me that I had a choice. He would help me quit. He'd be there right beside me, and yes, I could quit… but I had to make the choice. I had to make the choice not to drink every day. The Lord filled me with faith and confidence in Him that day that I had never known before, and THAT was when the idol of alcohol fell and got crushed out of my life.

I wish I could adequately explain the overwhelming impression the Lord put in my heart that day. It was like I knew all along that it was within me to quit. It was like I had a supernatural ability to see and understand that drinking wasn't who I was. Therefore, it wasn't a part of me like I had thought all those years. It was like all my prayers culminated into that one day and poured out over me like a cleansing rush of the Holy Spirit, and somehow, I knew, at that moment, I could do it! I made the choice to not drink again, and just like that, I was supernaturally delivered from an addiction I had worked to acquire and then fought for almost 20 years. That day, at that moment, when I made a choice, I broke a bloodline curse that threatened to consume me and then my children after me.

To most, it appeared that one day, I just quit drinking, and yes, technically, it was that way. But I must say, I was miraculously delivered. It was so much more than just making the choice to quit drinking. It was so much more than that. So much deeper. The Lord had to do a work in my spirit by teaching me and leading me from His Word, and then it began to get deep into my soul, which is the mind, will, and emotions. It was then that I could finally understand HOW to pray with faith. Then and only then was He able to expose that idol of Alcohol within me. Once I began crucifying my pride, and entirely depending on Jesus, the idol fell, and I finally got delivered!

I absolutely love hearing her tell this story because I witnessed her struggle for all of those years, but then I witnessed her growth in the Lord, in His Word, and this miraculous deliverance! I love how she says she had to crucify her pride! This is such a huge key here! God will not override our will, so we must crucify our pride to let Him come in and do the work He needs to do! I also love how she said it was so much deeper than just choosing to quit. Yes, first, she had to make that choice to partner with that, but then she decided to partner with God's Word every day! So good! I shared this with you because the Word will literally begin to expose every bad rotting fruit within you. This is a good thing! We cannot get delivered until we recognize what the good fruit is and begin learning what God says is good and what He says is evil.

APPLYING WISDOM TO YOUR DAILY LIFE

Prayer for the day:

Father God,

I ask You to show me a deeper understanding of Your grace and mercy to help me fully break free. Jesus, I need You to hold me through this journey and to show me your power through Your Word. Show me that Your power to overcome resides on the inside of me. Teach me how to be led by You. I surrender my will for Your will, Lord. Holy Spirit, guide me and continue to teach me through this healing journey that I am on. I give You full permission to expose anything hidden within my heart that needs to come up and out. I want You to be first in my life. I want to learn how to run to You more than anything else in this World. Help any unbelief within me, Lord. In Jesus' name, I pray, Amen.

Scriptures to meditate on:

1 Corinthians 15:33: *"Do not be deceived: "Bad company ruins good morals."*

Exodus 20:3: *"Thou shalt have no other gods before me."*

Exodus 20:4: *"You shall not make for yourself an image in the form of anything in heaven above or on the earth beneath or in the waters below."* (Back in the old days, many people carved images of gods to worship and some still do to this day but our modern day idols can look different. These can be our phones, the TV, people, self worship, pornography, alcohol, drugs, etc).

1 Samuel 15:23: *"For rebellion is as the sin of witchcraft, And stubbornness is as iniquity and idolatry. Because you have rejected the word of the Lord, He also has rejected you from being king."*

Isaiah 30:1: *"Woe to the rebellious children,"* says the Lord, Who take counsel, but not of Me, And who devise plans, but not of My Spirit, That they may add sin to sin.

Reflection:

1. Maybe alcohol isn't your struggle, but I'm sure there is some other idol in your life that you run to instead of God. I want you to be fully transparent here with yourself and with God. Make a list of the things you tend to run to instead of God? This can be in several areas. I'll give examples: Do you run to people for your fulfillment and identity instead of God? (I mean this in an unhealthy way; it is good to have friends and fellowship). Do you run to cigarettes, weed, or your vape pen to calm you down? (Idol of addiction). Do you run to pills to heal your pain instead of God? (Idol of pharmakeia). Would you rather binge-watch Netflix or read books instead of spending time with God? (Idol of entertainment). Do you run to your husband, wife, or kids for fulfillment in your identity? (Idolatry of Family). Do you run to porn or masturbation for a release or possibly a stronghold from your past instead of God? (Idol of Pornia). List any idols that you are aware of here:

____

____

____

____

____

____

____

____

2. Please do not get into any condemnation when answering these questions. This should be a good conviction exercise and know that this is between you and the Lord. He may not convict you on everything right away, but that is OK! This is a process that will continue through the rest of your journey here on planet Earth, but it is essential to see that we are growing. It is vital that as we read His Word and worship Him daily, we begin to see the good fruits of His Spirit being produced in our lives. We should also start to see Idols fall, recognize strongholds, and pull up poisonous roots that have been holding us back for too long.

3. After you have your list of idols, it is time to begin making them fall. We cannot do this on our own, but you must first make the choice to do it. God will always meet us where we are; however, He is all about relationships. He needs our "yes" and our obedience. Here are some practical steps to help you break down idols and break free from strongholds in your life.

A. Say out loud, " I do not want this in my life anymore." Father, please forgive me when I have run to this instead of you. Help me to overcome this idol in my life. I renounce all agreement with "(whatever it is you struggle with)" Write these here:

____

____

____

____

____

____

____

____

B. Now, find Scriptures to help you overcome whatever Idol it is in your life and write these below. Meditate on God's goodness in His Word and declare them out loud daily. This will begin to sink in and there is life and death in the power of our tongue, so the more you declare God's Word, the more these strongholds will begin to crumble.

____

____

____

____

____

____

____

____

____

____

____

C. Set guardrails for yourself. Two examples: 1.) If you struggle with pornography, get a flip phone and only be on the computer when you have someone near you that can hold you accountable. 2.) If you struggle with alcohol, do not go to bars or hang around people who want to drink.

D. Find an accountability partner if you are not strong enough to do this with just you and the Lord. This is totally OK!

| *Write your new biblical statements here for you to read out loud over yourself daily:* |

____

____

____

____

____

____

____

____

____

____

____

____

____

____

____

____

____

____

____

____

Declaration:

I take the time to read my Bible and spend time with God daily. Jesus is the Word; therefore, the Word of God is my life source here on earth. I partner with God's Word over every fleshly desire and every demonic report. God's Word has the final say in my life, and I abide by His Word. I love the Word of God, and it fills my soul and body daily. I am being made new by God's Word every day. I produce good fruit because I allow God to prune me with his Word daily. Not only do I read the Word, but I also live it out!

4 Beware of Deception

There is a warning that I strongly feel to release in this season and until Jesus returns. The Bible warns us about all the hype and confusion that false prophets will bring in these End Times. I have witnessed and personally experienced this. However, God showed me the dangerous doors that can be opened to deception by running after someone's supposed anointing instead of the true Anointed One. When we do not have daily intimacy with Jesus, it can open a door for deception.

When we do not read the Bible daily and study the Word of God, it can lead to deception. If we do not allow Jesus to continually heal our hearts and show us our blind spots, we can open even more doors to being deceived. This is not to promote fear in any way but to become very aware and get prepared. This preparation includes having daily intimacy with Jesus by being in His Word, worship, and prayer. I have seen many people in the body of Christ running after the anointings in people instead of Jesus, who is the Anointed One. Jesus is our answer to everything.

I see this manipulation happening within the church. Truly anointed and highly gifted people operating with a spirit that comes from the angel of light instead of the Holy Spirit. The angel of light looks extremely similar to the Holy Spirit, but it is a counterfeit. I have witnessed this over the past seven years from several "Christians." They can even see clearly in the spirit and have accurate words of knowledge, but they were listening through open doors in their minds from the enemy instead of the Holy Spirit. God revealed this to me in many ways. He allowed us to experience this firsthand with one of the churches we attended.

This is happening today more than you might think within the church. There are charismatic witches as well as false prophets who manipulate people by using their prayers and prophetic words to gain control. This is possible because God tells us in Romans 11:29 that the gifts and callings are without repentance. There can be powerful anointings and gifts upon a person, but we must continuously test the fruit of their spirit. We learned a difficult lesson a few years back that I'd like to share with you. There was a woman in our church who seemed to love the Lord, even knew the Bible, and had right-on prophetic words. Within a few months of getting to know this woman, she had no place to live so my husband and I opened up our home to stay with us temporarily until she found a place.

I won't go into full detail, but God revealed that she was a charismatic witch towards the tail end of her stay with us, and she had bewitched us from the start! It's a long story, but the door we had opened to allow this was that our hearts were not fully healed from past hurts within the church, and we trusted our "connection" with her first instead of being patient to truly get to know her by testing her fruit.

When God revealed these things to us, it was an arduous journey to navigate because this woman began to feel us sensing other spirits within her, and she instantly moved out. It became so awkward in our own home for about one week, and then, within one day, she was gone. She did it without even telling us. It was the strangest thing. Within days, she blocked me and tried to turn some of our friends and the church leadership against us. Let me tell you, this is a very manipulative and dangerous spirit that is operating within Christian churches right now, and we must be aware of it. This spirit is all about division, even though it portrays itself as having a heart for strong unity. This is total deception!

A few months passed after she left, and I finally went to the church where we all went to warn the leaders there. It took a couple of months for me to do this because I needed to make sure my heart was in the right place to speak out of love and not hurt or anger. These leaders did listen and seemed concerned, but I don't think they heeded the severity of the warning I was giving because a year and a half later, she ended up leaving with about 20 people from that precious little church. It is sad that one woman had the power to do this. But when you know the demonic spirits that were operating behind that woman, then you understand.

You may be thinking, how did you not know? How did the leaders in that church not know? Well, this is the dangerous thing about deception. You usually don't know when you're being deceived when you're in the middle of deception. This is another reason it is good to be plugged into a church where you have strong believers who operate in humility and the gift of discernment. This will help you if you get entangled in something you shouldn't. I will say that the first time I met this woman, I had a weird gut feeling about not trusting her, but I went against it because she was so charismatic and "loving." It was like you were just drawn to her. This was a harsh lesson to learn, but I am glad to have gone through it because it helped me grow in my gift of discernment even more.

The primary thing we must look for in these End Times when people claim to be Christians is the Fruit of the Holy Spirit. Take time to get to know people and test their fruit. Jesus has been drilling this into my head and my heart these past five years. I don't care how nice or how anointed a person seems anymore. I am looking for fruit! The Bible tells us in Galatians 5:22-23 that we will know people by their fruit. How do you know someone? By the fruit of their spirit! I highly recommend studying the Fruits of the Spirit and how a Follower of Christ is supposed to live. Also, I would advise you to make sure the people you are getting close to are hungry for more of God's Word and know His Word, which means you must know the Word!

There were some things that this woman would say and do that I would sometimes question, but I didn't go after it to see if what she was saying was actually in the Bible until after the damage had already been done. This is why it is so important to know God's Word and study His Word daily so that we can recognize counterfeit spirits. God is not calling every individual to be a Bible scholar, but He calls us into a deeper relationship with Him daily as He leads us through His Word.

I will say, though, that this experience, along with a few others, made me dig into my Bible like never before. I had always studied my Bible, but this experience made me hunger to know more and understand where and how I had become so deceived. It also made me wonder how other people who seem to want to love God could be doing these horrible things to the Body of Christ. It was so profound that it still pushes me to dig deeper into His Word daily.

These are things to ask and look for when getting close to fellow Christians during these End Times. Number one, "Do they believe that the Bible is true and the only Word of God?" Number two, "Do the fruits of their Christian walk line up with the Fruit of the Holy Spirit in the Bible? We must be aware of deep wounds and the damage they can cause if not dealt with. If people are vulnerable enough to share some of their wounds with you, honor that and be patient to walk through those with them because we all have wounds. However, please pay attention to the areas where they say they are healed and how they got their healing. Pay attention to the Fruit of the Spirit they should have gained by going through that supposed healing process.

I came to realize that this woman had only been "saved" for a couple years when I met her. She gave indication that she had been walking with God for several years due to the things that she knew, including enticing heavenly knowledge. However, she didn't have a church she planted in when she supposedly got saved. I say supposedly, not to sound rude or judgmental, but I genuinely do not know how someone can truly be saved by Christ and do the things that she did.

In the beginning stages of her walk with Jesus, she didn't have seasoned Christians around her to help sharpen her and grow. Instead, she read many books and watched videos from pastors and several charismatic leaders. She was enamored by signs, miracles, and wonders. She was also reading several spiritual books, which opened the doors for witchcraft and divination, such as astral projection, to begin operating in her life.

I share this with you because if you are a new believer, you must get planted in a church with a strong Biblical foundation operating in the leading of the Holy Spirit. We must know the Word of God and have like-minded believers around us to sharpen us. I realize now that I should have gone directly to the head pastors of our church right away when this woman turned against us out of nowhere. The Bible tells us if we cannot sort out a dispute with a brother or sister in Christ on our own, then we bring it to the council within the church with two or three witnesses, as it says in Matthew 18:15-17. This holds us and the person who harmed us accountable, and the ultimate goal is to bring healing and unity if possible.

Instead, I became even more wounded by this woman with past "people/church hurt" because I allowed myself to get too close to her in a short amount of time, which was not wise! I needed to lick my wounds for a while before I could get my heart right. I was also under extreme attacks of witchcraft that I didn't fully know how to deal with. This included days of severe vertigo, sickness, and a double-mindedness like I've never experienced before.

She also carried a full-on assignment from the enemy to destroy my marriage! So it took some time, to say the least. However, if I had gone to the church right away to expose what had been happening to the leadership with her there, maybe it could've helped expose her. Or perhaps God could have used the leadership to help her turn from her wicked ways right then and there because she would have had to face us with the pastors. I sometimes wonder, but I have to release and trust that God has a plan in all of it.

We must be in a constant place of humility, allowing the Lord to expose any wounds within our hearts because if we hold onto offense, unforgiveness, or bitterness, this can blind us. It is here where the enemy blinds us the most, and deception happens. Unfortunately, my husband and I were blinded for a season when this woman got close to us. This was due to deep wounds that we hadn't fully healed from the season before by people within the Church. One could say it came around full circle and bit us hard. I am sharing this story with you out of deep conviction because God has been sharing his heart with me on this very subject of His wounded Bride. I often travail in the spirit during prayer because I feel the Lord's heart for His Bride on this.

The main reason this woman continues to do what she does is because she is deeply wounded but will not admit it. Deep wounds that sear the heart to build pride is a dangerous place to be. I still pray for her because I know God has a mighty call upon her life. Unfortunately, she has chosen to keep hardening her heart by setting firm boundaries, which have become massive walls for her to live behind in total deception. She is still her own "god." She hasn't allowed God to fully become her everything to heal her and lead her. Someone in your church may be coming to your mind, or someone who has hurt you in your past within the church. I want you to release them to the Lord if you haven't done so already and pray for them.

I share this story with you because we have a responsibility once we become a Christian to walk out what it actually looks like to be Christ like! This means we must get to know who Christ is! How do we do this? By studying His Word, spending intimate time with Him, and allowing Him to heal and guide us. We also do this by hanging out with other like-minded believers so they can sharpen us by calling us out on our blind spots. I know we are far from perfect, and we may fail daily, but I have learned that humility is one of the primary keys to doing this! Humility can be a powerful answer to overcome so many trials in this life. Walking in this can expose things within us and help us see people through the eyes of Jesus. Humility can diminish arguments quickly, and it always produces great fruit that lasts. Humility is the one thing that can promptly mature us as well.

APPLYING WISDOM TO YOUR DAILY LIFE

Lord Jesus,

I am so incredibly thankful for Your precious Holy Spirit. Help me to be sensitive to Your leading in my life. I want to get to know Your voice so well that I can instantly discern the voice of a stranger. Help me in this area, Lord. I give You full permission to continue to peel back layers within my heart. I know I have wounds that need to be healed once and for all. Help me uncover any blindspots I may have, and I ask you to expose any hidden wounds within my heart that I may not want to admit. I trust you to lead me into victory through every hardship. Thank You, Lord, Amen.

Scriptures to meditate on:

Matthew 24:4: *"And Jesus answered and said to them; "Take heed that no one deceives you."*

2 Timothy 3:13: *"Evil people and imposters will go on from bad to worse, deceiving and being deceived."*

Matthew 7:21-23: *"One that day, many will say to me, Lord Lord, did we not prophesy in your name and cast out demons in your name, and do many mighty works in your name? And then will I declare to them, I never knew you; depart from me, you workers of lawlessness."*

2 Timothy 3:1-5: *"But mark this: There will be terrible times in the last days. People will be lovers of themselves, lovers of money, boastful, proud, abusive, disobedient to their parents, ungrateful, unholy, without love, unforgiving, slanderous, without self-control, brutal, not lovers of the good, treacherous, rash, conceited, lovers of pleasure rather than lovers of God— having a form of godliness but denying its power. Have nothing to do with such people."*

1 Corinthians 2:11: *"For who knows a person's thoughts, except the spirit of that person, which is in him? So also no one comprehends the thoughts of God except the Spirit of God."*

Galatians 5:22-23: *"But the fruit of the Spirit is love, joy, peace, forbearance, kindness, goodness, faithfulness, gentleness and self-control. Against such things there is no law."*

Key #8 Learn To Discern

The Bible says we are to judge others by their fruit. We are living in the End Times, where many will be deceived, and the number will only increase. We must learn how to discern God's voice as well as other spirits. When judging these other spirits, we must be careful about our judgments towards others and ourselves. We must ensure the discernment we are sensing comes from a place of love, not fear. Fear can make us run from a person instead of staying to love them through their battle if God leads us to do so. Fear comes from the enemy, but God tells us that His perfect love casts out all fear. I always say that with God's love residing in us, we have the ability to love the "Hell" right out of people. However, we must keep our hearts right and stay humble so that God can use us as His vessel, His way. Be very quick to forgive and walk in love with others at all times. This will involve setting healthy boundaries, and we can do this when our hearts are right with God. God will always reveal things to you when you seek Him! Ask the Holy Spirit to teach you about His discernment; he will lead you into all Truth.

All of these steps will begin to strengthen your gift of discernment

1. Begin asking the Holy Spirit all day long to reveal things about yourself, other people around you, and situations in your life. This could be anything. If this is new to you, start with small exercises like listening for that still small voice that says, "You might want to move that glass because it could fall, or put your keys here so you will be able to find them." Most people think this is our conscience talking, but the Holy Spirit is our helper, and He deeply cares about even the littlest things in our lives. When you begin walking in obedience to these little things, you will start to trust Him for the bigger things.

2. I'll give you another example that may initially seem a little scary but is super fun! It's a prophetic activation! Ask the Holy Spirit to provide you with an opportunity to pray for someone and listen to His leading as He gently nudges you by highlighting a person to you. If this doesn't happen right away, be patient, but you must act on faith and trust Him. Begin praying silently for that person and ask the Holy Spirit to reveal something special about them to you.

You might hear something or see a picture in your mind. Whatever it is, be obedient to trust that you saw or heard something, even if it doesn't make sense. It is usually the very first thing we feel, hear, or see. If you keep waiting, this gives your mind time to battle with the Holy Spirit and can lead you astray. So, it is best to stick with the first impression you get. Then be bold and ask that person, saying, 'Hey, I'm learning to hear God's voice in new ways, and I feel like He may have something for you.' Can I share it with you? Share it if they say yes, and ask them if any of the things you told speak to them in any way. If they say, "Oh my goodness, yes," then ask if you can pray God's goodness over them. If they say no, that doesn't make any sense. Say, Okay, thank you for letting me practice hearing God's voice. 'Can I still pray for you? Then pray a simple blessing over that person. God may give you more as you pray. It is all about stepping out in faith.

Another way you can do this is to automatically tell them that you feel like the Lord is showing you something for them because He loves them and then pray His goodness over them. This is a fun prophetic activation that teaches you how to hear the voice of God. Just watch how God will surprise you. Trust Him in this! He loves you, and He loves other people!

God will always speak to us but we are the ones who are too busy to take the time to hear Him. It is about patience and leaning into the "awkward." I was so nervous when I first began doing this, and to this day, I still get nervous doing this exercise due to the fear of man, but if I know the truth that God is Love, then I know God will provide a way. I have been so wowed by the accuracy at times of what God has given to me for people, but I also had to put my faith into practice. Humble yourself and trust your Heavenly Father to guide you.

3. I would like you to begin praying about big decisions if you aren't already doing so and wait to make a move until you hear an answer from God. If you are a new believer in Christ and do not receive a reply by the time you need it, then I firmly believe in going forth in whichever direction

brings you the most peace and follows God's Word. God tells us to follow after the peace that surpasses our understanding. It may not make sense, but you will still feel peace. I do want to say, though, that God will speak. As mature Christians, we should be hearing God's voice regularly. We need to take the time to pray, fast, seek out His Word, and be patient until we receive an answer. Pay attention to the signs and always ask God for direction along the way. We must remember that as long as we keep our hearts soft and right towards God, we cannot miss Him. He will always guide us and bring us into our destiny when we stay humble, allowing Him to lead. This is the goodness of the God we serve as Christians.

4. Be aware of becoming over-spiritual. I firmly believe in inviting Jesus into everything I do and giving thanks all day. However, we must use common sense. There is a balance and order in everything that God does, and He will help us stay balanced. I do not need to ask God what I am supposed to wear or if I am supposed to brush my teeth and shower for the day. I mention this because I have witnessed people get way off course in this area. Don't get me wrong, God speaks to many of us differently. He could tell you to wear something for a particular day, but we must be aware of not becoming double-minded about every little detail. This could lead to living in fear that we will not do the right thing. This is definitely an imbalance, and we must be on guard. The enemy loves to distract people with this, especially when they are learning to hear God's voice. We must align what we feel and do with the Scriptures. If it seems off, it probably is. God is a Loving Father who will always guide us in Truth! He is a God of order and divine balance. His Holy Spirit will guide you as you become sensitive to His leading.

5. Start paying more attention to your "gut feelings." This is a precious gift that God gives every human being, but once you are born again, this begins to accelerate. When you feel this, ask the Holy Spirit why you feel that specific way, then abide in whatever He leads you to do. Then, wait and see what happens. Nine out of ten times, I have realized that when I had a gut feeling about something, it was usually right, and I see that it was God trying to warn me and protect me in some way.

6. God's voice is usually small and gentle. I will say 90% of the time, I have felt like, "Hmmm, was that me or you, God?" But I now know that if I hear a quick thought that aligns with God's love, the Bible, and has nothing to do with selfish ambition, I quickly accept it and then abide. There have only been two times when I heard a loud "Stop" from God, and it was instantly for my protection. Most of the time, I have found His Voice to be still and gentle, giving us free will to listen to His guidance. Keep this in mind when practicing how to hear His voice.

Declaration:

I am healing because I am learning to walk intimately with my King Jesus. As I get closer to the Lord and obey His leadings, I hear His voice clearly. I can sense things in the atmosphere when His Spirit is moving and when things are not of His spirit because His word tells me I will know his voice. In John 10:27-30, Jesus says, *"My sheep listen to my voice; I know them, and they follow me. I give them eternal life, and they shall never perish; no one will snatch them out of my hand. My Father, who has given them to me, is greater than all; no one can snatch them out of my Father's hand. I and the Father are one."* Therefore, *My God will protect and guide me, for I am His!*

5 Make the Decision

I have a bold question for you to ponder. Do you believe that Jesus took every sickness, disease, and sin upon that cross? This means that Jesus took it all, every sin from today, from our past, and throughout our entire bloodlines all the way back to Adam. It was prophesied throughout the entire Old Testament that Jesus would come and do this exact thing for us one day, and it was confirmed in Matthew 8:17, as well as several other Scriptures throughout the New Testament.

Isaiah 53:4-9 *"Surely our griefs He Himself bore, And our sorrows He carried; Yet we ourselves esteemed Him stricken, smitten of God, and afflicted. But He was pierced through for our transgressions, He was crushed for our iniquities; The chastening for our well-being fell upon Him, And by His scourging we are healed. All of us like sheep have gone astray, Each of us has turned to his own way; But the Lord has caused the iniquity of us all to fall on Him."*

Matthew 8:17 *"This was to fulfill what was spoken through the prophet Isaiah: "He took up our infirmities and bore our diseases."*

We must get this truth so deep into our hearts and ask God for more profound revelation because it is here and only here when deliverance comes. We must believe that Jesus is our Deliverer. It is only by Him that true freedom comes. We must choose to believe that His Word is true no matter what our circumstances look like. I do not have it all figured out by any means, but the closer I come to Jesus in my daily relationship with Him, He reminds me of this fact constantly because He wants me to know how much He loves me and how much power resides in me through Him!

Why? Because He lives in me! And if you are a Born Again Believer in Christ, He lives in you too! We must learn to walk in a relationship of true intimacy with God because it is from this place where His grace, peace, and abundance flow into every area of our lives. Mentally, spiritually, and physically.

I need to ask you another bold question. Can you honestly say that Jesus is your everything? I know we worked on recognizing idols in an earlier chapter, but let the Holy Spirit do even deeper work here in this chapter. Does Jesus come before your spouse? Your friends? Your children? Your career? Your ministry? Your anointing? Do you want Him more than you want your healing or your breakthrough? I ask this not to condemn you but to check your heart to see if He comes first because this is where the power lies.

Jesus must become your everything! This is a process because we must learn to crucify our flesh and rewire our minds. This is our definitive answer to living this life in freedom. So, here's a question for you to constantly ponder: If you were stripped of everyone you love, every comfort, every freedom, but still had Jesus, could you be joyful and content? I know this may seem intense, but this is who God is raising up in these End Times, and He needs people to get to this place before He can powerfully use them for all that is coming. I believe Jesus is preparing His Bride at this time. He is stripping away the idols in our lives; however, it is up to us to allow Him to take them from us for good.

It is coming to a place of total surrender, and He is sharpening those who seek Him in this way. Sometimes, sharpening can be painful, but when we embrace it, we come out stronger than ever before. I encourage you to embrace the revealing of all Jesus wants to reveal within you. God will always shine the light to expose any darkness hiding within our lives. Darkness cannot hide in the light!

God is shining His light upon the darkness worldwide right now. He is exposing all evil. However, a lot of Christians are still blind. End-time prophecies are coming forth, and some are not paying attention. If one is led by the Holy Spirit, one can easily see the darkness being exposed all over the media in America and throughout the world. However, this light is also being shown upon any darkness still hidden in His Sons and Daughters. God is exposing the deep things within our hearts because He wants us to come out of all deception and into deeper revelation.

We cannot do this if we do not have an intimate relationship with our King Jesus. Intimacy reveals weaknesses; it brings vulnerability and humility like nothing else can, and your identity in Christ grows beautifully from this place. If you haven't done so already, it is time to decide to put Jesus first. Make Him Lord over every area of your life, and watch how He begins to use you. I promise you, it will be the best decision you ever make here on this earth! He will guide you and He will fight for you! I encourage you to make the choice to trust God no matter what, and you will begin to see amazing fruit come forth in your life.

Beware: when we don't make this decision to fully trust Jesus, deception can enter

I want to shift momentarily and dig in a little more from yesterday's teaching because our gift of discernment will increase once we get closer to Jesus. I previously mentioned the other spirits operating within the Church and how we need to discern them. However, I want to reiterate that excitement about signs, miracles, and wonders is okay. We should get excited for God to show up and blow our minds because more is coming in these End Times. However, we must be careful when chasing after the power of the gifts instead of the Gift Giver. This is how many will be deceived in the End Times. We must know who Jesus is intimately!

I have researched many mighty men and women of faith, like Smith Wigglesworth, John G. Lake, Derek Prince, and Kathryn Kuhlman, to name a few. They all had one thing in common: being so in tune with the Holy Spirit by having true intimacy with Jesus. They knew how important it was to spend time with God in His Word and prayer. They also learned the power of humbling themselves. It was here where the power of God flowed through them. We cannot take shortcuts when it comes to this spiritual life. We must work to build our relationship with Jesus and learn how to flow with His Holy Spirit. I encourage you not to take any shortcuts because the journey with Jesus is truly exhilarating! Take one day at a time and allow Him to lead you. There are always amazing lessons that come from our obedience.

I want to emphasize this because God has shown me that the Church has been allowing other spirits into its lives besides the Holy Spirit due to taking shortcuts. They haven't allowed God to crush them in order to walk in their specific anointings correctly, so rebelliousness comes just as it did with Satan. There are several reasons the Church has been deceived, but the one spirit I want to talk about is Lucifer, the angel of light. This is an anti-Christ spirit that brings many other spirits, but we must be able to recognize the deception happening because more is coming. I know God has burdened my heart to talk about this very topic. If we get too hungry for a move of God without first having intimacy with God, knowing who He is, and knowing His Fruit, we can open ourselves up to being misled.

Lucifer means light bearer, and 2 Corinthians 11:14 clearly tells us that Satan disguises himself as an angel of light. This means Satan can come in, imitating the Holy Spirit, and can mislead several people if we are not fully equipped with Jesus's Word and knowing His Spirit intimately. It says in the Bible that Satan was one of the most beautiful and alluring angels in all of Heaven, so we must be careful of his alluring tactics here on this earth. 1 John 4:1 tells us to test every spirit to see whether it is from God, but most people do not test the spirits because they are experiencing exciting emotions when witnessing signs, miracles, and wonders.

I am mentioning this because in order to carry God's wisdom and discernment, we must spend time with God. This comes from being intimate with Jesus and recognizing spiritual gifts to walk in victory, as the entire 12th chapter of First Corinthians tells us. The more time we spend with Jesus and listen to His ways, the more purified we will become. This allows us to be His willing vessels here on earth.

To bring this week full circle, I will reiterate once more that Jesus is our primary key! Jesus and everything He did on earth and on the cross is the answer to complete freedom in every area of our lives. We cannot make up formulas trying to complicate the Gospel. We must be cautious when going back under the Law and trying to work for what Jesus already paid the price for. God has shown me that this is a twisting of the truth that only brings you deeper into a place of confinement by trying to work for your deliverance.

I am sharing this with you because I have gone down several paths trying to receive full healing in my body or get rid of thoughts from my past, and God constantly brings me back to the simple Gospel, which is His Love! Let me ask you this: How did you become a Christian? You just had to believe in what Jesus did on that cross and that he now has the power to live inside you through the Holy Spirit, right?

Well, it is the same for every other type of deliverance we need in this life! As we grow in faith through intimacy with Jesus, we will become more free and wise. We must stay humble, though, and remember that God is Sovereign. He has a time for everything, and in the waiting, we can embrace long-suffering, which brings patience, which then brings endurance, and endurance brings perseverance. This helps build the right kind of fruit in our lives. We must believe that God turns everything around for our good, no matter what we may face or have to walk through.

Galatians 3:22-25 *"But the Scripture declares that the whole world is a prisoner of sin, so that what was promised, being given through faith in Jesus Christ, might be given to those who believe. Before this faith came, we were held prisoners by the law, locked up until faith should be revealed. So the law was put in charge to lead us to Christ that we might be justified by faith. Now that faith has come, we are no longer under the law."*

There is a difference between "works" and obedience. Getting into a "works" mentality will only bring you into more bondage. What I mean by this is that no one can earn their way into heaven by working their way into a relationship with Jesus. It is a gift freely given once we receive Jesus as Lord. We technically become free from that moment in our spirit, but the soul and body still need deliverance. So it is here, when we start to get to know Jesus by reading His Word and worshiping Him, that we begin wanting to obey His every word because we start to get drawn by His love. Jesus came to conquer the law and sin that separated us from God. We will grow in every area of our lives as we are obedient to Him.

It is important to remember that we should not go back to living under the law of rules and regulations. Still, we must have a revelation of living under God's love through this powerful relationship with Jesus Christ. John 3:16 is an excellent representation of God's love for us. Galatians 5:1 says, *"It is for freedom that Christ has set us free. Stand firm, then, and do not let yourselves be burdened again by a yoke of slavery."* The entire book of Galatians gives great insight in how to walk in the freedom of Christ and to be aware of anything that tries to bring you back into bondage.

I will leave you with a couple questions to ponder. First, are there any areas in your life where you feel like you must work harder to get your deliverance? Take a few minutes to write these down in your journal. I want you to know that you are not alone if you are experiencing this. I used to get entangled in this trap all the time. However, I will give you some advice that will help you. It is crucial to remain completely surrendered in your everyday life. Most times in life when we feel any pressure, this is a good indication that what we are dealing with is from the enemy, not God.

Throughout my years of walking with Jesus, I have learned that He is never in a hurry and walks me through things peacefully. It is usually my wrong thoughts that cause anxiety. If something is taking much longer than we anticipated, He probably wants to grow us out of some unhealthy things that no longer need to be there. You see, you cannot put new wine into an old wine skin; it would burst. God's plan is never to burst us open and hurt us. He is gentle and will always lead us to the truth if we trust Him. I encourage you to embrace all that you are going through and keep trusting Jesus every step of the way. I have several chapters that will help you in this exact area along this journey, so do not get discouraged.

The second question I want you to ponder is this: Are you living in the freedom Christ died for you to have? I want you to write down your answers to specific situations you currently face and then ask the Lord to show you what lies you have been believing. Because it is the lies that we believe that keep us in bondage. Again, I want you to know that this is not to condemn you but only to reveal the traps that the enemy uses to hold us back in life. I hope that you will begin to experience breakthroughs each week by applying these keys to your daily routine and thought process.

APPLYING WISDOM TO YOUR DAILY LIFE

Prayer for the day:

Father God,

Please come in and show me who I am. Holy Spirit, I ask for your comfort and strength to truly begin putting You first in my life, and Jesus, I repent for not making You Lord over every single area in my life. I want to experience a genuine relationship with you as my Heavenly Father here on this earth, and I want to be sensitive to Your Precious Holy Spirit. Help me, Jesus, to understand Your Word with deeper revelation and power and grasp the fact that YOU live inside of me. Help me steward my body well as the temple of Your Holy Spirit. As I give my life and my time to You, God, I expect You to show me areas that no longer serve me and areas that You want to grow and stretch me in. I am Your living vessel, God. I am here on this earth to partner with You so we can work together towards Your divine purpose for my life. Lord, I know your plans for me are good, so I trust you to walk me through this life with Your power, peace, love, and discernment! I surrender my will for Yours. Have Your Way, God. In Jesus' Mighty Name, I pray.

Scriptures to meditate on:

2 Corinthians 4:6: *"For God, who said, "Light shall shine out of darkness," is the One who has shone in our hearts to give the Light of the knowledge of the glory of God in the face of Christ."*

Isaiah 12:2: *"Behold, God is my salvation; I will trust and I will not be afraid; for the Lord God is my strength and my song, and he has become my salvation!"*

Proverbs 3:5: *"Trust in the Lord with all your heart, and do not lean on your own understanding."*

Romans 8:28: *"And we know that for those who love God all things work together for good, for those who are called according to his purpose."*

Proverbs 3:6: *"In all your ways acknowledge him, and he will make straight your paths."*

James 4:8: *"Draw near to God and He will draw near to you!"*

Hebrews 11:6: *"And without faith it is impossible to please God, because anyone who comes to him must believe that he exists and that he rewards those who earnestly seek him."*

Reflection:

I know we are diving deep this week, and we even burned up some deep things that were hard to let go of last week, but is there anything else you need to release today? Each week will be precept upon precept, so pay attention to things that need to be released. You may find yourself doing this again and again, and this is OK! Some of this may seem repetitive, but our hearts are like an onion. They have several layers, and it can take time for each layer to be peeled and revealed. All these action steps in this book give you tools to live in freedom. It takes time, but freedom will come.

1. What areas in your life are you not fully surrendering to God?

____

____

____

____

____

____

____

____

Are there any idols that you are still putting before the Lord? This could be your children, your husband, your finances, social media, etc:

____

____

____

____

____

____

____

____

Let the Holy Spirit search your heart and continue to work on allowing God to crush any idols in your life by partnering with His word and His love to then walk it out in obedience to whatever it is that He is telling you to lay down. Humility, vulnerability, and obedience to the Lord will help you through every step of your journey until you leave this Earth!

2. Do you feel like you are in control or are you allowing Jesus to lead your life?

____

____

____

____

Have you surrendered the deepest places in your heart to Jesus? The places of deep shame, fear, or bitterness?

Are there any areas in your life where you are still not trusting him fully?

Are you in control or is Jesus? Take a few minutes to journal anything that may be revealed to you:

Declaration:

I fully trust Jesus in every area of my life! I trust His Word over every diagnosis the world tries to give me. I trust His love for me and that He will make way for me no matter what difficult situations may arise against me. Jesus made the ultimate sacrifice for me, which means I will crucify my flesh daily for Him so that I may be entirely led by him. I am God's beloved. He protects me. He strengthens me. He always helps me to persevere. I am His!

WEEK 5

Choose To Believe That God Is For You

1 Do you believe God is good?

This chapter will begin challenging you in every area of your life. There is one question I want you to honestly ask yourself, do you believe God is good? Most of us would say instantly, of course, God is good, just speaking out of what is the right thing to say, but I have learned that to fully thrive in this life, you must believe this. This is a crucial statement to hold onto and get into your heart in order to walk in complete freedom. You see, after going through all the hardships in my life since I was a child until now, this question has challenged me. I'm sure many of you can relate to this if your life has been dealt some difficult cards.

One of the most significant areas where the enemy holds us back is here. If we think God is against us how can we trust Him to move powerfully on our behalf or into all He has for us? Unfortunately, we cannot and it is here where you must be vulnerable and begin asking God to heal your heart. Ask Him to show you whenever you felt He was against you, and now ask Him to reveal to you what He was working on in your heart at that time. Also, ask the Holy Spirit to show you that He was actually right there with you. Now, take a moment to see how God ended up protecting you or allow Him to show you how He turned it around for your good and possibly the good of others.

It wasn't until this past year that I finally broke free from a lie that plagued me. This lie was that God was against me. This can be so subtle that you are not even aware that you are being held in bondage to this very thing. I mean that sometimes, in this Christian life, we can speak many good things but not allow them to truly get into the depths of our hearts and believe them. One of the famous lines from a believer is this: "God is good. . . all the time, and all the time, God is good!" This is the truth; however, have you learned how to partner with this so deeply in your heart that even when all hell comes against you, you still believe that God is good? This is where you trust His goodness and know that He will bring you through no matter what.

God has shown me that many Christians don't believe He is good, and this one thing is holding them back from so many wonderful things that God has in store for them. Make the choice today to lay down all offenses toward God. Make Him LORD over every area of your life and give Him access. There is an excellent tool in today's reflection homework to begin fully trusting God. Give Him the reins to everything in your life. As He leads, step out in faith, trusting Him to turn everything around for your good. Remember, no matter what it looks like, choose to trust Him and watch how He will turn it around for your good! This will begin building your trust in God even more. It is a heart condition that I am talking about here. You must surrender your will for His to start seeing and trusting in His goodness.

This may be challenging some of your minds and your hearts right now, and for some of you, you may say, "Amen!" Why? Because you have learned how to walk through the fire and still believe that God is good. However, if this challenges you, ask God to reveal any areas that need healing because He wants His children free from this bondage. He wants you to walk out your full potential in who He has created you to be. The time is now to arise and break free from this lie. God, your Heavenly Father, is for you and wants the absolute best for you! He created you to have intimate fellowship with Him. He knows you better than anyone else because He is your Creator. He knows all that He put inside of you. He knows the strength inside of you, and He knows all that you can and will walk through. However, you were not meant to walk this journey alone. Let your heavenly Father come in and hold your hand. Let Him carry you when you cannot carry yourself. He is a good Father who has amazing and wonderful things in store for you, but He needs your trust and your complete surrender.

APPLYING WISDOM TO YOUR DAILY LIFE

Prayer for the day:

Father God,

I humbly ask You to show me any areas in my heart where I believe lies about You. I ask You to show me Your goodness and how You have always been there for me, even when I didn't think You were. Help me to heal from any mother and father wounds that have made me put up walls within my heart against You. I ask You to start tearing down these walls once and for all, Lord. Please forgive any mistrust I have towards you and help me with any unbelief that is within me. I trust that Your ways are higher than mine. Help me see all the times when I couldn't see Your protection. In Jesus' Name, I pray.

Scriptures to meditate on:

Isaiah 41:10: *"Fear not, for I am with you; be not dismayed, for I am your God; I will strengthen you, I will help you, I will uphold you with my righteous right hand."*

Romans 8:38-39: *"For I am sure that neither death nor life, nor angels nor rulers, nor things present nor things to come, nor powers, nor height nor depth, nor anything else in all creation, will be able to separate us from the love of God in Christ Jesus our Lord."*

Hebrews 12:11: *"For the moment all discipline seems painful rather than pleasant, but later it yields the peaceful fruit of righteousness to those who have been trained by it."* (A good Father will always discipline His children to raise them in a healthy way)

Romans 5:8 *"But God shows his love for us in that while we were still sinners, Christ died for us."*

John 3:16-17 *"For God so loved the world, that he gave his only Son, that whoever believes in him should not perish but have eternal life. For God did not send his Son into the world to condemn the world, but in order that the world might be saved through him."*

Jeremiah 29:11: *"For I know the plans I have for you, declares the Lord, plans for welfare and not for evil, to give you a future and a hope."*

Key #10: Believe That God Is For You No Matter What!

If we partner with the truth that God is always for us, that means even when the attacks come, we can stand firm on this foundation that God will bring us through! God knows who He created us to be and He knows the end from the beginning, so don't you think it is vitally important to build trust and intimacy with Him? It is here, and only here, where we can truly learn how to discern, how to cope, how to fully heal, how to thrive through hardships, and so many other things while we live here on this earth. I know we have been working on this through the past weeks, but I encourage you to choose today that God is for you! Let this get so deep into your heart that you know, that you know, that God is good and He wants the best for you! When you begin walking this out, you will be able to overcome every obstacle the enemy throws at you, and you will start to step into your destiny.

1. You worked through some of this in week 3, but we are going deeper today. I want you to write down all the times when you may still feel like God was not there for you. Be extremely honest with yourself here. It is ok to feel mad at God when you think He wasn't there for you, especially when you do not understand why something so terrible had to happen to you or someone close to you. Do not feel bad about writing these down. God already knows your heart and wants you to be fully transparent here. You will probably begin to find some instances here that are keeping you from having intimacy with your Heavenly Father, your husband & closest friend, Jesus, or your precious leader and comforter, Holy Spirit:

____

____

____

____

____

____

____

____

____

____

____

____

2. Once you write these down, I want you to spend time in prayer and worship. This might take you hours or even weeks to get through, which is ok, but please do not skip this step! This is a crucial step I do with people during inner healing sessions, and this helps break people free immensely. Please spend an hour/day searching this out with Holy Spirit. During your worship & prayer time, I want you to ask Holy Spirit to show you where Jesus was during the exact situations you wrote down from step one. If you need to forgive anyone at this moment, do so. List them here now and release them:

____

____

____

____

____

____

Unforgiveness can block you from hearing God clearly, so make sure you release people daily if needed. Total forgiveness can take time, so be patient with your heart. Then, ask the Holy Spirit to fill your heart with anything that was stolen from your soul at that moment. Make a list of anything God shows you here. These could be words you hear, a scripture, or a vision. Write down whatever you hear, see, or feel from the Holy Spirit:

Stay in one situation until you feel healing and a release, then move on to the next if you feel ready. This has been one of the most powerful things that has helped me heal and see God's love for me even through all my abuse. Jesus showed me where He was in the exact rooms of the abuse that was happening to me. I saw Him weeping and how hard He was interceding for me. Ask Him to do the same for you. He will show you His goodness.

We serve a loving Father who wants you to know He is always there for us! It may not be in the way we think. We must keep in mind that God has to work through so many pieces of the puzzle down here on earth due to generational curses, demonic spirits, people's free will, our parent's inability to parent well, whatever, you name it. God Almighty is not a genie. He doesn't grant wishes or say, poof, you don't remember that trauma anymore, but with time, He heals. He protects us in His sovereign ways and uses our suffering for our good. His will is to help deliver others & bring people into Heaven through our healing!

3. Do not expect to get a complete understanding of all of your situations at once. It all depends on where you are in your healing process. God may show you something you disagree with; however, humble yourself and surrender to His sovereignty, knowing He is God and you are not. Choose to trust that His plan is good and that He will use everything you have been through for your good and to help others. This entire exercise is good to do about every three months because new wounds can develop. So, these simple steps will help you clear out any baggage trying to latch onto you. I call this my "spiritual oil change." It helps me keep my heart right and take inventory of what I need to release.

Declaration:

I declare that I am a child of the most high God and my God loves me more than I can even think or imagine. I serve a supernatural Father and have supernatural encounters with the Holy Spirit weekly because the God of the universe loves me and is for me. Oh, how humble this makes me and how thankful I am to serve a loving, merciful God who meets me where I am. I am loved, and I am healing because I know my God is for me. I know that if he has brought me to something challenging, He will powerfully bring me through it. I can overcome anything because Jesus overcame it all!

2 Ask For God's Perspective

It is essential to ask God to give you His eyes to see, even if He tells you it is not for you to understand yet. We must surrender to His will and know He is our good father who sees the end from the beginning. Getting on board with God's perspective is the most excellent tool we can use throughout this life. When we begin seeing life situations through God's eyes, everything changes. Our fears begin to fade away because we see the bigger picture and grasp His mighty Love.

When we invite God into our situations, we can have peace in every area of life. You must choose to trust God no matter what! You may be saying to yourself that this is easier said than done. I am here to tell you that there may be some truth in that. However, we can train our brains to do this, and there is divine power when we choose to trust God's will and His plan for our lives instead of trusting our own will and ways. When you do this, there can literally be a supernatural shift in the spirit from your mind into your heart.

We must come to this place where we fully surrender and lay down our will for God's will. This is hard, but I'm not going to lie to you. It is worth it! I am a walking testimony that this works, and I have witnessed so many others get instant freedom once they do this. Jesus tells us several times throughout Scripture that this is the way. There is a price and Jesus paid the ultimate price for us on that cross, so we can live forever in eternity with Him. To live a successful Christian life here on earth, we must lay down our lives and die to what we want because the reality is that we were bought with a price!

I want to encourage you that once you do this, you will begin to trust and see God's goodness because, at the right time, He will show you how He turned every bad situation around for your good. You will begin to trust that you can do all things through Christ, who gives you strength, endurance, perseverance, and peace while going through hell. If you want to begin living your best life now, this is a great strategy to start using every day. You must lay down your will for His will. He knows exactly why you are here on earth at this exact time, and He wants to partner with you to display His glory! It is truly the greatest gift we can receive to be a vessel for the great & almighty God of the universe!

I want to give you some examples from my life so you can apply them to every area of your life. I will talk about a small, less important example and some big ones to give you insight into keeping the proper perspective that God is good when the unexpected happens. On Thanksgiving day of 2020, God was training me in this. I had a tire blow out on a highway bridge, and it was in a construction area with only two lanes. This was incredibly nerve-racking, and I could've begun to go off on a spiral of negative emotions, saying, "Oh great, really?" "Why God?" Do you ever notice how we tend to blame God for many things that probably have nothing to do with Him?

In this instance, I chose to go with the perspective that, Ok, God, You are good, even though I was highly irritated because I was heading home from the grocery store to grab last-minute items for our Thanksgiving meal. But I began praising Him anyway within seconds of this happening. Then, within minutes, I had a couple of men stop off the side of the road who started helping me change my tire; one of the gentlemen even followed me to a gas station to make sure I could put air in my spare tire.

I share this small instance with you because our circumstances can begin changing rapidly when we choose the right perspective from the get-go. We begin tapping into frequencies from heaven and favor begins to pour out, especially when we immediately speak the Word over our situation. The Bible says that we have the mind of Christ once we become born again. 1 Corinthians 2:16 says, *"For who hath known the mind of the Lord, that he may instruct him? But we have the mind of Christ."* When we listen to the leading of the Holy Spirit, we can tap into every quality that Jesus represented because the Bible also says that we have Christ living within us!

I want to dwell here momentarily, elaborating on this very key. We must understand that God is good no matter what happens in this life! I want you to be encouraged that this is easy to do when you make Jesus Lord over every area of your life. When you do this, you will start choosing to allow Him to guide you and then be obedient when He leads. John 15:14 clearly states when you abide in Jesus, He abides in you. Galatians 2:20 says, *"I have been crucified with Christ. It is no longer I who live, but Christ who lives in me. And the life I now live in the flesh I live by faith in the Son of God, who loved me and gave himself for me."*

I want to elaborate on this Scripture for a moment because some people can take this out of context. It is not about dying for Christ because He is the one who died for us. But it is about dying to our will and how we want to live our lives as if we are in charge. God wants us to lay down our lives so we can then live for Him once we come to Him. Why? Because He is God, and again, He knows His plans and purposes for us. We won't know those plans until we surrender all to Him, including laying down our will for His will.

I know we dove into this question last week, but we have to ask ourselves every day when we are faced with difficult situations: Do we believe the Word of God is true? This can apply to so many areas of our lives. If we know who is living inside of us and we begin listening to His leadings, then I promise you, you will begin seeing amazing turnarounds in your life. With every trial you face, you will see how God brings you through powerfully every time.

We must choose to partner with this first, though; if we believe the Bible is true, then we can partner with the facts that God is Love, God is just, and God is good. This means He is good in every area of our lives, even through the devastating parts. Why? Because the Bible shows us there is a purpose in everything, and it is always for His glory. One larger example of keeping the perspective that God is always good that I want to share with you is something I've had to walk through recently.

I have experienced several gut-wrenching miscarriages. With my first miscarriage, I instantly partnered with fear, abandonment, and anger, which led me through a long process of hardening my heart unknowingly. With my second miscarriage, I chose to trust God in the bigger picture of things, trusting Him to walk me through the pain of enduring this again. I had to truly lay down my will and trust that He knows best no matter what. That His ways are higher than mine. It happened in the middle of the night, and I knew I was losing the baby because this was now my second time going through this.

I chose to allow God into the deep places that were hurting in my heart, screaming to ask Him why, but instead, I partnered with who my God is and that He is good. As I began my three-hour laboring process, I chose to praise Him, literally singing and crying simultaneously, allowing my heart to stay open this time and not become hard. It was truly a miracle that by doing this one act of trusting God, even though I didn't understand why I had to lose another baby, I was able to completely heal in two weeks.

I chose to invite Jesus into my healing process and asked Him to do it His way this time. My first miscarriage took me over a year to fully surrender all the hurt and trauma over my womb until I got pregnant again. Then, I invited him into my pain through my second one. I have endured even more miscarriages since these first two, but I still choose to trust that my God is good and that His timing is perfect.

I share this because there is power when we choose to say, "God, You are Sovereign, and I trust you." I may not understand, but I trust that you are good and that you are for me! This takes an immense amount of humbling, and it stripped me to the core, but every time I choose to do this through intense suffering, I find myself closer to Jesus than ever before. He sees the end from the beginning. We must surrender every area of ourselves to live in complete freedom, choosing to heal, grow, and be a light in other people's lives. It is rarely just for us when we go through suffering. It is usually because once we overcome the hard things with the Lord, we will then carry an anointing to help others get through their tough times.

I have recognized how God always uses me to encourage others because God has brought me through complex trials. I now choose to embrace suffering because I know it is always for me to grow somehow, some way. I choose to trust Him through the process by speaking His promises and truth about my situation, and then I know He will show up mightily in His timing. I can confidently say this because I have been walking this out and have seen his goodness too many times in my life now to stay mad at Him. I'm sure you feel this way too if you have learned how to do this, but for those of you who are new to trusting God like this, I pray for you to be encouraged. Once you begin to do this, you will start to see how God shows up for you time and time again. Our God will not fail!

<u>APPLYING WISDOM TO YOUR DAILY LIFE</u>

Prayer for the day:

Father God,

Forgive me for any hardness I may have in my heart towards You and others. Give me Your eyes to see and Your heart to feel, Lord. Help me to get out of my selfish ways and take time to ask You if there is anything you'd like me to say or do to a particular person whom I may be irritated with. Help me to humble myself and do Your will instead of wanting my own. Help me to see people through Your eyes with love. I want to mature in You, Lord. Help me to be sensitive to the leading of your Holy Spirit when there are things that You need me to be aware of. I am honored that You want to partner with me and be a blessing to others. Thank You for Your love, Your grace, and Your mercy. Amen.

Scriptures to meditate on:

Joshua 1:8-9: *"Keep this Book of the Law always on your lips; meditate on it day and night, so that you may be careful to do everything written in it. Then you will be prosperous and successful. Have I not commanded you? Be strong and courageous. Do not be afraid; do not be discouraged, for the Lord your God will be with you wherever you go."*

Psalm 145:9: *"The Lord is good to all, and all His tender mercies are over all His works."*

James 1:17: *"Every good gift and every perfect gift is from above, and comes down from the Father of lights, with whom there is no variation or shadow of turning."*

Psalm 27:13: *"I would have lost heart, unless I had believed that I would see the goodness of the Lord in the land of the living."*

Psalm 34:8: *"Oh, taste and see that the Lord is good; blessed is the man who trusts in Him!"*

Psalm 145:7: *"I will meditate on the glorious splendor of Your majesty, and on Your wondrous works. Men shall speak of the might of Your awesome acts, and I will declare Your greatness. They shall utter the memory of Your great goodness, and shall sing of Your righteousness."*

Reflection:

1. I want you to begin asking God for His eyes to see in every situation you face, the good and the bad. He will show you the bad or evil things, usually to teach you how to pray against them or help others break free. This will help you begin to see God's goodness in everything. Begin to thank Him for every situation you face, good or bad, because this will help you grow more than anything when you abide in Him.

2. I want you to begin doing this with people as well. This includes any offenses that arise towards other people. As soon as you get upset or feel offended, quickly ask the Holy Spirit to show you where the

area of your heart may need to be healed like we have been doing. But this time, I want you to ask the Lord for His eyes and heart to see and feel where that person may be coming from. A lot of times, people are rude because they are hurting. Hurting people hurt people. This convicts me deeply because of how many times we have allowed our flesh to get in the way and be rude back instead of being a blessing to that person who is probably wounded.

3. These exercises will help you grow in your Christian walk like nothing else. They will humble you and actually begin to heal you in many ways. Once you train yourself in these, you will start to look introspectively and grow in a fantastic level of God's compassion and love. This has radically changed my life!

Declaration:

I declare that I see people through the eyes of Jesus. I have His compassion and I carry His understanding for others. I am patient and kind even when things or people irritate me. I am humbled to see what areas in me still need healing so I can truly walk in love with others no matter what. This humility helps me to yield to what my Father in Heaven is saying instead of what I may be feeling. I can do all these things through Christ because I have the help of Holy Spirit, in Jesus' Name!

3 Trust the Process

I firmly believe that we only go through difficult times so we can grow and then help bring others through their difficult times and teach them how to live in complete freedom as well. You see, Paul said we would suffer upon this earth, but we should consider it all joy because there is a greater purpose in all of it. We must choose to partner with the perspective that God is good! No matter what we are going through. We must know that God will powerfully bring us through every situation if we allow Him to do so. The choice is ours. God gave us free will from the beginning of creation. It is up to us to partner with His truth and not the lies that try to defy us.

I can hear some questions arising now within your spirit, asking the why questions, and I understand entirely, but I encourage you to seek out God's heart. We must never forget that we live in a fallen world, and there are several spiritual factors that we may not be able to see, but God will give you comfort if you choose to receive His will for your life. We must humble ourselves, release the reigns over our lives, and fully give them to God. It is through the testing of our faith that we finally believe and truly know that God is good. It is also important to remember that God allows difficulties in your life for good reason. They are always there to strengthen us in some way so we will produce good fruit from the Holy Spirit. This prepares us to steward more powerful anointings in the future, well.

I love how the passion translation puts it in James 1:2-4, it says, *"My fellow believers, when it seems as though you are facing nothing but difficulties, see it as an invaluable opportunity to experience the greatest joy that you can! For you know that when your faith is tested it stirs up in you the power of endurance. And then as your endurance grows even stronger, it will release perfection into every part of your being until there is nothing missing and nothing lacking."* God is producing endurance in you whenever you face a trial, so humble yourself, trust Him, and embrace all that He has for you.

I love this one saying that God dropped into my spirit after my miscarriages. He told me, "Kristin, the world has a fight or flight system, but I have a fire system." It is our human instinct to go into a fight or flight response when pain comes upon our hearts, but when we offer God a place to go into these hurts, He brings us into the fire. This fire then begins to refine us, burning up every wrong thought, every hurt, every wrong belief system, and you start to burn with a holy reverence for Jesus. You also begin to see through the eyes of Jesus instead of your own understanding or wounds. Jesus is Lord over my life; therefore, I surrender every area to Him. If something doesn't belong there, He wants to burn it out of us. He wants to bring us into a purification process of becoming one with Him by allowing Him to come into the innermost parts of our being. He wants full access to our hearts.

There will be seasons in our lives once we say yes to Jesus, where we will go through sanctification and chastisement. These usually happen during the long waiting processes throughout life. It is always of our free will to surrender, though, because God will continually ask us to sanctify ourselves. This is because He wants an intimate relationship with each of us and the absolute best for us. The Holy Spirit will begin to give you simple nudges when you shouldn't be doing something or if God is leading you to do something. Either way, He will always lead us through a process to bring us into His good and perfect will for our lives if we humble ourselves and allow Him to lead.

I have come to learn about chastisement in these past few years. I didn't really understand the meaning of this until the Lord began walking me through what this looked like. You see, God is outside of time, but we, being here on earth, are always in the realm of time ticking away. With this being said, God wants us to continually learn and grow. He is a good Father who wants the best for His kids. We will continue learning even more about Him and His kingdom once we enter Eternity. However, here on earth, He revealed to me the importance of the chastisement seasons. Chastisement will always bring us closer to Him.

For many years, I had a wrong perspective on chastisement. When you research this word Biblically, it looks as if it is a word for harsh punishment, and in most cases in the Bible, it is represented this way. However, in the past few years, I have faced some intense seasons that were non-stop, and I remember crying out to the Lord and asking him why. He answered me with such love and conviction by telling me this was for my good. I didn't understand precisely what He meant and almost wanted to get mad at Him. But I chose to partner with the fact that God is good!

During one of these intense seasons, I had a video pop up on my YouTube feed from Derek Prince, who was teaching on seasons of chastisement, and it changed my entire perspective of difficult seasons. The Latin root of chastise is castigare, which means "to set or keep right" or "to make pure." There are a couple of definitions for chastisement, which mean to rebuke for making a mistake, to criticize harshly, or to punish severely. This doesn't sound like a good thing but stick with me here. After I got this revelation, it empowered me greatly. I began to look at going through trials as a true honor because I knew that I was getting an upgrade in the Spirit once I got through it.

God tells us that we grow from glory to glory with Him. What does this mean? This means every difficult season could be considered a season of glory! Again, we must get God's perspective on this and watch what a powerful tool this is in your spiritual tool belt. The Lord showed me that there will be sanctifying seasons when we will be called into a deeper level of purification and holiness. This would be considered as being set apart or made pure. There will always be seasons of this because the closer we come to Jesus, learning to crucify our flesh, the more pure we become. It is during these seasons of sanctification that we should be learning. Learning to guard our eye, ear, and mouth gates. This is a season of sensitivity, stripping, and intense learning.

Then comes the season of chastising. They may not happen back to back because certain sanctification processes can sometimes take years, but eventually, there will come the chastisement season. The Lord showed me that this is a season where we will be tested in the things that we have learned. In order to grow, we must have accountability. Think of a chastisement season as if God is your powerful life coach, holding you accountable for all that He just taught you in the seasons before this one.

Certain situations will begin to arise in your life to see if you have learned from your last seasons of hardship. If we pass these so-called tests, then we get promoted, so to speak, in the Spirit. Know that these tests are always to reveal our character, strengthen our faith, and ultimately refine our hearts to long for the things of God.

This is prevalent if you look at the Scriptures from Revelation back to Genesis. Every influential person God used in the Bible went through intense seasons of sanctification and chastising. They all had to go through extreme processes to learn to steward the anointing upon their life well for the next season. The gifts are already within each of us when we are born, but it is by going through the harsh seasons of life with Jesus that the anointing begins to flow in these gifts. The anointing is what it is all about. Why? Because Jesus is the Anointing.

The anointing is the indwelling presence of the Holy Spirit in the life of a believer. This indwelling powerful presence of God came only because Jesus was crushed for our sin, iniquities, and transgressions. Anointing comes with Jesus once we accept Him into our hearts. Then, it is by us yielding to Him that His power can flow through us. By allowing our flesh and souls to get crushed through harsh seasons, His anointing oil can flow powerfully out of us because this life is not our own.

Now, don't get me wrong, God can use people immediately if they are willing vessels. But as I have learned through my walk with Jesus, the anointing will get stronger as we sanctify ourselves to become closer to Him. Why? Because when we stay close to Jesus, we become more like Jesus. I'm bringing this up because Isaiah 10:27 tells us that it is only by the anointing that the heavy yokes of bondage are broken. People can have the most beautiful voices when they sing or speak on stage in a church, but if they are not anointed to allow the power of Jesus to flow through them to stir up other people's souls to get saved and set free, then what is the point?

I will close with this. Try your hardest to look at difficult seasons as opportunities to grow in the Lord and to come up higher into your destiny. Know that every hardship in your life can be an amazing opportunity if you allow it to. I have learned how to trust Jesus through the process. I may not fully understand many things, but I have learned how to surrender. When I fully surrender to Him, allowing Him to love the Hell right out of me through all the Hell that is trying to destroy me, I always come out stronger when I choose to trust Him through it.

I have always come out more refined, more humble, and wiser. One of the beautiful things I recognize is that there is a higher level of anointing upon my life after every crushing season. So now, I embrace them. I encourage you to trust God like never before. Be open to the crushing processes. Get eternally minded and know that you have nothing to lose. This is a powerful thing to partner with. I hope this blesses you and encourages you if you are in a crushing season right now. This Christian life is seldom about us. Great purpose comes from our crushing.

APPLYING WISDOM TO YOUR DAILY LIFE

Prayer for the day:

Lord Jesus,

I need You. I know You, more than anyone else, understand the crushing and gut-wrenching pain. Help me fully trust You, and know that You will bring me through the crushing season that I am in and equip me for the next one. I want Your will over my own. I am learning to trust You more and know that You have the absolute best for me. So I ask You to help any unbelief or fears that I may have. I break all agreements with every spirit of fear, control, manipulation, and rebellion. Jesus, I give you permission to search my heart and humble me so I can see life through your eyes. Help me, Lord; in Jesus' name, I pray. Amen.

Scriptures to meditate on:

2 Thessalonians 2:13: *"But we ought always to thank God for you, brothers and sisters loved by the Lord, because God chose you as firstfruits to be saved through the sanctifying work of the Spirit and through belief in the truth."*

Acts 26:18: *"To open their eyes and turn them from darkness to light, and from the power of Satan to God, so that they may receive forgiveness of sins and a place among those who are sanctified by faith in me."*

Isaiah 10:27: *"And it shall come to pass in that day, that his burden shall be taken away from off thy shoulder, and his yoke from off thy neck, and the yoke shall be destroyed because of the anointing."*

1 Corinthians 1:30: *"It is because of him that you are in Christ Jesus, who has become for us wisdom from God—that is, our righteousness, holiness and redemption."*

Isaiah 40:31: *"But those who wait on the Lord Shall renew their strength; They shall mount up with wings like eagles, They shall run and not be weary, They shall walk and not faint."*

Philippians 1:6: *"Being confident of this very thing, that He who has begun a good work in you will complete it until the day of Jesus Christ."*

Psalm 138:8: *"The Lord will perfect that which concerns me; Your mercy, O Lord, endures forever; Do not forsake the works of Your hands."*

James 1:4: *"But let patience have its perfect work, that you may be perfect and complete, lacking nothing."*

1 Peter 1:6-9 *"In all this you greatly rejoice, though now for a little while you may have had to suffer grief in all kinds of trials. These have come so that the proven genuineness of your faith—of greater worth than gold, which perishes even though refined by fire—may result in praise, glory and honor when Jesus Christ is revealed. Though you have not seen him, you love him; and even though you do not see him now, you believe in him and are filled with an inexpressible and glorious joy, for you are receiving the end result of your faith, the salvation of your souls."*

Reflection:

Too many times, we put so much pressure on ourselves to work our way out of a situation when really it is all about learning to trust and rest in God's goodness through that situation. When we do not operate from a place of resting in His goodness, we often end up manipulating a situation or ultimately not finishing that race the Lord has graciously set before us. God does not want us to give up. It is not His will for you to feel defeated like you cannot make it through whatever you may be going through. All I want you to do, if you are going through a trial, is to rest in His goodness. Do all you know to do by spending time in His Word with worship & abiding in His Word. But my primary step for you to implement into your life this week and for the rest of your life is to do everything out of knowing that you are fully loved by God. Choosing to rest in the fact that He is God and He is for you. If He has brought you to something, He will bring you through that something.

1. No matter what thought comes against your mind that you may be battling with, I want you to say, "Ya, but God loves me!"

2. No matter what situation arises against you, say, "I can get through this because my Almighty God is backing me. He loves me, and He is for me! He will guide me!"

3. We must come to a place where we truly know how much God loves us. This will radically change how you look at intense seasons when they come.

4. You can begin to test yourself with God in this. What I mean is when you feel the Holy Spirit leading you to do something, trust it, then obey. If it is genuinely from the Holy Spirit, you will see how God will show up for you. This can take some time, so be patient. However, If it is not from the Holy Spirit, then at least you were obedient to step out in faith, and God will still honor that! As long as you keep your heart right towards the Lord and continue trusting Him, I'm telling you that He will make a way for you. Either way, you cannot miss God's goodness for your life when you keep your heart soft in love towards Him. He is that good! There have been times of such distress, anger, and rebellion in my life, but as long as I got my heart back into right standing towards Him, He always showed up for me. He will do the same for you!

5. We must get to the end of ourselves. This is why the Bible tells us to die to ourselves daily. It is a process, but this is when God shows off His best work in our lives. Rest in the Father's love. Abide in His love (This means to do whatever it may be that He tells you to do). Then, just release and trust.

Declaration:

I am a daughter (or son) of the most high God! He put everything inside of me when I was formed in my mother's womb to be able to overcome. I put my trust in Jesus. Therefore, I am led by His Holy Spirit, who guides me and strengthens me when trials arise. I know every difficult season I go through equips me for my destiny. I find God in my most significant weaknesses, and He constantly shows up mightily for me. When I am weak, He is strong! I can face any trial because I know God has allowed it for a reason, and He is backing me.

4 Who Told You

Once we begin to truly love ourselves by knowing how much God loves us, we can establish a strong relationship with Jesus. We can start to let go of all jealousy, insecurities, co-dependencies, the fear of missing out, the fear of man, and so on. This is a huge key to living His Kingdom way here on earth. You are commanded to love God, love yourself, and love others. If you struggle with doing these things, this means there are still roots of wounds in your heart. Allow God to help you recognize this and deal with these roots. It is imperative that we come into the Love of God, the true Awe and Reverence of God. We must learn to walk in such a reverential fear of Him daily that we begin to fear nothing else in this life.

God began revealing to me how important it is to truly grasp the meaning of His Agape Love! This will help you to walk in God's Love in all areas of your life. The word Agape comes from ancient Greek, a Greco-Christian term that refers to unconditional love. This Love is the highest form of love, charity, and the Love of God for man and man for God. Agape is considered to be the Love originating from God or Christ for humankind.

I am still unraveling this profound revelation and to be honest, God challenges me in this quite a bit. However, God lovingly reminds me that there are two places to operate out of in this earthly realm. We can operate out of love or fear. When we operate from the place of Agape Love, we partner and align our hearts fully with God in total humility and with whatever He says. This gives us all authority because Love truly forgives, heals, and brings freedom. When we partner with Love we partner with Heaven. There is only Love in Heaven! There is no fear or darkness of any kind.

You see, God always operates from Love. Even while correcting or placing His judgment, it is always from Love. His pure Love brings justice. God is not a God who can lie (Titus 1:2), and Jesus knew no sin (1 Peter 2:22). This means He is perfect in all His ways! It clearly states in Romans 8:28 that He turns ALL THINGS around for our good IF we love Him. The choice is always ours to come into our divine partnership with Him. Jesus came to be the ultimate sacrifice for us to finally be one with God, but the choice is ours (2 Corinthians 5:21).

Think about the very beginning when God created Adam and Eve. They were one with Him in every way. There was no division among them or anywhere in their environment. They participated in the full glory of God! This was how God intended for us to live, fully one with Him. But Adam and Eve had free will, just as we do. We all have a choice. Unfortunately for them, and, us, they literally disrupted everything here on earth, but thank God He sent His only Son to redeem it all!

God gave Adam and Eve authority over every living thing on earth. As I've mentioned, I believe Adam and Eve could talk with all the animals and every living being on earth and in Heaven. I also think every creature on earth lived in divine unity before the fall. There was no hate, evil, killing, circle of life, etc. Everything was in divine alignment. Let this sink in again, and think about it. It must have been normal for Adam and Eve to talk to animals. Otherwise, if that wasn't normal, don't you think she would've been alarmed when the snake spoke to her instead of being deceived to eat the fruit?

I am sharing this because a more profound revelation needs to take root in our hearts; we were designed to be one with God! Fully loved, fully identified in ALL He has for us, but we cannot do that if we don't love Him or ourselves. We must learn how to enter this place, spend time with Him daily, and invite Him into our every minute. He wants to share His heart with us and with everyone who will receive it! He does not want one person perishing, as He tells us in 2 Peter 3:9!

Hell was not made for humans. Hell was created for Satan and all of his demons (2 Peter 2:4). The choice to go there is up to us, and it breaks my heart that most Christians are not operating from this place of Agape love. This makes it difficult for others to see God's Love and goodness and want to come to Him. It all starts with you and me, (Mathew 28:18-20).

I want to share a little story about when Jesus really got onto me about comparing myself and trying to prove myself to other Christians. He was working immensely on my identity in Him this particular season. We have to be so careful of the deep insecurities caused by wounds in our hearts because this can thwart the plans of God for our lives. I have been through a ton of "church hurt." This type of hurt, in all honesty, can happen anywhere, but people tend to put a higher standard on Christians even though they are just regular people who will fail daily!

However, the hurt from other Christians was intense, and these wounds caused my husband and I to shut down for a season. It messed with the tremendous love anointing upon our lives, and we began looking at people differently. Our view was now through the lens of wounded hearts instead of God's loving heart. During this season, I found myself rebelling against Religion. Honestly, this is okay in some instances because God is not for religious acts by men; He is all about intimate relationships. However, the wounds started giving me a rebellious spirit, which became dangerous.

God was so gracious in this season. He began gently rebuking me and even showed me where I was getting off balance by showing me the spirits I had started to partner with. Even though these were the exact spirits that were raging against me. It is ironic to think about, but the more I learn about how demonic spirits operate, this is extremely common. This is why it is imperative to allow God to start healing you immediately as soon as an offense occurs. If you do not, this is where deception can enter into your heart. I had to humble myself immensely to hear God's voice clearly.

One night during this season, I was awakened by an audible voice speaking to me. The words I heard were, "Who told you you were naked?" I instantly got out of bed because I knew the Lord was dealing with me, but I wasn't sure exactly what that question meant. So, I began to seek God out on this question in prayer and by diving into His word. I started studying those exact words, and God gave me a deep revelation.

You see, I wonder sometimes if Adam & Eve would have been quick to repent as soon as God asked them questions in the garden instead of rebelling. Do you think God would have forgiven them and brought them right back into oneness with Him? I ponder it because His ultimate will is to be with us, and He sent his only Son to do this for us. It leads me to consider this question: "Who told you that you were naked?" I hope it makes you ponder every time God asks you to do something that has to do with coming back into alignment with Him. I hope we are quick to repent instead of rebel.

God was asking me this question because it was the same exact thing He was asking Adam and Eve in the beginning. "Who told you that you were naked?" As in, "Did I tell you that?" I believe God was telling them and was telling me to examine the person who told you those things because that did not come out of My mouth, and if it didn't come from Me, you should not go into agreement with it.

God always has the final say. He has the final word, and it is so important that we know His Word and what He says about us. This helps us to begin to understand our identity in Him through Christ! This may seem easier said than done, and it does take practice, but it is attainable. We must learn how to rewire our brains from every curse spoken over us by meditating on God's Word. We are His children first and foremost; that is the most important thing in this life.

We must get this! Have grace for yourself if you have been through a lot of abuse and wounds because this takes time, but it is up to you to take a stand and choose to believe God's Word over every other word someone has said or thought about you. You must decide to come back into right standing with God as a Daughter or Son of the Most High God because that is who you are! You do not have to stay in a shameful, wounded heart condition any longer.

To wrap this day up, I want this "Who told you" question to begin stirring in you from here on out. If a wrong belief comes to your mind, ask yourself, does God think that way of me? Did He tell me those things? Or, if someone tells you something out of judgment and not loving correction, ask yourself, "Does God say this about me?" "Should I be partnering with this if God did not say this?" We must learn how to combat the negative condemning thoughts and other people's judgments. This takes time, and it takes some seeking out in God's Word to know what He says about you, but you can do this! This is attainable.

APPLYING WISDOM TO YOUR DAILY LIFE

Father God,

Forgive me if there is any place in my heart where I still do not trust You or do not fully believe in all You have put inside of me. I know I am Your creation, so help me see what You see. Help me to believe in what You have created within me. Open my eyes to see, my heart to feel, and my ears to hear from You, Lord. I ask You to show me what You think of me and give me a glimpse of what You have created me for. I trust You, God, to speak to me through Your Spirit and Scripture. Thank You for loving me and making me. Amen.

2 Corinthians 5:21: *"God made him who had no sin to be sin for us, so that in him we might become the righteousness of God."*

Titus 1:2: *"In the hope of eternal life, which God, who does not lie, promised before the beginning of time."*

John 1:12: *"But to all who did receive him, who believed in his name, he gave the right to become children of God."*

2 Corinthians 5:17: *"Therefore, if anyone is in Christ, he is a new creation. The old has passed away; behold the new has come."*

Isaiah 43:1: *"But now, this is what the Lord says—"He who created you, Jacob (make this personal for you, and say your name here),he who formed you, (and here) Israel: Do not fear, for I have redeemed you;I have summoned you by name; you are mine."*

Matthew 28:18-20: *"Then Jesus came to them and said, "All authority in heaven and on earth has been given to me. Therefore go and make disciples of all nations, baptizing them in the name of the Father and of the Son and of the Holy Spirit, and teaching them to obey everything I have commanded you. And surely I am with you always, to the very end of the age."*

2 Peter 3:9: *"The Lord is not slow in keeping his promise, as some understand slowness. Instead he is patient with you, not wanting anyone to perish, but everyone to come to repentance."*

1. I want you to spend time with the Lord today seeking out more Scriptures on your identity in Christ. Find out what God says about you and write those down. Then, I want you to look up the meaning of your name in the Bible. You can google this. The origin of your name might be depicted in Hebrew or Greek, but it will be powerful! Do this for your first, middle, and last name. After you write those down, I want you to put this into a prayer declaration. Write this declaration out so you can begin reading this out loud every morning, every night, and every time the enemy

is attacking your identity. Read this aloud to remind yourself and the devil who and whose you are. This will help you begin to fully believe who you are in Christ. You are the Lord's, and He has a mighty plan for your life! His Word will not return void!

Here is an example that I have created for myself:

My Name is Kristin (Believer in Christ) Lynnea (Linden Tree) Taylor (cut). I did some deep research on the history of the Linden Tree, which brought me deeper revelation. You may need to do the same thing when you research and pray into your God-given name.

I am a powerful believer in Christ, and God uses me in multifaceted dimensions. I have a heart that can flourish in several different types of environments. I have been nourished and grown in fertile grounds from Heaven, and I always succeed in rich soil, even though I was born into dark, rough grounds. I carry a powerful anointing in helping others align with their divine giftings and help them find balance during their growth. My spirit is larger and more powerful than I can even think or imagine. I have an anointing to help set both men and women free by bringing them back to their true identity in Christ. I operate in immense healing when the time is needed most for others. I have the ability to cut through the enemy's lies and help set people free from his chains. And with all of these things, it is because I have been cut from above and clothed with divine righteousness to carry out the plans my Heavenly Father has for me upon this earth! I am fearfully and wonderfully made, and the enemy knows it! This helps me to always persevere through every attack because I am an overcomer, and I can do all things through Christ, who gives me strength. God uses every attack to stretch me, strengthen me, and to bring me up higher into the divine calling He has upon my life! My Heavenly Father knows what I can handle, and He knows my purpose. So I trust in His timing and His plans for my life, for I know that they are good!

Write your powerful name declaration here:

____

____

____

____

____

____

____

____

____

____

____

____

____

____

____

____

____

____

____

____

____

____

____

Declaration:

The Lord had a mighty plan and a purpose for my life before I was even in my mother's womb. Even though my parents may not have known the true meaning and impact of my name, God did! I am who God says I am! I am love because God is love and He is within me! I trust the plan that God has for my life and I am excited to embrace everything that comes my way to bring me higher into my divine purpose!

5 Choose Truth

I hope this week has challenged you because it challenges me even as I am writing it. We will always be in a process until the day we leave this earth, but this one key to partner with -the fact that God is for you- will dramatically change your life! I know it can sound incredibly cliche for me to keep telling you to look at life with a positive Biblical perspective, but it is true! This is where the power lies. God tells us to live with joy and to burn with a zeal for life, as it says in Romans 12:11. James 1:2 then tells us to consider it pure joy whenever we face trials of many kinds. How do we do this? By fully trusting God, leaning on His promises to bring us through our trials, and relying on Him for our happiness. Nothing else will fulfill us.

You must choose to believe what He says about you. He says you are the head and not the tail, that you are above and not beneath. You are an overcomer, and you can do all things through Christ! You are, first and foremost, a spirit being who does not have to submit to the fallen flesh! You have the Holy Spirit living inside you to guide you every step of the way! You are a victor and not a victim! My point is this: YOU ARE POWERFUL, AND YOU HAVE THE POWER TO MAKE POWERFUL CHOICES, SO CHOOSE WISELY! How do we do this? By going to God's Word, choosing to agree with Jesus, and being led by His Holy Spirit.

It truly is as simple as this. We usually hold ourselves back from our destiny because we are not partnering with Truth. You can choose to partner with the Truth that God is good all of the time, and when we do this, we begin to go to His Word for wisdom and direction in our lives. This means through every circumstance in your life, God is good. You can choose to be happy even when your world is collapsing around you. You can choose to love even when hatred comes against you. You can choose to forgive even when the offenses keep coming.

On the other hand, though, you can choose to hate or be miserable and partner with a victim mentality. The choice is ultimately up to you. You have a free will that God will not override. So it is essential to choose wisely. Allow yourself to feel whatever it is you may need to think about to process something. Then be quick to let that go, repent if you have to, and get back on the bandwagon of fully trusting God and declaring His Truth over your situation. The ultimate goal is to declare His goodness and promises right when the trial comes. This will be good to help you train in fully trusting Him.

I have now learned how to partner with God in every situation that arises in my life. I let myself feel the emotions I need to feel in order to process. Then I release them because feelings lie! I then run to my Father by encountering His Love and choosing to stand on His Truth, the Word of God! We have a choice to look at life with the right perspective, and if you begin to do this, you will begin to see wonderful fruit being produced in your life.

I am living proof that this works. The Word of God works! It is powerful, alive, and active! Apply it to your life in every area and believe it until you see the promise come forth. This is not about naming and claiming it. This is about having a healthy heart relationship with Father God, Jesus, and Holy Spirit. It is about choosing to trust in His goodness and having faith to trust His timing.

You must choose to believe that God is for you. If bad things are happening in your life, it's okay to ask him what is going on. He will show you, maybe not right away, but it is up to you to change your mind and trust that He has a plan even through the suffering. You must trust Him to walk you through your process, whatever that may look like!

Once you begin to grasp this Truth that God is so eminently for you, you realize that you cannot fail! You just can't! You can have God almighty backing you in everything you do as long as you partner with His Word and obey any instruction that He has given you. This makes life so much easier when you truly know that God loves you and He is for you. You begin to encounter His love and start believing in every bit of who He has created you to be. This means you truly start loving yourself because you know God loves you. It is only from here that we can then truly love others.

If you find yourself having difficulty embracing the Truth that God is good, I encourage you to go through that "why" exercise from week 1 again. Spend time with Holy Spirit and ask him where the lie came in for you not to trust God. Once you find it, do as the Holy Spirit leads you. He may have you repent or forgive someone or have you rest and embrace the Father's Love for you. Whatever it is, God leads you to do, be obedient. I want to encourage you that this is not a one-and-done thing. We must exercise this daily to build trust with our Heavenly Father, Jesus, and Holy Spirit.

<u>APPLYING WISDOM TO YOUR DAILY LIFE</u>

Prayer for the day:

Father God,
I ask You to help any unbelief that may still be within me. Help me to feel and know Your Love on a daily basis. I know what Your Word says, and I know that You gave one of the greatest loves there is, and that was Your only Son. I love you because You first loved me. Thank You for coming after me and rescuing me out of the pit. I cannot live my life without You and Your love. Help me to encounter Your love in more profound ways, Lord. I choose You in every area of my life! Thank You for loving me and helping me grasp Your amazing Agape Love. Amen.

Scriptures to meditate on:

James 1:17: *"Every good and perfect gift is from above, coming down from the father of the heavenly lights, who does not change like shifting shadows."*

Exodus 34:6: *"The Lord, the Lord God, merciful and gracious, longsuffering, and abounding in goodness and truth."*

Deuteronomy 28:13: *"The Lord will make you the head (leader) and not the tail (follower); and you will be above only, and you will not be beneath, if you listen and pay attention to the commandments of the Lord your God, which I am commanding you today, to observe them carefully."*

Psalm 145:5-7: *"I will meditate on the glorious splendor of Your majesty, and on Your wondrous works. Men shall speak of the might of Your awesome acts, and I will declare Your greatness. They shall utter the memory of Your great goodness, and shall sing of Your righteousness."*

Key # 11: Know Who God Is And Who He Says You Are:

Ask God daily to begin showing you who He is throughout His Scripture. Ask Him to show you how He has been there for you, specifically throughout your life. Then start asking Him daily to show you Who He says you are. Seek this out in His Word! Do you truly know the character of God? Do you know everything He says about you and why He created you? Ask the Holy Spirit to give you glimpses into your destiny. This key is something that can and should be used over and over again throughout every season of your life. God is always speaking, and we should constantly grow. This means that as we grow, God will give us more insight into our destinies and His plans and purposes for us. If there are things that you believe about yourself that do not line up with the Word of God and all He says about you, choose to let those things go. Choose to believe in who God made you to be. Choose to see all that God has put inside of you. Choose to believe that you were destined to walk this earth in glory to glory (2 Corinthians 3:18).

Reflection:

---

1. Write down any wrong belief systems you may have about God (ex: you may feel God is a manipulative father b/c your father was manipulative).

____

____

____

____

____

____

____

____

____

Now, look up scriptures that combat those lies. This could include how God is truthful, loving, kind, patient etc.

____

____

____

____

____

____

____

____

____

____

____

Then take time to repent for any wrong belief you may have towards God and ask Holy Spirit to come and fill any wounds in your heart.

2. Write down every time when God has protected you. Be humble here. Some outcomes may not have been how you wanted, but look for God's protection. I am a firm believer that rejection is usually due to God's protection, even though it hurts. In the long run, it was always for our good. If you cannot find His goodness and protection in a bad situation, spend time soaking with Jesus and ask Him where He was in that particular situation. God will show you if you spend time with Him. Keep your heart soft and humble here:

____

____

____

____

____

____

____

____

____

____

____

3. Make a list of who and what you believe you are, both good and bad. Be honest and vulnerable here. We need to expose any lies that you may be believing about yourself:

____

____

____

____

____

____

____

____

____

____

____

4. Then I want you to cross through every bad thing you just wrote about yourself. Replace it with God's promises and truth about who you are here:

____

____

____

____

____

____

____

____

____

____

____

5. I want you to look at this list every morning and every night reminding yourself who you are in Christ! Continue to do this until you start believing it with all your heart and soul. This is a process and can take time but your mind will begin partnering with God's truth over you. This will help you recognize the lies when they try to come in.

Declaration:

I am chosen, and I am a child of God! I am an heir to His throne, seated in heavenly places, and a conqueror through Jesus Christ. I love because God first loved me. I may not be where I want to be, but I am learning and growing daily. I am coming up higher in my God-given authority because I trust everything God has put inside me. The almighty God of the universe is for me! If God is for me, who can be against me! I know that God loves me. Therefore, I love others well! God is perfect and good!

WEEK 6

Christians Must Walk In Unity

1 We must Forgive

I want to touch base on something that may be a stumbling block for you if you find this week challenging. Laying down our will is one of the most difficult things we must do on this earth because we live in a prideful fallen world. The flesh and our soul will fight us on this almost every time, so we must train daily. The main reason for all the exercises throughout this book is to train your mind because this is where the main battle lies. Some of you possibly had some very difficult things happen to you while growing up. Unfortunately, this has probably caused you to mistrust people, which in turn causes you to mistrust God. Let's face it: our formative years are critical for healthy relational development. If those years were chaotic or abusive for you, this task of trusting people is probably not the easiest for you to do.

I have mentored and coached several people throughout my life and this is one of the hardest things to break through. Most people say they forgive, but in reality, there are deep places still within the heart they hold on to. They expect a particular person who hurt them to say I'm sorry or to change their ways. Unfortunately, most people have given in to the lie that it gives them a sense of power not to release those who hurt them. When forgiveness doesn't happen, we create self-defense mechanisms that some may call boundaries. In all reality, they have become walls, and have created deep bitterness within our hearts that we may not even recognize. We must be cautious of this.

I experienced this when my father passed away. I always felt like I forgave him and would keep forgiving because the enemy used him mightily to keep trying to hurt me. But it wasn't until he passed away that I became filled with rage, anger, and bitterness. These things were buried deep due to all the past wounds from him. This exposing of unforgiveness brought up some other areas that I also needed to deal with.

Sometimes, it takes a major crisis to finally face the hard truths we have been hiding from due to self-defense mechanisms. Grief can be a powerful tool because it usually exposes roots within our hearts that have been dormant for several years. I encourage you when these roots begin to show their ugly heads, and you start to feel all the nasty emotions, to invite the Holy Spirit in to help you go through the stages of grief. Usually, when trauma happens, we go into fight or flight, never really entering into full healing mode with the only true Healer, who is Jesus.

In a later chapter of this book, I go into more detail on how to receive deeper healing. Please reflect on your homework with the Holy Spirit for today and this entire week. As people and specific memories come up for you to expose any areas of unforgiveness or bitterness, I want you to search your heart with the Holy Spirit. Ask Him to lead you through any natural feelings of grief that come up to the surface.

The first thing that will probably come up is denial. If you think you have truly forgiven every person in your life and all difficult circumstances, you may want to humble yourself. Ask Holy Spirit to help you get rid of any denial and begin to crucify your pride. Please do not get offended, but if we want freedom, we must be willing to be completely honest with ourselves and with God. Being vulnerable and honest will help us receive God's love, truly love ourselves, and walk in love with others.

When anger starts to rise, ask God why you feel angry? Where is this stemming from? Then, ask Him to lead you through a forgiveness exercise. What does that look like for you? Does it mean role-playing as if that person is sitting before you? Or do you feel God is leading you to go to that person to forgive them? Forgiveness is strictly between you and God; you do not have to do this as an in-person act. However, deeper healing can sometimes occur by physically and vocally releasing that particular person in the flesh. I am sharing this so you can lean in and listen to how the Holy Spirit guides you through your forgiveness process. This process is between you and the Lord.

If you do not want to face these people or circumstances with an open heart, ask the Lord, why do I not want to take responsibility here? I am not saying you have to go to that person physically, but we should eventually be able to walk in God's love and peace with the person who harmed us. We are choosing to forgive them in our hearts and minds. We have a responsibility as Followers of Christ to forgive. Jesus commands us to forgive in Mark 11:25. I want you to ask yourself some questions because these will help you find some lies that are keeping you bound. Am I blaming anyone for how I act or react in life? Do I find myself bargaining with God in certain situations? Am I bargaining for a specific healing or wanting to save someone?

I find it interesting that these are the patterns we all tend to go through when we do not fully trust God. We are left with unhealed places in our hearts when we do not trust Him through a healing process. The patterns that tend to repeat in our lives usually involve some level of unhealed wounds, and not properly walking through the stages of grief. This tells me that most of us did not have the luxury of "knowing how to" or being able to sit with God to go through our healing process healthily. This includes knowing that God is good and being able to walk through every stage of our grief with the Holy Spirit when trauma happens in our lives.

The five stages of grief are denial, anger, bargaining, depression, and acceptance. So, when you begin going through all these exercises with the Holy Spirit at the end of each day, pay attention to these five areas. This will help you recognize areas of trauma in your life that you haven't fully dealt with. Once you acknowledge these and allow Holy Spirit to lead you through this, I think you will be amazed at how quickly you will begin to recognize the enemy's tactics that try to keep you bound.

I am giving you this opportunity to face any trauma you haven't fully dealt with now. This was "my why" when I started this book. I have a deep, burning desire to help the body of Christ heal. If we do not get healed, we will continue to wound our brothers and sisters and continue to keep creating division within the Church. The Bride of Christ cannot afford to do this any longer! God has called us into wholeness through the blood of Jesus Christ. It is up to us to come into this wholeness by receiving His love, mercy, and grace for us. We can then demonstrate this to others, especially being a light unto unbelievers.

It is a beautiful ebb and flow that happens, but unfortunately, hurting people will hurt people because they just haven't learned how to heal. I am not saying I am fully healed in every area but I sincerely desire to step into God's Wholeness. I am still in the process, but I have learned how to love others with God's love. It is all about dying to ourselves. I have also allowed the Lord to train me on how to fight the enemy because God has given us the keys to open and close doors. We must remember that Jesus already won the battle against Satan. He finished it at the Cross. This battle we are now in is not between God and the devil. Since Jesus went to the Cross, this battle is between the Church and the devil.

Jesus took back the keys that Satan stole from Adam in the garden. He then went to Hell and fought against the demonic entities and rose from the dead on that third day, breaking the curse over man! It is now time for the Bride of Christ to arise and shine into all she was created to be. Jesus gave us the keys when he left us with His Holy Spirit before He rose into Heaven. Jesus is constantly interceding for us at the right hand of Father God, and we have the power through the Holy Spirit to walk in our whole identity in Christ. Jesus is waiting to bring His Bride to Heaven to be with Him forever. We must do our part in presenting the loving Gospel to the brokenhearted to help save as many souls as possible. Are we walking this out in our daily lives?

We need to grasp this! Our mission should be to get healed so we can love well. This happens by aligning our hearts with Jesus so we can be a clean vessel where the Holy Spirit can work through us to help lead others to the Lord. Once we become Christians, this life is no longer our own. So why are we still sitting in a place of selfishness, holding onto our past and justifying any unforgiveness? It is time to let go, my dear brothers and sisters in Christ. We can no longer allow the enemy to hold us back in our fears or hurts. These will blind and distract us from walking out the Gospel of Jesus.

<u>APPLYING WISDOM TO YOUR DAILY LIFE</u>

Father God,
Help me to fully release every person who has harmed me in any way. I give them to You Lord and I ask You to come in and help me heal every broken part of my heart. Holy Spirit, I give You full permission to show me any time unforgiveness tries to take root and to expose any areas of bitterness that I may still have. I am open and surrendered to Your will, Lord Jesus.

Scriptures to meditate on:

Matthew 6:14-15: *"For if you forgive other people when they sin against you, your heavenly Father will also forgive you. But if you do not forgive others their sins, your Father will not forgive your sins."*

Matthew 18:21-22: *"Then Peter came to Jesus and asked, "Lord, how many times shall I forgive my brother or sister who sins against me? Up to seven times?" Jesus answered, "I tell you, not seven times, but seventy-seven times."*

Matthew 5:43-45: *"You have heard that it was said, 'Love your neighbor and hate your enemy." But I tell you, love your enemies and pray for those who persecute you, that you may be children of your father in heaven. (Praying for our enemies keep us in the right place of right standing with God)."*

Proverbs 16:7: *"When a man's ways please the Lord, he makes even his enemies to be at peace with him."*

Luke 6:27-28: *"But to you who are listening I say: love your enemies, do good to those who hate you, bless those who curse you, pray for those who mistreat you."*

1 Timothy 2:1-2: *"I urge you then, first of all, that petitions, prayers, intercession, & thanksgiving be made for all people - for kings and all those in authority, that we may live peaceful and quiet lives in all godliness and holiness."*

Psalm 147:3: *"He heals the brokenhearted and binds up their wounds."*

Mark 11:25: *"And when you stand praying, if you hold anything against anyone, forgive them, so that your Father in heaven may forgive you your sins."*

Luke 17:3: *"So watch yourselves." If your brother or sister sins against you, rebuke them; and if they repent, forgive them."*

Matthew 5:23-25: *"So if you are offering your gift on the altar, and there you remember that your brother or sister has something against you, (or you have something against them) leave your gift there in front of the altar. First go and be reconciled with your brother or sister, and then come and offer your gift. Reach a settlement quickly with your adversary while you're on the way with him to the court, or your adversary will hand you over to the judge, and the judge to the officer, and you* *will be thrown into prison. Truly I tell you, you will never get out of there until you have paid the last penny."* (Jesus was talking about the physical and spiritual legalities here. The spiritual is IF we do not forgive and get right with people, we will allow the enemy to keep us in a prison within our minds).

Romans 12:17-21: *"Do not repay anyone evil for evil. Be careful to do what is right in the eyes of everyone. If it is possible, as far as it depends on you, live at peace with everyone. Do not take revenge, my dear friends, but leave room for God's wrath, for it is written: "It is mine to avenge; I will repay," says the Lord. On the contrary:"If your enemy is hungry, feed him; if he is thirsty, give him something to drink. In doing this, you will heap burning coals on his head." Do not be overcome by evil, but overcome evil with good."*

Key # 13: You Must Forgive

Reflection:

Feel free to break these questions up over a couple of days because we are digging deep!

- I want you to take time to add anyone that may have come up in your mind today after reading this section. Sometimes, I still have to do this in my own life to check my heart. Some wounds can go so deep that we may not recognize any unforgiveness or bitterness inside us because we have lied to ourselves for so many years.

Remember that total forgiveness takes time. The first step is to forgive in your heart and openly forgive with your mouth out loud. This is considered *attitudinal* forgiveness, which is discussed in *Mark 11:25*. Jesus tells us, "When you stand praying, if you hold anything against anyone, forgive them, so that your father in heaven may forgive your sins." This means we are commanded to forgive within our minds and hearts; we are choosing to forgive anyone who wrongs us. It comes down to a choice and to our will. We all have free will, but when you choose to forgive, this is where so much freedom begins to blossom within you.

You must decide to humble yourself and realize that we are not God. He can deal justly with the other people who may have harmed us. It is not our job to retaliate. We must forgive and continue to release. We must constantly remind ourselves that we have done this by making the choice to forgive. We must continue to do this when any hurts, or anger may arise towards the person that we have forgiven due to past hurts or anything that comes against us in the future.

Now, I would like to touch base on *relational forgiveness*, which is discussed in *Luke 17:3*. In this Scripture, Jesus tells us, *"If your brother or sister sins against you, rebuke them: and if they repent, forgive them."* This is talking about having a covenant relationship with someone. For example, when you are in a marriage, and you are having trouble healing because your spouse has not repented, and they continue to hurt you through the same behavior patterns. This comes with guidelines that are different from those for attitudinal forgiveness. Why? Because you are in a covenant relationship with that person under God, yet they are not repenting. To keep our hearts right, we must still forgive them attitudinally, which we are commanded to do in *Mark 11:25*. But *Luke 17:3* tells both parties to repent, then forgive.

Relational forgiveness requires repentance and helps us to move forward into a healthy relationship. You both should be able to rebuke one another gently. Then tell each other what the other person has done that hurt you. Then, you should repent before one another, forgive each other, and work on not doing the same thing again. I highly recommend Biblical marriage counseling if you cannot get to this place of true repentance within your relationship. True repentance and forgiveness make life so much better! The bottom line is to ensure you repent and forgive within your heart and mind. This frees you from any bondage that comes with holding onto unforgiveness, which then turns into bitterness.

Luke 17:3 and Matthew 18:15-20 also ring true with brothers and sisters in Christ within the Church body. It is truly time to mature and be able to face one another head-on instead of running away. The time is too short to have petty disagreements that cause so much division within the Church.

1. Ask God if you need to forgive Him for anything. Doing this may surprise some of you, but God showed me that I had to do this and that this was blocking my intimacy with Him. I'm sure you have been through some difficult times throughout your life, and sometimes, the enemy can creep in and allow our hearts to become hardened towards God. This is a massive stronghold that keeps many Believers in bondage because the religious spirit wants to tell you, "Who am I to forgive God?" But God gives us free will, and He wants to allow us to come to a place of humility and forgive Him, then ask Him to forgive us for holding Him in contempt for all the things that the enemy has actually done. We must remember that God only allows things in our life to strengthen us, grow us, and allow our roots to dig deep so we can bear the weight of the fruit that is to come. I do want to be clear, though: whenever I say God allows, this means He is sovereign. It does not mean He has done anything evil to you or makes you go through evil things. The devil and his demonic spirits are the ones who bring evil and all the pain we have to go through in this life. God is the one who will get us through powerfully and train us along the way on how to overcome the schemes of the devil.

2. Now, I want you to take some time and allow the Holy Spirit to go deep into your heart to help you recognize any roots of bitterness that have formed due to this unforgiveness. Allow the Holy Spirit to show you any walls that you have built within your heart due to self-defense mechanisms. A lot of times, choosing not to forgive will block us from hearing from God and receiving His blessings.

<u>Here are some things to look for within your life to see if you have any roots of bitterness in your heart:</u>

- Do you have difficulty resolving conflicts?

- Do you struggle with any outbursts of anger: this includes going from 0-10 within seconds

- Do you tend to withdraw from people before you truly take the time to get to know them?

- Do you ever give the cold shoulder to others when you feel threatened or offended in any way, but have not talked to them about a certain situation that possibly upset you?

- Do you ever find yourself giving the silent treatment to someone or are you passive aggressive in any way?

- Do you act out with vengeance at times? Giving people a taste of their own medicine with possible spiteful remarks, back biting or gossiping, without thinking first?

Write down anything you see, hear, or feel here and then repent for holding onto any unforgiveness and bitterness:

____

____

____

____

____

____

____

____

____

____

____

____

____

____

____

____

____

____

____

____

____

____

Holding onto unforgiveness creates deep wounds that can create bitterness. This bitterness turns into hardness within our hearts, and this is dangerous because it can lead to deception. It comes from being wounded, and we then start putting up blockades in our hearts to protect ourselves instead of allowing God to protect us. You must choose to start bringing these walls down and trust God. Forgiveness is a choice. I encourage you to choose forgiveness every day until any and all bitterness is fully released.

Unforgiveness and bitterness can block the good relationships God is trying to give us. They can also block intimacy with the Holy Spirit and the ability to hear God clearly. As Jesus clearly says in *Mark 11:25*, this will ultimately block our prayers. God should be our ultimate protection over our hearts. He is our shield, our strong tower, because we have learned how to yield and put our trust in Him. When we grasp this, we no longer have to put up walls or blockades. However, I find many Christians still operating out of a place of woundedness, and this is dangerous. Be patient with yourself. Do not expect this to happen overnight, but allow yourself to feel and recognize any anger, hurt, bitterness, or unforgiveness.

- This exercise will likely take you the rest of our time together and even further. I want you to begin to meditate on the Scriptures about forgiveness, bitterness, resolving conflicts, anger management, gossip, etc. Anything you struggle with, look up how God says to deal with these things. You must begin to see how God wants you to think and live when it comes to these areas of conflict in your life. We cannot do that without studying topics in His Word that we struggle with. The Bible is a powerful guide showing us how to live successfully here on earth. When you meditate on Scripture, this will help you memorize and hold onto God's Word when more harmful situations arise in your life. This will prepare you for battle in such a powerful way.

Remember that God is God, and we are not! So, a huge key to getting free while doing these exercises is to lay down your will and choose His ways instead of your own! If the Bible says it, that is it! No, and, if, or buts. This makes it easy for you to say, "OK, God, I choose to do it your way. Help me."

Declaration:

I give you my will and any justifications I may harbor in my heart. I release every person (Name them out loud) to you again. I forgive them, and I bless them. Thank You, Lord Jesus, that You are a redeemer of all things, even those that deeply hurt me in my past. I know that You use every negative situation and turn all things around for my good God, because I love You! I trust You and know that I will be fully healed with time. In You, Christ Jesus, I am healed! I choose to be no longer led by my feelings. I choose to believe Your Truth! You took every hurt, every sickness, every disease, every sin upon that cross. I trust You, Jesus!

2 It is up to us

Early on in my walk with the Lord, God was showing me that unity is a key to seeing God's power flow through the Bride of Christ. This chapter holds some valuable keys for unlocking the tangible presence of God, and I believe it may even pave the way for revival to pour out upon all flesh before Jesus returns. I have yearned for this since the first time stepping into church after fully surrendering my life to Christ. It still stirs my spirit deeply even as I begin to write this chapter.

I remember the first time I felt this way as if it were yesterday, and I have come to realize that this is one of the primary callings in my life. I am called to break up any hard ground in people's hearts as well as combat intense demonic atmospheres. I recall looking around during one church service and feeling overwhelmed by numerous insecurities, which created a divisive atmosphere. This spiritual atmosphere weighed heavily on me, and I could sense the sadness of the Holy Spirit.

Mind you, this was 14 years ago, and I'm still seeing this today. This is not to place the only blame on us as Believers in the congregation, but also upon the leaders of churches. We must all come to a place of humility, forgiving others and praying for one another, knowing we are far from perfect yet digging deep into our identity in Christ. We must operate from the place of loving God and loving who He has created each of us to be individually. It is essential to believe in all that God has placed within us. I genuinely believe that when this happens, the church will begin to flow in the fivefold ministry again, and a new era of the Church of Acts will begin to emerge.

Please read through the entire book of Acts and see how the Holy Spirit quickens your spirit for the times that lie ahead. Be open to hearing new and exciting things from Him. In *Acts 2:42-47*, it says, *"They devoted themselves to the apostles' teaching and to fellowship, to the breaking of bread and to prayer. Everyone was filled with awe at the many wonders and signs performed by the apostles. All the believers were together and had everything in common. They sold property and possessions to give to anyone who had need. Every day they continued to meet together in the temple courts. They broke bread in their homes and ate together with glad and sincere hearts, praising God and enjoying the favor of all the people. And the Lord added to their number daily those who were being saved."*

I want you to think about the word 'devoted' mentioned in verse 42. Devoted means to have strong loyalty, affection, or dedication to something. Another definition suggests that something is given over to, displayed, studied, or discussed. Can we honestly say that we are entirely devoted to Christ and the work He has given us to do? Please do not succumb to any condemnation here, feeling defeated, but let it stir something so deep that it inspires you to burn for Jesus and all that He has in store for you in these end times. God chose you to be alive on this earth at this exact moment.

I must say, when I talk to some believers about the verses above, I get a deer in the headlights look, and I know what they are thinking, "Wait, what? You want me to share my finances with other people besides my immediate family?" However, I will say that I do get a few who are awakened to all that is coming and are eager to begin jumping on board. I truly believe we will return to a time when all Christians will have to do this. In these last days, persecution is going to come to Christians and Jews like never before, and we must be ready.

How do we arrive at a place of surrendering all and coming into unity? By first purifying ourselves and sanctifying ourselves to Jesus. This will help us discern and hear God's voice clearly. Then, be obedient to all that He tells us to do. The remnant will be the first ones who begin preparing in this way. They will be the "Josephs" to all other believers who won't be prepared when things in this world start to get even more chaotic. This remnant represents the forerunners of Jesus Christ, and they will be the ones to lead other believers in the End Days. Do you know if you are a part of this remnant? I know that I am, and I encourage you to seek God like never before to get on board!

It is time to move beyond our self-centered ways and start realizing what the Body of Christ is called to represent. It's not about what you or I want, but it's about what Jesus wants to do through you and me. I find it interesting that God designed the human body to function in perfect unity with all its components, including nerves, blood vessels, organs, bones, muscles, ligaments, and more. However, when something is off, it can disrupt your entire body due to a single tiny defect.

This unity within our bodily system is the same way we should look at our brothers and sisters in Christ. God calls us The Body in several Scriptures, but there is an excellent depiction of this in *Ephesians 4:16, "From him, the whole body, joined and held together by every supporting ligament, grows and builds itself up in love, as each part does its work."* We need to start acknowledging the powerful giftings in one another and realizing that we need each other! Our walk with Jesus here on earth is not just about focusing on our gifts or what the leaders in our church possess. It is all about looking deeper within and helping to bring out the gold in others so they can rise higher and feel included in God's Kingdom. We all have a part to play here. If we want to see a move of God like never before, we are going to have to start "doing Church" differently.

APPLYING WISDOM TO YOUR DAILY LIFE

Prayer for the day:

Lord,
I repent for any area within my life where I do not want to surrender. I give You permission to search my heart and show me these areas, Lord. Help me to soften my heart to fully begin to trust You in any area where I feel that I don't want to surrender. In Jesus Name, I fully surrender!

Scriptures to meditate on:

Galatians 2:20: *"I have been crucified with Christ. It is no longer I who live, but Christ who lives in me. And the life I now live in the flesh I live by faith in the Son of God, who loved me and gave himself for me."*

Romans 6:1-11: *"What shall we say then? Are we to continue in sin that grace may abound? By no means! How can we who died to sin still live in it? Do you not know that all of us who have been baptized into Christ Jesus were baptized into his death? We were buried therefore with him by baptism into death, in order that, just as Christ was raised from the dead by the glory of the Father, we too might walk in the newness of life. For if we have been united with him in a death like his, we shall certainly be united with him in a resurrection like his."*

John 12:24-26: *"Truly, truly, I say to you, unless a grain of wheat falls into the earth and dies, it remains alone; but if it dies, it bears much fruit. Whoever loves his life loses it, and whoever hates his life in this world will keep it for eternal life. If anyone serves me, he must follow me; and where I am, there will be my servant also. If anyone serves me, the Father will honor him."*

Key #14: Die To Yourself Daily

Some of the scriptures from above may strike a chord within you. I promise that if you allow God to search your heart here and show you His goodness and mercy, your fears and/or rebellion will begin to dissipate. I am still learning how to die to myself daily, but I have trained myself to be conscious of this, which helps me to humble myself to do it.

Reflection:

1. Start paying attention throughout every day from now on and begin examining your heart each night before bed. If you find any place where you did not humble yourself or where you were not obedient to the Lord, repent and ask the Lord for an opportunity to make it right. Get ready. The Holy Spirit will stretch you in this area, and He will begin giving you opportunities for redemption. We must learn to choose His will over our own every time. When I do this, I am never disappointed, and God always amazes me. His ways truly are so much better than my own.

I declare today that I no longer live for myself. I live for my King Jesus, my Father in Heaven, and His mighty Holy Spirit, who have good plans for my life. I lay down my will for God's will. I am His vessel, and I allow myself to be used by Him for His glory daily. Even when I feel my flesh raging, I will crucify it every time because I am God's willing vessel.

3 Let Holy Spirit lead

I want to provide you with an example of this type of unity so you can begin to stir your heart with excitement. My husband and I started hosting worship nights at our home back in 2017. These worship nights consisted of people from all walks of life. Some Catholics, some Lutherans, some off-the-wall Charismatics, some young, some old - you name it - whoever we felt the Holy Spirit would tell us to invite, we did. I was hesitant about doing this at first because it meant crucifying my flesh. However, we knew the Holy Spirit was telling us to do this, so we were obedient. As soon as we held our first night of worship, we immediately began to see the fruit of what God was leading us into.

He began showing us what would happen if people came to church hungry for an encounter with God—coming with no agenda except to meet with their King Jesus and soak in deep fellowship with the Holy Spirit and fellow Believers in Christ. As leaders, we had no agenda besides loving those who came into our home and completely trusting the Holy Spirit to lead us. I didn't know how to play any instruments at this time, but I knew God was asking me to lead this. As I obediently led us in acapella worship, completely allowing God's presence to guide me, powerful moves of the Holy Spirit began to happen.

Once we began these worship nights, it became increasingly evident how God was yearning to move in each of our lives. We went from having two-hour worship nights to having 7 hours of complete intimacy with Jesus, being able to enter into visions, as well as people's gifts popping out of them like popcorn. I renamed these worship nights 'Popcorn Worship Nights' because they always brought total excitement to see what God was going to do next.

People who didn't know they had the gift of prophecy would get a vision or hear a word of knowledge in their spirit to share with someone else in the room. Spiritual eyes began awakening like never before. People began having encounters with angels and seeing in the spirit realm for the first time. You can find proof of these Spiritual Gifts of unity and diversity in *1 Corinthians 12*, and really throughout a lot of scripture. Powerful things happen under corporate anointing, especially when there is a total hunger for unity, being one in Christ.

I finally learned how to truly worship with Heaven, to be so incredibly led by the Holy Spirit that I can flow with new songs that only come from Him, the true King of Kings. We must learn to be led by the Holy Spirit in all aspects of our lives, but especially for worshipers. Worshippers have always been on the front lines before battle and the true worship of God confuses our enemies. It is only when we go where the Holy Spirit leads that we will flow in the anointing, and it is only the anointing that breaks the chains that bind us (Isaiah 58:6)!

I have learned that this is where the power lies, and we have barely scratched the surface yet! I believe it is when we take our eyes off the clock and completely surrender our time and agendas to God that He will show up mightily. We have only experienced a small amount of His grace thus far, not the true power of His glory that He is wanting to pour out through us. We must get this revelation because we do not want to miss this powerful move of God that is coming! We need to be diligent in seeking Him, listening to His voice only, which includes studying His Word and then walking it out in full surrender and obedience. This is what unity looks like with us, God the Father, Holy Spirit, and Jesus.

This is what we should be encountering within the church walls but unfortunately, most are not. I've asked God several times why this is not happening in the Church today, and He has bluntly told me that it's because they keep looking at the clock, care too much about what other people think, and try to keep me within the walls of their own church and their agendas.

I am a true believer that when we give time and space for God to move, He will. It may not be on our timing but our willingness and hunger for intimacy with Him, will bring His Holy Spirit to move. Please know that I am preaching to myself as I speak to your hearts. I speak out loud daily for God to come and bust out of every box I have tried to place Him in and to be open for Him to use me as His willing vessel.

We only held these worship nights once a month back then for a year; however, I am hearing the Lord say that this needs to be every week. The Body of Christ needs this! Imagine if we were achieving those miraculous results from just meeting once a month. What would it be like if we met all the time? It will be just like, if not better than, the days of ACTS! Pursuing daily intimacy with Jesus and yearning for God's presence is a key to achieving unity and genuinely helping people feel free in their calling.

We are entering a time when God wants to pour out His Spirit upon all flesh and do the miraculous! We can expect to see more people get healed in the years to come than we have ever seen before. We must be aligned with the leadings of the Holy Spirit. God is not just going to be known for being in the walls of the church, but His fire is going to burst forth through the streets, the fields, and the forests reaching all walks of life. It is our job as His Bride to be ready when this outpouring happens.

APPLYING WISDOM TO YOUR DAILY LIFE

Prayer for the day:

Lord,

I ask You to give me the hunger, the want, and the desire to seek You more with my brothers and sisters in Christ. Help me understand the importance of unity within your church and how I can be a catalyst to initiate this outside of my church walls, within my neighborhood, and/or my community. I want to learn how to fully surrender to You and experience Your flow within and through me and my fellow believers in Christ. Open the doors for me to do this, Lord, and I ask You to kill any fear that may be coming up right now. In Jesus' Name, I pray.

Scriptures to meditate on:

Galatians 5:25: *"If we live by the Spirit, let us also walk by the Spirit."*

1 Corinthians 1:10: *"I appeal to you, brothers, by the name of our Lord Jesus Christ, that all of you agree, and that there be no divisions among you, but that you be united in the same mind and the same judgment."*

1 Corinthians 12:13: *"For in one Spirit we were all baptized into one body—Jews or Greeks, slaves or free—and all were made to drink of one Spirit."*

Romans 8:26-27: *"Likewise the Spirit helps us in our weakness. For we do not know what to pray for as we ought, but the Spirit himself intercedes for us with groanings too deep for words. And he who searches hearts knows what is the mind of the Spirit, because the Spirit intercedes for the saints according to the will of God."*

2 Corinthians 13:14: *"The grace of the Lord Jesus Christ and the love of God and the fellowship of the Holy Spirit be with you all."*

John 17:21-23: *"That all of them may be one, Father, just as you are in me and I am in you. May they also be in us so that the world may believe that you have sent me. I have given them the glory that you gave me, that they may be one as we are one—I in them and you in me—so that they may be brought to complete unity. Then the world will know that you sent me and have loved them even as you have loved me."*

Matthew 18:18-19: *"Truly I tell you, whatever you bind on earth will be bound in heaven, and whatever you loose on earth will be loosed in heaven."Again, truly I tell you that if two of you on earth agree about anything they ask for, it will be done for them by my Father in heaven."*

Ephesians 4:11-13: *"So Christ himself gave the apostles, the prophets, the evangelists, the pastors and teachers, to equip his people for works of service, so that the body of Christ may be built up until we all reach unity in the faith and in the knowledge of the Son of God and become mature, attaining to the whole measure of the fullness of Christ."*

Philippians 2:3-5: *"Do nothing out of selfish ambition or vain conceit. Rather, in humility value others above yourselves, not looking to your own interests but each of you to the interests of the others. In your relationships with one another, have the same mindset as Christ Jesus."*

Reflection:

1. I want you to be intentional to start praying & worshipping with a friend or a group of friends at least once a month. This may stretch some of you, but it is so important to see how the Holy Spirit shows up when we set aside time to be intentional about praying and worshiping with our family in Christ. Remember to come together in unity and make your main agenda about worshipping God, praising Him, studying His Word, and praying.

2. After you have spent this time with your friend or friends, I want you to take a moment to journal about how God showed up for you during your worship time together. Genuinely ask him to show up even more the next time you all meet. We must create hunger from deep within ourselves!

3. This will help you begin to hunger for deeper intimacy outside of the church walls. We are called to do this. This isn't just about coming together as a small group within your church to fellowship. That is important, but this is about coming with an intentional purpose to meet with your friends to worship and pray and learn to allow Holy Spirit to lead and bounce off of all of you who come together. It's about coming together in such unity that you experience becoming one in the Spirit.

Declaration:

I decree and declare that I am a kingdom builder for Jesus! I make a difference within my church, outside of my church, and within my community. I am a conduit for Jesus, bringing love and creating unity wherever I go. As I begin to create a space for my brothers and sisters in Christ to come together and build community and unity, we will make a massive difference in this world. I know how essential unity is, and I am taking the steps to make this difference within myself and the lives of others.

4 The Sifting has begun

Being led by the Holy Spirit includes letting go of all offenses. One of the greatest commandments Jesus gave us is found in *Matthew 22:37-39, where Jesus replied, "Love the Lord your God with all your heart and with all your soul and with all your mind." This is the first and greatest commandment. And the second is like it: 'Love your neighbor as yourself."* I believe this is stirring deep within the Bride of Christ at this moment. Chosen believers who once walked in religion and were bound by offense are beginning to awaken and release from these bonds.

God showed me that a dividing line began in 2019 within the spiritual realm, and it is still happening to this day in 2024. God is weeding through the church right now to see who will truly become His Bride. He showed me that a great shaking will come to His people and that purification is happening, whether people want it or not. It will be beautiful for those who want it and are ready for it. This will bring us closer to Jesus and each other than we've ever been before. Get ready!

When I look back at all that the Lord showed me in 2019, I am in shock and awe of all that has transpired, but I know that more shaking is yet to come. The Church became rattled in 2020 when the governments decided they were not essential. Families were divided by the intense deceiving spirit that came with COVID, but unfortunately, all of this chaos wasn't enough to make people humble themselves and truly seek out God for answers.

There was a remnant who stood their ground for the Lord, humbly abiding by the Holy Spirit's lead instead of the government's laws. I believe God began a mighty work in their leadership. I can only imagine the levels of trust they had to go through to stand up against that demonic agenda. This was all preparation because I know more is coming. Covid was just a trial run that the enemy unleashed, but we must remember that God allowed it, and He is going to enable the Church to be sifted even more.

Christians who did not stand well in those times will hopefully have a resounding cry of repentance burning inside of them. I saw a massive "exposing" that would begin happening, and this was back in 2019. We are now, in 2024, beginning to see God at work in both the Church and the world. We are only scratching the surface. God holds leaders within the church to a higher standard, and we will be judged accordingly. We should also be more aware of the voices we are listening to and what comes out of our mouths from here on out.

I want to mention this powerful Scripture again, where Jesus says, *"Do not suppose that I have come to bring peace to the earth. I did not come to bring peace but a sword."* I honestly didn't recall this Scripture until my husband saw it in his mind one day while we were praying for America. I began to study this, and it will help us in these End Times. This Scripture is *Matthew 10:34*, and it goes on to discuss further division that will occur between close family members in its following verses, *35-36*.

Now, we all know that Jesus is the King of Peace and that we can find peace through Him, even amidst the most perilous storms in our lives. This Scripture reveals another aspect of Jesus, which is important to take note of. You see, when Jesus came to the earth for the first time, there came a lot of division, especially within the religious people. As Jesus prepares His Bride in these End Times, I believe we will see even more division, but this time within the Church.

I know this whole week has been focused on unity within the Bride, but some intense division and cutting away from the flesh and the world must happen before we, as believers in Christ, can come together as one Bride. Have you ever noticed how the Word of God can deeply offend people? Or, have you ever been offended by the Bible? I know I have, especially when I was first coming to the Lord and when I've gone through difficult seasons. Why? Because the Word cuts deeper than a double-edged sword. It is the ultimate source of Truth and it will offend our fleshly desires, our worldly ways, and our cultural behavior.

Again, Jesus says, *"I have not come to bring peace but a sword."* He is dividing the Kingdom of Light from the kingdom of darkness and we are in a very intense spiritual battle right now. Too many Christians are trying to live in the world to be liked or accepted, and this is not OK! The Bible clearly tells us that we, as Followers of Jesus Christ, are to be set apart from the world! We are to live very differently from how the world lives!

God has been personally dealing with me in this area for the past four years. It has been challenging to humble myself and fight against the spirit of religion as well as the flesh to fully come into profound revelation of who God is calling His Bride to be. We are in the End Times, and this is one of the ways God is preparing His Bride, so we should be obedient to every conviction He brings to us. We must realize that it may cause us to be separated from our family, friends, or culture. God is separating the wheat from the tares right now and I don't know about you, but I want to be the pure wheat.

I want to focus once again on being offended. Being offended is one of the most significant barriers to hearing the voice of God clearly and unifying within the Bride of Christ, and ultimately, it affects our intimacy with Jesus. Jesus commands us to forgive and let go and let Him be the Judge. Now, I will be the first one to admit that I have not done well in this area throughout my past. I have not judged others accordingly, and God still convicts me when I look at other Believers with a hardened heart in any way. We must keep our hearts soft every day and allow God to bring conviction to us. We must be aware of any offenses we may still be holding onto because this can fester into unforgiveness and bitterness.

How can we be the change we want to see if we aren't allowing God to change us first? 1 Corinthians 10 says this: *"I appeal to you, brothers, by the name of our Lord Jesus Christ, that all of you agree, and that there be no divisions among you, but that you be united in the same mind and the same judgment."* Once we allow the Lord to deal with our hearts, we should then be able to walk this Scripture out, not caring what anyone thinks of us because it's all for His glory anyway. We must get to this place! Many times, we, as human beings, get intimidated by man. However, when we know that it is Almighty God speaking to us, then we must be confident in walking out whatever it is that He is leading us to do.

Once we fully give God the reins over every area of our lives, especially within the church body, then and only then will we see His Kingdom come. We must begin to look at other Believers as our faithful brothers and sisters in Christ, always seeking to bring one another higher. When Jesus found us in our muck and mire, He didn't leave us there. He pulled us up and out, bringing us to higher levels. We, as Believers in Christ, are called to do the same for others.

We may not get along ideally, but we can still love them well. Loving them well includes being honest when God wants us to share something with them that may convict them or go against some of their ways.

This also includes allowing other believers to convict us when we need it as well. It goes both ways, and we must be humble to receive those words and seek the Lord.

When sharing the Truth with others, it is crucial to ensure that God is guiding us in this area. Do not try to tell someone they are wrong out of the hurt places within your own heart; this will only make a person feel condemned instead of convicting them with God's love, which always leads to a place of repentance and freedom. It is essential that we continually strive for improvement in our daily walk with Jesus. We must allow the Lord to continue healing our hearts daily so that we can be His vessel and an example of His love. Love will always help us see other people through God's heart and not our own understanding.

***The Body's identity has to first start with individual identity in Christ,
and then come together as one powerful union in Christ.***

APPLYING WISDOM TO YOUR DAILY LIFE

Dear Lord,

Please help me to recognize every time I feel an offense rising and help me to extinguish it instantly. Help me to look inward at myself and allow You to heal any wounds that the offense may be festering. Help me to start looking inward instead of blaming others, Lord. I want to walk in love and live an unoffendable life. I know my flesh is weak, but I also know that I can do all things with You, Jesus, and You, Holy Spirit. I give you full reign to tug on my heartstrings when offenses try to rise in my life. Deal with my heart accordingly, Lord. In Jesus' Name, I pray.

Proverbs 19:11: *"Good sense makes one slow to anger and it is his glory to overlook offense. A person's wisdom yields patience and it is to one's glory to overlook an offense."*

1 Corinthians 1:10: *"But I urge you, believers, by the name of our Lord Jesus Christ, that all of you be in full agreement in what you say, and that there be no divisions or factions among you, but that you be perfectly united in your way of thinking and in your judgment [about matters of the faith]."*

Roman 14:19: *"So then, let us pursue [with enthusiasm] the things which make for peace and the building up of one another [things which lead to spiritual growth]."*

Luke 17:1-4: *"Then said he unto the disciples, It is impossible but that offenses will come: but woe unto him, through whom they come! It were better for him that a millstone were hanged about his neck, and he cast into the sea, than that he should offend one of these little ones. Take heed to yourselves: If thy brother trespass against thee, rebuke him; and if he repent, forgive him. And if he trespasses against thee seven times in a day, and seven times in a day turn again to thee, saying, I repent; thou shalt forgive him."*

Matthew 18:21-22: *"Then Peter came to Jesus and asked, "Lord, how many times shall I forgive my brother or sister who sins against me? Up to seven times?" Jesus answered, "I tell you, not seven times, but seventy-seven times."*

Matthew 5:38-39: *"You have heard that it was said, 'Eye for eye, and tooth for tooth.' But I tell you, do not resist an evil person. If anyone slaps you on the right cheek, turn to them, the other cheek also."*

1 Peter 4:8: *"Above all, love each other deeply, because love covers over a multitude of sins."*

Colossians 3:13: *"Bear with each other and forgive one another if any of you has a grievance against someone. Forgive as the Lord forgave you."*

Key #15 : Live Unoffendable:

Every time you feel offended, please start looking inward with the guidance of the Holy Spirit. This will help you grow immensely in the Lord. If you have an offense, I want you to begin asking the Lord, what wound is still inside of me that needs healing? We should be able to walk this earth unoffendable as Christians because our identity has become so rooted in Him. We begin releasing and allowing any attacks from the enemy (who loves to use people) to bounce off of us because we are so rooted in Christ's love that we can humble ourselves to pray for that person instead of getting angry and offended. This will help you to no longer allow unforgiveness and bitterness to take root as well. This is a compelling thing to begin implementing in your life.

Spend time with God and ask Him to reveal every situation where you still hold offense in your heart. Then, ask Him where the truth lies in that situation (God will always reveal His goodness, even in the worst of conditions, if we trust Him). Ask Him to show you where the root is in your heart that allowed you to partner with offense in the first place. Unforgiveness and bitterness often hide within the walls of offense, holding you back from the promises of God.

Reflection:

1. Make a list of any and all offenses you still have in your heart:

____

____

____

____

____

____

____

____

____

____

2. Make a list of people you still have unforgiveness towards:

____

____

____

____

____

____

____

____

____

____

____

3. Now spend time in prayer and worship, asking God to give you His heart and His understanding towards those people. Keep in mind hurting people hurt people; this helps me release those who have hurt me. God has shown me that they are just incapable of love because they do not know the love of God. We must have grace, and we must forgive. This is a huge commandment in the New Covenant that Jesus gave us before He left this earth.

4. Ask God to help you to forgive. I know this will be difficult for many of you because I, too, can still struggle in this area at times. But say this day after day until your heart begins to fully release it: "As an act of my will, I fully surrender _________(the person) to you, Lord, and I forgive them."

Declaration:

I decree and declare that my flesh is being crucified daily. I look inwardly now every time an offense arises within me. This helps me to walk in love and humility with others and to forgive quickly. I do not need to prove myself to anyone because I am a child of the most high God. God knows my heart, and I know that He is a just God. He will deal justly when the time is right. Every battle belongs to the Lord. My job is to keep my eyes fixed on Jesus and keep my heart soft to the Holy Spirit's conviction. I have the Holy Spirit working in me daily, and I yield my life and my will unto Him! I walk in the Spirit and not in my flesh.

5 Unity within the Bride

God gave me a powerful vision at the end of 2020, and I would like to share it with all of you because I believe it was a prophetic sign of what the Body of Christ must do in the end times. This time is upon us now. However, I would like to say this first. Christians must begin walking out their whole identity in Christ by allowing God to refine them so they can arise into all that Christ has put within them. We must die to ourselves so Christ and His will can live through us. This is where true identity in Christ begins to form. It is from this place that we can begin walking in unity with our brothers and sisters, for there is no need for competition or division. It is time to lay aside any differences we may have with each other because the time is short. The time is now to unite and begin aligning ourselves for all that God has in store for us to do in these end times.

The vision began with me standing in a Heavenly realm. I was standing in an open area when all of a sudden, a beautiful white horse appeared beside me (*Revelation 19:11*). I looked to my right and my left, and suddenly all these Believers, my Brothers and Sisters in Christ dressed in all white, came alongside me as far as my eyes could see. Then, several more white horses appeared on the side of each of them. Our minds were so in tune that we did not even need to speak to one another; we could read each other's minds. Within an instant, we knew we were to get onto our horses. Then, just as in sync as a military move together, we all jumped up onto our horses.

As soon as we did this, we all locked arms, knowing this was a key that would win the battle ahead (*Acts 2:44-46*). This locking of arms was another intricate militant act, and we became entirely in sync with each other. We aligned our hearts in unity and love towards our One True King, Jesus, and the heavens opened up at the exact moment when black and red billowing smoke began to come towards us. We all knew to keep our focus on God and all that He was doing in the Heavenlies (*Isaiah 44:22*), (*Psalm 20:1-9*).

As we continued in worship, staying focused on our King, this beautiful liquid began pouring out of the skies with such intricacies for each one of us. This exquisite liquid consisted of pure gold, white gold, and what appeared to be liquid diamonds. As it came down, it began to mold into the most elaborate and magnificent pieces of armor. Angels placed each piece of armor onto every one of us! Not one piece of armor was the same. It was truly miraculous to see, and it was terrific! There was not one ounce of jealousy among us, only the pure awestruck wonder of what was happening through the goodness of God.

After the armor was supernaturally placed upon us, we all could feel what was coming. We stood our ground, never loosening our arms for even a second, because we knew the power came from our unity with Jesus and with one another. We continued to worship our King, trusting Him and all that He had placed within each of us for this exact moment. All of a sudden, our horses grew enormous, majestic wings. As we stayed locked together in prayer and worship, the horses moved forward and began to grow arms out in front of them, carrying every type of massive weaponry imaginable.

As this dark red and black billowing smoke came closer, we all saw the demons beginning to rage against us. But, we were not shaken. We knew who was fighting this battle for us! (*Isaiah 59:19*) We continued to stay in unity, in love, in worship and prayer. We kept our arms locked this entire time, and these amazing horses began to fight off the evil effortlessly for us!

It is essential to share this vision because it is for the Body of Christ right now and until Jesus returns for us. This vision applies to everything we do in life! It began with all of us dressed in white. I find this significant because Jesus is calling His Bride into purity and sanctification like never before. The times we are living in are not a time to be messing around by "playing" Christianity. Jesus says He is coming back for a Bride who is ready, pure, and has been storing up her oil (*Matthew 25:1-13*). This purification is key to being bold and immovable for all that is coming in the times ahead of us.

The divine unity in this vision tells me that we need each other, and we must keep our eyes fixed on our King, Jesus! God began speaking to me about the importance of His Body coming together at this time, and I find it very interesting because there is immense division within the Body of Christ right now. But God! I believe it is up to us to shut the mouths of lies, deceit, and gossip. We must rise above by humbling ourselves and sharpening one another to present a Bride who is going to be ready for her Bridegroom.

It is time to stand upon the Word of God, not backing down from all that is going to come against us. It is important to remember this vision and how we must work together to take back what the enemy has stolen and is still trying to steal. There is a reason Jesus calls us the Body. We are His church, and The church is called the Body of Christ. Every human body is designed to work in unity with the other parts of the body. I believe our bodies should exemplify a powerful example of how He wants His Church to operate. God began speaking to me about His Body. He showed me that even when one person is "off" or feels left out, it can affect the purposes of His Bride. We truly need one another, and if we are going to live the Kingdom way, wanting to bring Heaven upon this earth, we better understand this and get a deep revelation on how to become unified.

God will appoint people to run beside us and with us because we are not meant to run this race alone. However, we must be confident in who God has made us to be so that we do not fall into jealousy or cause division any longer! It is time for us to surrender all our pride and insecurities. When we come low, dying to ourselves daily, we can push one another up higher. We need to encourage one another into all that Christ has made us to be. We do not want to miss the great opportunities that are coming to advance His Kingdom!

Once we know our identity is in Christ, we can help others discover their own identity and begin living on this earth the way God intended us to. Think back to the Garden of Eden when God first created the world, man, and every living creature. God's intention for creation was for us to live in unity and for humans to subdue every single thing on earth by partnering with God. This means partnering with His Word, which is the only truth we can firmly stand upon. We have authority when we know who we are in Christ!

When we have our identity rooted in Christ, we can then have unity! We will finally look at each other in awe of our giftings and the anointings that are upon us! All jealousy and insecurities bow to the power that comes from within you once you know who you are in Christ! I can tell you this because I am living proof. Yes, thoughts still come to try and thwart my actions, but I know that free will is an extremely powerful gift. I have a choice to partner with God's Truth. I encourage you to get right with your neighbor, get right in your heart with anyone who has hurt you. Where we are going, you cannot take these poisonous things with you. It is time to release every hurt and choose to forgive. It is time to walk powerfully alongside one another into all that God has for us. It is time for unity, my dear brothers and sisters in Christ! We must come together!

APPLYING WISDOM TO YOUR DAILY LIFE

Father God,

I know that You care about every detail of my life and forgive me for not being humble enough to ask You for Your direction. Holy Spirit, I ask that You help me to be sensitive to You. Please help me recognize when you lead and guide me to follow when I hear or sense your guidance. Please help me hear your voice clearly and discern the voices that come into my mind. Help me to discern the voices of the enemy. Lord, I give You full permission to reprimand me when I need it. Help me to humble myself and recognize that what You are allowing in my life is to strengthen me and train me in preparation for all You have in store for me in the future. Help me to fully believe that Your plans are good for me and others. Help me see other people as You see them, Lord. Help me to fully forgive those who have hurt me and help me to grasp Your Agape love. Teach me daily, Lord, and show me areas within my own heart that I need to release and allow You to heal fully. I cannot do it on my own, Lord, so help me. Help me to love myself and others the way you do, Lord. Give me insight to see with Your heart and Your eyes. Give me the strength to love the unlovable as You do and help me to set healthy boundaries in my life. Help me to stay humble and wise so I can be a part of the unity You are calling your Body to have. In Jesus' Name I pray.

1 Corinthians 1:10: *"I appeal to you, brothers and sisters, in the name of our Lord Jesus Christ, that all of you agree with one another in what you say and that there be no divisions among you, but that you be perfectly united in mind and thought."*

2 Corinthians 13:11: *"Finally, brothers and sisters, rejoice! Strive for full restoration, encourage one another, be of one mind, live in peace. And the God of love and peace will be with you."*

Acts 4:32: *"All the believers were one in heart and mind. No one claimed that any of their possessions was their own, but they shared everything they had."*

Ephesians 4:22-24: *"You were taught, with regard to your former way of life, to put off your old self, which is being corrupted by its deceitful desires; to be made new in the attitude of your minds; and to put on the new self, created to be like God in true righteousness and holiness."*

Galatians 3:26-28: *"So in Christ Jesus you are all children of God through faith, for all of you who were baptized into Christ have clothed yourselves with Christ. There is neither Jew nor Gentile, neither slave nor free, nor is there male and female, for you are all one in Christ Jesus."*

John 13:34-35: *"A new command I give you: Love one another. As I have loved you, so you must love one another. By this everyone will know that you are my disciples, if you love one another."*

Philippians 2:3: *"Do nothing out of selfish ambition or vain conceit. Rather, in humility, value others above yourselves."*

Key #16: Stop Comparing Yourself To Others: Love Who God Has Made You To Be!

Stop comparing yourself to other people. Let this key seep into your brain and your heart so deeply that you never again think poorly of yourself. The fact is that there is only one of you in this entire universe! Only you can do what you can do! God has destined something specific just for you to do here on earth. This is why it is essential to draw close to God and truly begin to discover who you truly are. Not who the world made you into through the trauma of life, or the way you were raised, etc. Truly allow God to show you who you are and all that you have been created for! Be secure in Christ! Be secure in who you are in Him!

Reflection:

1. Write down a list of things that you believe God has gifted you with and why you like these things about yourself. (This will help you begin seeing the gold inside of you!):

____

____

____

____

____

____

____

____

____

2. Now write down a list of things that you desire to have and become in your life:

____

____

____

____

____

____

____

____

____

3. Then take time to pray and ask God which of those things you should begin going after right now. (this
   is important to seek God because He has times and seasons for us):

____

____

____

____

____

____

____

____

____

____

For example, if one of your desires is to become healthy and God says it is time, then begin setting a schedule to meal prep, eat healthier, work out, etc. Another example is perhaps pursuing your own business. If God gives you the green light, then take the first steps toward creating your own business. Use wisdom and hold onto your current job until you are established in your own business. My point is that we need to pursue the desires of our hearts and all that God has put within us. We should update our goals every six months to take a self-inventory and ensure we are moving forward. Amen?

4. Set some realistic goals for the things that the Lord just showed you to begin going after for this season.
   (I highly recommend creating a vision board for your goals!)

____

____

____

____

____

____

____

____

____

____

____

5. Then write down anyone whom you have compared yourself to in the past or possibly are comparing yourself to now:

____

____

____

____

____

____

____

____

____

____

____

____

____

____

____

____

6. Then write down why you are comparing yourself to them:

____

____

____

____

____

____

____

____

____

____

____

____

____

____

7. Now I want you to sit here for a minute and check your heart. Is this comparison coming from a victim mentality or a coveted mindset? If so, quickly repent and ask God to show you where you need some healing. Then come back into right standing as a child of the most high God and begin going after what it is that you desire. (Comparison usually comes from a lack inside of us where we are not being fulfilled in some area of our lives).

8. If you find yourself getting into comparison in the future, I want you to rewire your brain into a positive wavelength instead of a negative one. Often, comparison leads us to defeat, but we usually compare because we desire what that person has. Again, we must be cautious of developing a covetous mindset, but if it is something we truly desire and could attain, then we should pray and pursue it. We have the power to seek the Lord on this and see if it is the direction He wants us to go. If it is, then begin working towards your goal to become whatever it is that He has put within you. If it is not, then stay in your own lane for that season and be happy with where God has you for the time being.

9. Knowing your identity in Christ is such a vital key because it helps you to get out of comparison, and you begin looking at others with a desire to come up higher instead of feeling defeated.

Declaration:

I love who God has created me to be, and I enjoy meeting others who are different from me. There is always an opportunity for me to come up higher in my destiny. I can do this by looking at others with the heart of God. I am sensitive to the desires that God has placed within my heart, and I am setting attainable goals to achieve these desires. I am learning daily how to lean into God's direction for my life.

WEEK 7

Learn To Balance Your Life Within The Spirit Realm

1 The Flesh & The Spirit

Last week, we touched on how to live an unoffendable life, but this week will provide deeper insight and strategies on how to live it out daily. We are currently living in times that the Bible has talked about for thousands of years. Isaiah 5:20 says, *"Woe unto them that call evil good, and good evil; that put darkness for light, and light for darkness; that put bitter for sweet, and sweet for bitter."* As I look around, I am astonished by what is happening all over the World but especially within America.

I know that God says in the End Times, things will get dark, so we, as Believers in Christ, will shine brighter. However, I didn't know if I would see all of this transpire within my lifetime. We are here now, though, and with this comes a desperate pleading from my heart for people to be awakened—especially Christians, who are called to lead God's Endtime Army. I see the hearts of many people who are radically deceived right now. This deception has been allowed due to unhealed emotional wounds. These wounds often conceal themselves behind pride, which ultimately stems from fear. I see this fear that has been built into control through manipulation, feeding the simple pleasures of humanity, which stems from the fallen nature of sin.

I believe everything that has been happening since 2020 throughout the World is because we are living in times where God talks about in the Bible sifting the wheat from the tares. The time is now when the shaking has begun and will continue to prepare the Bride of Christ for Jesus' return. There will be even greater things that will come to deceive us, so we must be on high alert. There will be severe consequences for those who do not draw near to Jesus in these times. I can personally say that I long to be as close to Jesus as I can every single day. This will help us to be led correctly for the times that are coming.

I titled this week's chapter around "Learn to balance the flesh and Holy Spirit" because I see the World and even Christians running rampant after the desires of the flesh. These desires include pride, lust, perversion, selfishness, sexual immorality, sensualism, and a list of a whole lot more. Unfortunately, I also see the Church as imbalanced. I am not saying this to pass judgment or complain, but we must recognize these things so we can be prepared for what is to come. We cannot sit back, expecting different results, if we continue doing the same things we did before we knew Jesus. Once we give our lives to Jesus, we must change our actions and let our lives lead by example, which will help lead others to Jesus.

There are consequences that come from our spoken words and our actions. These consequences can come from unforgiveness, rebellion, and offenses we carry within our hearts. I believe that, as a whole, human nature has felt these consequences increase in some way over the past few years, both in the World and within the Church. God is preparing His Bride right now because, unfortunately, the Church does not know who she is, and she must awaken to the Truth. This insecurity in her identity has allowed a ton of wickedness to take over and corrupt the Earth. However, the exciting thing to look forward to is that a powerful Bride will arise in the time to come.

I believe we will see some of the mightiest moves of God in these End Times. It is going to be a new era of the Acts Church. We will see great signs, miracles, and wonders like never before. We, as the Church, should not want to miss this, but we need to prepare. I felt an urgency to write this book to help awaken and raise the Body of Christ to its true identity. It is, unfortunately, our fault that all the chaos is occurring within the Earth, especially in America. God gave Adam all authority over the earth and every living thing within it, and then, as humans, we lost that authority when the Fall of Man occurred. However, Jesus took back that authority and gave it to us, believers in Christ, to reclaim dominion here on earth until we reach heaven. We must start taking responsibility for our actions. We must humble ourselves and acknowledge where we have fallen short, repent, and get back on track. It is imperative to start preparing now for the times that are coming.

The Church needs to arise into all that she was created for, so the shaking and the sifting have begun. I hope that this chapter opens your eyes to the real enemy and that everything that happens in this life first occurs in the spirit realm. This is why our spirits must be awakened to what God is doing and what we are meant to do in this time and the times to come. We must allow the Holy Spirit to lead us rather than following the pleasures of our flesh. How do we do this? God tells us (Believers in Christ) that we died and our old spirit man was crucified with Jesus. Once this happened, we were born again. However, it is our job to continue to crucify our flesh and renew our souls daily so that we may walk in the new life that was given to us (Galatians 5:16-26 & Romans 12:2).

One of these pleasures of the flesh is pride, and the key to overcoming the temptation of pride is humility. We must train ourselves how to be humble and meek. There is such power in these two Gifts of the Spirit, but we must train ourselves in these gifts. When we choose to humble ourselves, it allows us to see things from God's heart and His perspective. We are going to need humility for all that is coming! The spirit of offense has escalated to another level since 2020, and I see the divisive spirits reveling in it. Unfortunately, the Bible tells us that things are only going to get worse, but it also says to hold on to hope because we will always overcome in the end. We, as believers and followers of Christ, must not give into the temptation to argue and try to prove ourselves, lest we fall into prideful, foolish ways. When we stay humble, we receive wisdom from the Holy Spirit on how to proceed in a conversation or a difficult situation. It is imperative to learn how not to react but to wait for the Holy Spirit's guidance in how to move forward.

Waiting for confirmation from Him may be awkward at first, but I'm telling you, this will help you so much in this life. I always tell people to follow after peace no matter what, so if your reaction is going to cause an upheaval, then don't do it. Keep your lips sealed tight and humble yourself. This is called self-control, and we can all achieve it, especially if the Holy Spirit is living within us. The choice is always our own. We must remember that the battles we face in this World are not against flesh and blood, but we are against spirits and principalities, as it says in *Ephesians 6:12*. This helps me to get rid of any offense towards others because I remember that this is not the true identity that God has for this person who is being rude to me. When I stay humble, God helps me see the woundedness in others when they get angry, and this helps me recognize any woundedness within myself as well. I then end up having grace for the person and begin praying for them instead of criticizing them. When I feel offended, I always ask God, where is the root inside of me, Lord? Help me to get rid of this and be able to walk out Your love with people, Lord.

God will always fight for us if we allow Him to, and He is our true Vindicator. So, we must ask ourselves, why are we so hard-pressed to prove our points if it will ultimately lead to total division? You see, we are all wounded. There is no perfect human being, but when we stay humble and learn to lean on the Holy Spirit, God says that people will be drawn to us because of His light and His love within us. His love is perfect. Without Him, we will fail. I am deeply convicted in this area, and I try to allow God to help me daily.

I am not saying we shouldn't have our own opinions and stand our ground when we need to; all I am saying is that there is great wisdom in learning how to discern situations and allow the Holy Spirit to lead us in conversations and dealings within this world. He sees things that we do not, and there is power when we do not give our pearls to swine (*Mathew 7:6*). There is also power when we walk in His ways rather than our own (*Isaiah 55:8-9*). Do we want ourselves to be glorified, or do we want Christ to be glorified? This is a great question to ask yourself consistently.

Think about that for a moment. Please understand me here; God loves you, and His grace is something we cannot fully fathom. We can all be set free from this selfishness by having intimacy with Jesus, daily, which leads us closer to our destiny. Do you ever realize how there is always a fight against your time with God? Something that always tries to interrupt it or steal it? Or how about the plain fact that sometimes we don't "feel" like reading our Bible or listening to worship music or praying? Do you know why this is?

It is because we are the by-products of the fall of man. We live in a sinful, fallen World with an enemy who hates us. But if you get the revelation of who you are in Christ, you no longer have to bow to the things from the fall because Jesus took back every key that Satan stole from Adam, and He gave it to us! It is stated in *Galatians 5:17* that the flesh is always at enmity with the Holy Spirit, and in *Romans 6:19 and 8:7-8*, that the flesh is never inclined to do what the Spirit desires. This means there is a spiritual war going on over you daily, but you have a choice in whether you want to win this daily battle.

We must make our flesh submit to the Holy Spirit. However, God showed me that too many Christians grieve the Holy Spirit because we give the flesh more dominion than His Spirit. It is stated in *Genesis 3:21* that God made garments of flesh for Adam and Eve after the fall of man occurred. The battle with the flesh originated from the fall, but Jesus came to break the curse of the fall by bringing us back into right standing with God. We, as Christians, must get this revelation! We were first created in God's image, but then the fall happened, separating us from God. Then, when we were born again, we received Jesus' Spirit, which came to live within us. We truly do have all the power we need right at our fingertips when we submit to Jesus and His Spirit's leading.

Unfortunately, this is one of the main reasons why most Christians are looked upon as powerless. Some Christians do not know who they are in Christ, meaning they do not recognize the power that resides within them, nor have they truly learned how to be led by the Holy Spirit. Again, knowing your identity in Christ is crucial to everything in this life as a Christian. We must submit to the sovereignty of God and His timing, but through this, we experience the strengthening of every gift of the Holy Spirit. God will allow us to go through the tests of this life to build the character within us to be able to carry out the calling that He has upon our lives here on this earth.

Remember the vision I shared with you about becoming one with Jesus in Chapter Three? I want to elaborate on one vital aspect of that vision. When Jesus brought me back to the Garden of Eden, before the fall had happened, Adam and Eve were glowing. They were radiantly beaming with light. They had the form of beautiful human bodies, but they didn't have flesh as we have now. I believe it wasn't until after the fall that the flesh came upon them. This was a huge revelation to me. It helps remind me that I am, first and foremost, a spirit being because Christ lives inside of me. This means that I have the power to override my flesh and everything that comes with this fallen world system! We need to grasp the revelation of how much God loves us! This revelation will carry us through every trial that we face in this life.

<u>APPLYING WISDOM TO YOUR DAILY LIFE</u>

There are some long Scripture readings for today & tomorrow but I need you to recognize the importance of getting into the habit of feeding your spirit more than your flesh. This is a huge key to walking out your freedom daily. We must choose to read, hear, and come into agreement with God's Word!

Prayer for the day:

Lord,

I repent for every time I give into my flesh instead of walking in obedience to your Holy Spirit. I know you want the absolute best for me and that your plans are good for my life. I know that you are a good Father who leads me well. I know that Your wisdom is far greater than any of my thoughts, so I ask You to lead me, and I give You full permission to humble me in the areas where I am still rebellious. Help me in my weaknesses and open up my eyes and heart to see why You are telling me not to touch something or do something. Make it plain upon my heart so I do not ever want to touch that particular thing that feeds my flesh and leads me astray. Thank You, Lord, for guidance and your mercy.

Scriptures to meditate on:

Romans 8:1-16: *"Therefore, there is now no condemnation for those who are in Christ Jesus, because through Christ Jesus the law of the Spirit who gives life has set you free from the law of sin and death. For what the law was powerless to do because it was weakened by the flesh, God did by sending his own Son in the likeness of sinful flesh to be a sin offering. And so he condemned sin in the flesh, in order that the righteous requirement of the law might be fully met in us, who do not live according to the flesh but according to the Spirit. Those who live according to the flesh have their minds set on what the flesh desires; but those who live in accordance with the Spirit have their minds set on what the Spirit desires. The mind governed by the flesh is death, but the mind governed by the Spirit is life and peace. The mind governed by the flesh is hostile to God; it does not submit to God's law, nor can it do so. Those who are in the realm of the flesh cannot please God. You, however, are not in the realm of the flesh but are in the realm of the Spirit, if indeed the Spirit of God lives in you. And if anyone does not have the Spirit of Christ, they do not belong to Christ. But if Christ is in you, then even though your body is subject to death because of sin, the Spirit gives life because of righteousness. And if the Spirit of him who raised Jesus from the dead is living in you, he who raised Christ from the dead will also give life to your mortal bodies because of his Spirit who lives in you. Therefore, brothers and sisters, we have an obligation—but it is not to the flesh, to live according to it. For if you live according to the flesh, you will die; but if by the Spirit you put to death the misdeeds of the body, you will live. For those who are led by the Spirit of God are the children of God. The Spirit you received does not make you slaves, so that you live in fear again; rather, the Spirit you received brought about your adoption to sonship. And by him we cry, "Abba, Father." The Spirit himself testifies with our spirit that we are God's children. Now if we are children, then we are heirs— heirs of God and co-heirs with Christ, if indeed we share in his sufferings in order that we may also share in his glory."*

Galatians 5:19-21: *"Now the works of the flesh are evident: sexual immorality, impurity, sensuality, idolatry, sorcery, enmity, strife, jealousy, fits of anger, rivalries, dissensions, divisions, envy, drunkenness, orgies, and things like these. I warn you, as I warned you before, that those who do such things will not inherit the kingdom of God.*

Galatians 5:16-17: *"But I say, walk by the Spirit, and you will not gratify the desires of the flesh. For the desires of the flesh are against the Spirit, and the desires of the Spirit are against the flesh, for these are opposed to each other, to keep you from doing the things you want to do."*

Galatians 5:24: *"And those who belong to Christ Jesus have crucified the flesh with its passions and desires."*

Matthew 26:41: *"Watch and pray that you may not enter into temptation. The spirit indeed is willing, but the flesh is weak."*

Reflection:

1. Are there any areas in your life where you know you are still being rebellious? This could be anywhere from knowing that you overeat and have lazy tendencies even though you know you need to get healthy. Or, how about watching TV or scrolling on your phone more than spending time with God? Or, how about learning how to keep your mouth shut instead of reacting in offense or anger? I know we've touched base on some of these over the past few weeks, but remember, we're dealing with precept upon precept each day and each week. We are not going to eliminate all of our negative thinking in one day or even fully in these nine weeks while going through this book. However, this book provides you with tools to learn how to walk in freedom daily if you so desire. List any areas of your life where you may still have Rebellion:

____

____

____

____

____

____

____

____

____

____

____

2. I want you to establish a daily routine for yourself if you haven't already, over the past few weeks. Writing down a routine and setting goals will help you keep track of your time and progress. For example, you write down that the 1st hour of your day will consist of you drinking your morning coffee or tea with Jesus and His Word. This will help you set aside a specific time for Bible study, prayer, and journaling. Now, if you find yourself waking up and gravitating towards something else, ask the Holy Spirit, is this my flesh, or is there a deeper wound I need to tend to? Begin paying close attention to the pulls of your flesh. We must learn to crucify our flesh by telling it to shut up and then begin doing the opposite of what it wants. Additionally, when creating your schedule, I recommend being very precise. The example below is quite vague. I want you to be intentional about your day and every hour of it while you are awake. It is essential to be precise because this will help hold you accountable at the end of your day, ensuring you accomplish the tasks you set out to do. Be realistic about the time you have so you don't feel overwhelmed or condemned if you don't accomplish your daily goals. The primary purpose of this is to hold you accountable and help you work towards achieving your goals.

<u>Here is an example of a simple daily routine Monday-Friday:</u>

6:30 - 7:30 am: Coffee & Bible time with my husband
7:30 - 8:30 am: Time alone with Jesus ~This includes reading my Bible, journaling, praying
8:30 - 9:00 am: Eat Breakfast
9:30 - 11 am: Exercise either at home or at the gym
11:00 - 12 pm: Shower and get ready
12:00 - 6 pm: appointments with clients
6:00 - 7 pm: Cook and have Dinner with Family
7:00 - 9 pm: Catch up on business Emails and Social Media Posting
9:00 - 9:30 pm: Get Ready for bed
9:30 - 11pm: Read my Bible and then go to bed

<u>DECLARATION:</u> I decree and declare that I am no longer bound by my flesh or my emotions. Jesus took every single fleshly desire and sinful deed on that cross for me to live freely. Therefore, I will not allow my flesh to rule nor lead my life any longer. I have the power of the Holy Spirit living in me and guiding me. I am obedient to His leadings. I am organized. I have the mind of Christ. I follow through on the goals and steps I have laid out for myself and my family. I am becoming healthier with every day that I live because I am crucifying the desires of my flesh. My precious and mighty Holy Spirit leads me daily.

2 Make your flesh & Soul Bow

There is immense power in Scripture when we read it, believe it, and begin to walk it out. We must apply it to our lives daily. It is essential to reach the point in our lives where God's word has the final say. It doesn't matter how I feel or what's coming against me, I choose to trust my God! My life is beginning to change, revealing deeper levels of the truth that we are, first and foremost, spirit beings. We must learn how to balance this while living in this fallen, fleshly world, but there is a breakthrough to be had here.

God is testing me with this, but I am quickly learning that this is true! The enemy constantly attacks our flesh and our soul (mind, will, emotions). I have suffered through several physical ailments throughout my life. I may continue to do so, but God has given us dominion over the flesh. He also gave us dominion over every living creature on this Earth, and he says that He will make your enemy your footstool.

The flesh is, and even your soul can be, in enmity with God's Spirit. So it is up to us to make them our footstool! It is up to us to honestly believe what God has said and then walk it out both in our minds and our bodies. With all of this being said, it is extremely important to be led by the Holy Spirit and not engage in the works of the flesh. God has a specific timing for our healing and deliverance because He is the only one who knows all that it will produce within us. If you are suffering in any way, hold on tight to the promises of God. Declare those promises out loud over your life and continue to praise Him through it all in worship. He will bring you through your trial mightily!

We must also acknowledge the revelation that God gave us dominion over the Earth. It is stated in Psalm 115:16, *"The highest heavens belong to the LORD, but the earth he has given to mankind."* I'm telling you, Christians need to rise into their identity in Christ because once we do, the Church will have the power we are supposed to be operating in! Why? Because we will realize who we are in Christ! We will come together in unity like never before, and we will begin to see God move in profound ways. God is waiting for us! You and me! He has given us authority, so we must stop blaming God and take action to bring about the changes we long to see. When we recognize our authority through Jesus Christ, we can boldly face any challenge that comes our way.

I want to share a few additional tactics that the enemy often employs against us. I have learned these things over the years, and hopefully, this will help you become aware of these tactics so you can break free, too. One of the first things God revealed to me is how the enemy always seeks to make you feel rejected. The devil and his minions will constantly use this because this is how he felt when he was thrown out of Heaven. This is one of the enemy's most significant tactics. He wants you to feel rejected and alone, so he will constantly try to use people to get you to feel this way. He loves to exploit any insecurities to manipulate your emotions and hold you back. He will use circumstances, especially within your childhood, to allow the seeds of rejection and abandonment to take root. Then, he will use it for the rest of your life if you do not break an agreement with it.

Unfortunately, this tactic of his is powerful because it prevents people from experiencing genuine encounters with the Love of God, as well as unity with other believers. If you have felt rejected by the people closest to you, chances are you have felt or may feel rejected by God. Even though this is the furthest thing from the Truth, it tends to keep people isolated, never feeling as if they can truly be themselves because they have learned how to hide extremely well behind the walls they have built over the years. If you can relate in any way, ask God to reveal these roots to you and begin breaking agreements with them. It truly is that simple. Just as in the chapter on free will, it is the same here. You may have to continue doing it until it moves from your mind to your heart, but freedom will come.

God always gives us a choice, and what Jesus did on that Cross thousands of years ago says that we are free. Choose to be free today, my friends! Choose to overcome every tactic that the enemy uses. When we learn to grow through the trials of his tactics by submitting to Jesus and crucifying our flesh, we then have power and dominion over the exact thing that has attacked us for years! It is powerful!

I have learned to now look at any rejection that comes my way as God's protection. If something doesn't work out in my life, I know that God has something better in store for me. I choose to believe this because I know that God is for me! Begin applying this motto to your life every time the feelings of rejection want to rear their ugly heads. Choose to face it head-on with the power of God's love. Knowing that He is allowing this for your growth and, ultimately, for your protection. Somehow, someway, I know that God is protecting me, even when the pain feels like it is too much to bear. We will never fully comprehend the ways of God, but we must acknowledge that He is good and His plans for our lives are good. He sees the end from the beginning, and He knows how to guide us through this life with power and success.

This is why I have emphasized throughout this entire book the importance of getting incredibly close to Jesus, learning your identity in Him, and being extremely careful about what you come into agreement with. When we choose to draw close to Jesus, freedom comes. The Truth comes, and we finally start seeing things in a whole new way because we are aligning our souls with God's Word. Our flesh, which has to do with the desires of our body, begins to align with His Spirit because we are training our mind, will, and emotions to agree with Truth. We finally start to understand God's word and hear His voice clearly. When we come to this place, we can crucify our flesh regularly, and we can better discern the tactics of the enemy. This is how sensitive we should become. When we abide in Christ, we will go where He goes, and we will do what He wants us to do (*John 5:19-20*).

Another tactic the enemy always uses is within our minds. If he can get us riled up emotionally, he can use this as leverage. Remember that this is within our realm of the soul. The enemy will always try to get you to partner with pride, manipulation, and control. This strategy is a huge one because once I explain it, I bet you will be highly aware of all the things that try to entangle you in this web. The enemy uses this one thing constantly. I gained a deeper understanding of this during the first two years since the Covid pandemic. All hell began to break loose all over the World with the crazy division that happened through propaganda.

I find it interesting that when I discuss anything related to COVID with others who seem to have a different opinion than mine, they often want to argue with me and sometimes even end the relationship if I disagree with them. What happened to the good old healthy conversations where we could listen, learn from one another, and then agree to disagree? Something has truly changed within these people. Some people have become angry and rigid, so blinded by their own views that if you disagree with them, they act as if you are the enemy instead of seeing the actual enemy at work. As Christians, we should be very aware of His mode of operation.

This, my friends, is called a spirit of manipulation and control. The spirit of Jezebel and Leviathan love to hide behind these tactics, bringing confusion, manipulation, and division. We should always be able to have conversations with people to see and respect where others are coming from, even if we disagree. It is about making the feelings of our flesh and soul realm submit to the wisdom of the Holy Spirit. Unfortunately, this is not how the world operates today, and the Church needs significant help in this area as well. It starts with us. We must be aware and learn how to walk in love by crucifying our flesh daily, amen?

God revealed to me in 2019, before this whole "plandemic" came upon the Earth, that a demonic spirit was coming to the entire world that would twist everything. Please know when I say "plandemic" that I am speaking of the evil powers that brought this wicked scheme into being. I saw pieces of wood being twisted into black wicker that covered the entire earth, knowing that the word 'wicker' means to twist. God specifically used the phrase twist when He revealed to me what was coming to the world. It is my prayer that God's people will be awakened to the twisting that has been going on for years within the powers that are and will be. Again, it is just as the Bible describes in *Isaiah 5:20*, where good will be called evil and evil will be called good. We must stay alert by thoroughly learning to abide in Jesus.

APPLYING WISDOM TO YOUR DAILY LIFE

Lord,

help me to humble myself so I can hear from You clearly. Help me to continue healing any wounds within my soul that are causing me to rebel or fear You in any way. I trust You with my life, Lord Jesus. I trust you to lead me well and to give me wisdom with discernment. It says in Your Word that discernment is a gift You give to Your saints, so I am asking You, Lord, to stir this gift within me and teach me how to steward it well. Help me to bow to You always so I can then make my flesh and my soul bow to Your spirit. Holy Spirit, I give You my will. Help me, teach me, grow me, strengthen me in Jesus' name, I pray! Amen.

Scriptures to meditate on:

Romans 8:13-14: *"For if you live according to the flesh you will die, but if by the Spirit you put to death the deeds of the body, you will live. For all who are led by the Spirit of God are sons of God."*

Romans 7:18: *"For I know that nothing good dwells in me, that is, in my flesh. For I have the desire to do what is right, but not the ability to carry it out."*

Romans 8:5-7: *"For those who live according to the flesh set their minds on the things of the flesh, but those who live according to the Spirit set their minds on the things of the Spirit. For to set the mind on the flesh is death, but to set the mind on the Spirit is life and peace. For the mind that is set on the flesh is hostile to God, for it does not submit to God's law; indeed, it cannot."*

Galatians 6:8: *"For the one who sows to his own flesh will from the flesh reap corruption, but the one who sows to the Spirit will from the Spirit reap eternal life."*

1 Peter 2:11: *"Beloved, I urge you as sojourners and exiles to abstain from the passions of the flesh, which wage war against your soul"* (remember that the soul is your mind, will, and emotions. When we feed the flesh, it will make us feel double-minded because our new spirit only wants to please God, which already has begun to rewire our minds, but when we feed the fleshly desires, this will cause dissension within your entire being. Be very aware of this).

Reflection:

Dying to our flesh and our soul realm is difficult because the flesh always wants to rule. Imagine a child being raised as a spoiled little brat getting every single thing that they ever wanted and there were no boundaries or discipline in their life. This child would be set up for disaster as they grew into adulthood. They would rebel against authority and likely develop a victim mentality, which hinders all growth. Well, this is precisely how it is with our flesh. If we continue to let our flesh do what it wants, our old self (our fallen spirit before we got born again) will begin to manifest. We will not come into the fullness of all that Christ has for us. With this being said, we must crucify our flesh and its desires daily. This means telling our flesh to shut up and training ourselves to walk out what God's Word tells us to do instead.

A great example of this is when you set a goal to begin getting healthy. You rarely want to go to the gym, and you don't usually like to give up your favorite unhealthy foods. However, when you become diligent in doing these things and begin to see good results, it becomes easier for you to maintain that consistency. You also start to feel amazing in your body and your mind because our bodies were created to be healthy. It craves a healthy routine. It craves good food that fuels our body to keep us healthy. It craves movement and sound sleep. You get my point. It is the same, actually, for a child. A child craves discipline even though they don't know it. We must keep in mind that we were first created as spirit beings (in the image of God, Genesis 1:27 & Psalm 104:1-2) with supernatural bodies (Philippians 3:21 and 2 Corinthians 5:1-10), but then the decaying flesh was given to us as a result of the fall of man. Therefore, our spirit craves what is good from God, while the flesh always wants to rebel. We must crucify our flesh and feed our spirit daily.

1. I want you to begin paying attention to how much your flesh and your soul try to control you throughout your day, week, and month. Here are some examples to help you know what to look for: This could be not wanting to wake up early to spend time with God before your day begins. Not wanting to pray, worship, or read your word. Not wanting to be kind to someone who is rude to you. Or, how about staying in the place of lies that keep repeating themselves over and over in your mind when an offense rises against you? I hope you get my point, but I want you to start paying attention to these things so you can be intentional about crucifying the desires of the flesh. It is time to rewire your soul to align with God's Word and fully come into the new creation that God promises we can be. Amen? Write down what tries to rule you throughout your journal each day so you can begin to recognize these desires and get into a habit of crucifying them.

2. When you recognize these things, make a simple shift in your heart and mindset. Be quick to repent for whatever the Lord convicts your heart with. Then, make a plan to follow through with whatever things will bring you into a deeper intimacy with Jesus. I encourage you to find an accountability partner to hold you accountable for these things. Consider finding someone who shares your desire to do this so you can hold each other accountable and grow together in your faith in God.

____

____

____

____

____

Declaration:

I am no longer bound by my flesh because Jesus took it all for me upon that cross. Jesus gave me His Holy Spirit once I made Him Lord over my life. Therefore, I am learning how to be entirely led by the Holy Spirit! I command my mind, will, emotions, and body to come into alignment with the Holy Spirit! This includes learning how to crucify my flesh daily and every selfish desire it has. I am an overcomer and conqueror through the blood of Jesus! I am in a process of continual improvement until I leave this earth, going from glory to glory! Amen!

3 You carry Power to overcome

Before the whole world shut down in 2020, I had four months of intense dreams where I had to go back into prison. These dreams felt so incredibly real that when I would awake, I would pray in the spirit all night long. I was seriously wrestling with the Lord because I thought I was possibly going to have to go back to prison. I didn't realize it then, but God had me interceding for people all over the World for all that was coming. The burden was almost too much for me to carry, as I felt a great weight from the Lord. I honestly thought God was going to send me back to prison. This was how real the dreams in that season were to me.

I don't believe it was a coincidence when the entire World shut down, and most had to be confined to their homes. God was allowing me to feel what was coming. God always allows us to go through challenging circumstances to prepare us for what is coming if we are listening to His guidance. We can find examples of this to be true when examining every influential person in the Bible, such as Paul, Job, Joseph, Daniel, Ezekiel, and Jesus, among others. You see, these dreams were warning dreams for the entire World! Life in 2020 reminded me of the same chaos I endured when I was in prison.

Nothing made sense or added up. Now, this world system is saying things that we are supposed to adhere to even though there is no truth backing what is being said. However, the huge tool that the enemy has used in this to control and manipulate is fear. The Body of Christ must partner with love, not fear, in these End Times. We must be like Joshua and Daniel, taking a stand and stepping out boldly, knowing Who is backing us!

I could tell you many things about the spirits of manipulation and control, as I have become highly aware of their ugly tactics over the years. The tricky thing about these particular spirits is that you do not always know that you are getting entangled with them. It isn't always as apparent as someone arguing with you and trying to manipulate you. Let me give you this example.

I have certain people in my life who are not saved yet who are within my family, and of course, I want them to go to Heaven. Not only that, but I want to see them live a life full of power and freedom. Recently, God showed me that my emotions were deceiving me because I wanted them to be saved so badly. I realized how I was being prideful and manipulative by thinking I was the only one who could be a positive influence in their life to lead them to Jesus. I was also trying to manipulate them due to unhealed areas in my own heart. I had to humble myself right away and repent, saying, 'Oh God, who am I?' You are God, and You know how to reach them better than I do. I fully surrender them to you. Help me, Lord, to love them where they are and lead by your example.

This manipulative spirit arises whenever you attempt to exert control over a situation or person. This could be as simple as trying to get someone to like you or having to over-explain yourself about a particular situation. Trying to prove yourself typically comes from a spirit of rejection. Still, past trauma can allow the door to be open to partner with a spirit of manipulation and control as well. Every time something rises against you, and you feel yourself losing control, ask yourself, 'What am I choosing to partner with here?' Then, ask the Holy Spirit to guide you into your next steps.

If you know who you are in Christ, it becomes much easier to recognize these tactics because you no longer have to prove yourself to anyone or try to make things happen as you fully trust God. You trust who you are in God, and you know that you no longer have to try and manipulate anyone or anything in your life. Why? Because God is a good God who wants the absolute best for you! Your identity in Jesus is key to becoming aware of everything you need to be mindful of. God will always give us insight when we abide in Him and ask Him for direction.

Another tactic to watch out for is false humility. Be very aware of this one because it opens the door for the enemy to use you and can also block your blessings. When you know who you are in Christ, false humility cannot stay. There is only true repentance and genuine humility that comes along with our Identity in Christ. Ask yourself this question: when someone compliments you, do you truly receive it? Do you know deep in your heart that you can respond with bold humility, or are you saying thank you from a false place of humility within your heart?

How about when someone wants to bless you with a gift or money? Do you joyfully receive it as a blessing from the Lord, or do you say thank you with false humility, allowing shame and unworthiness to creep in, or possibly do not accept it at all? Ask the Holy Spirit to reveal to you areas in your heart where this tactic may be hindering your progress. There is such freedom when we allow the Holy Spirit to reveal everything that needs to be healed inside of our hearts. This is where freedom can finally flow, and God's power can be used in a mighty way through you.

There are so many tactics the enemy uses that I could write an entire book to expose them. However, the last one I want to chat about is distractions and excuses. I hear many people in the body of Christ talk about being so busy with work, kids, school, ministry, and other responsibilities that it is challenging for them to find time to spend with God. Let me tell you a secret. This is a lie from the pits of hell, and unfortunately, a lot of us have bought into it! I used to be one of them. Once you have an intimate relationship with Jesus, He should be with you every second of every day. There is no separation between time for Jesus and time for kids, work, hubby, wifey, etc. You should always bring Jesus into everything you do in life! When you do this, it fosters a deeper relationship with Him, and you become excited to spend more intimate one-on-one time with Him. It no longer feels like a chore to read His Word or to set time aside to be with Him.

The excitement begins to come because you start getting more profound revelations within His Word that you never heard before, even if you've read that same Scripture. This is how awesome Jesus is! When we have encounters with Him daily, we begin to grow daily. If we continue to use the excuse of being too busy, the enemy will always win, and we will have a difficult time stepping into our true identities and destinies. We must be strategic with our time and our intentions.

We do not want to be like the Israelites, going around the same mountain repeatedly. I encourage you to make the choice today to say, "I will no longer use this as an excuse and allow Satan or any of his minions to steal my destiny!" The choice is yours! You are powerful! You have the option to get distracted, and you have the choice to use excuses. Justifying why you can't or won't will always hold you back from your destiny. One thing I have learned, and it has helped me immensely, is to own my faults and stop making excuses for them. I have asked my husband and my closest friends to hold me accountable in this area, as I want to succeed with excellence in life. I want to live a life of abundance, and Jesus wants this for us too! If the devil can distract us, he can destroy us. We must become very aware of distractions in our lives.

Many distractions in the world mask what is really happening right now. The enemy has been setting things up for a very long time for all that is happening all over the World. I encourage you to seek God for deeper revelation on all that is coming and how you can walk through it without being scorched. I prophesy that you will walk through this time and the more difficult ones to come being fully on fire, but not have one hair on your head scorched, nor will you even smell like smoke. You will only beam with the radiance of God being purified along the way!

God showed me that Isaiah 60:1-7 is coming. He showed me that these things have already happened in the spirit. Those who grasp this revelation will begin to see the blessings from these verses manifest in their lives. The hearts of people are being awakened to the Truth, and they will arise and shine into all that God has called them to be. This is not a time to be deceived by hardening our hearts and bowing to wicked schemes of the enemy. But it is time to bow low in humility to our King Jesus so He can lead us powerfully. It is through discernment and humbling ourselves that we can be trained up in every Fruit of the Spirit. We must begin walking like Jesus so we can be the light that Jesus wants us to be in these times.

The wealth will be transferred from the wicked to the righteous! We are made righteous all because of Jesus! We cannot work for this righteousness, nor can we work for what Jesus has already paid the price for, but we can walk with Him in obedience to wherever He leads us. We are truly living in some of the most exciting times and we were born for a time as this! However, it is up to us to grow in our identity in Christ and discernment to recognize the times and seasons.

Do you know what God is calling you into this season? Do you know what you have been destined for here on this Earth? Do you know what God has anointed you to do in these times? I encourage you to seek God's heart in these matters and allow the Holy Spirit to reveal His Truth to you! Be ready! Be Aware! Do not fear; the time is now to come and arise into all He is calling you to be!

APPLYING WISDOM TO YOUR DAILY LIFE

Father God,

Thank You for giving me more profound revelations of Your Word and training me to hear Your voice only. Thank You for showing me how to be keenly aware of the enemy's tactics so I can fight correctly. Holy Spirit, thank You for strengthening my spirit as I come to you in the secret place. Jesus, I give you full permission to come into every area of my heart and within my life to have your way completely. Show me Your ways, God. My life is Yours; it is not my own. I give You all of me! Show me the things that I need to still release unto You that I have held onto too tightly. Show me areas where I have allowed the enemy to hold me back and show me how to break all ties and agreements with his evil ways. Lord, I thank you for every rejection that has happened in my life because I am learning that this is your protection. Thank You for every protection throughout my future. I trust You with my life, Lord. Thank You for helping me apply these keys to my life daily. Thank You for delivering me from every root that has tried to hold me back in bondage by the flesh, by curses, or any spiritual attack. I know the power that resides inside of me, and I know that I have the power to break every stronghold, every curse, and every lie off and out of me by the precious blood of Jesus! Amen!

Scriptures to meditate on:

Proverbs 1:7: *"The fear of the LORD is the beginning of knowledge; fools despise wisdom and instruction."*

Proverbs 3:5-6: *"Trust in the LORD with all your heart,and do not lean on your own understanding.In all your ways acknowledge him,and he will make straight your paths."*

James 1:5: *"If any of you lacks wisdom, let him ask God, who gives generously to all without reproach, and it will be given him."*

Ephesians 5:6-10: *"Let no one deceive you with empty words, for because of these things the wrath of God comes upon the sons of disobedience. Therefore do not become partners with them; for at one time you were darkness, but now you are light in the Lord. Walk as children of light (for the fruit of light is found in all that is good and right and true), and try to discern what is pleasing to the Lord."*

2 Timothy 1:7: *"For God has not given us a spirit of fear, but of power and of love and of a sound mind."*

Psalm 25:12-14: *"Who are those who fear the Lord? He will show them the path they should choose. They will live in prosperity, and their children will inherit the land. The Lord is a friend to those who fear him. He teaches them his covenant."*

Key #16: Choose To Partner With God's Love Instead Of Fear

It is time to begin partnering with God's love and His Faith. Let go of fear! I'm not talking about the healthy fear that God gives to us, as wisdom and warnings like, "Don't touch that it's hot, or don't go down that street, it's not safe." This actually comes from God's love and protection. But what I am talking about is partnering with a spirit of fear that begins to make you feel double-minded and question whether God is truly for you. We must continue training ourselves to have faith and trust God's Word like never before. God is always in the business of protecting us, even though we may not see it at the moment. God is sovereign, and when we choose to "fear" Him (which means to love Him and have a holy reverence for Him) more than anything else in our lives, we can begin to live in total freedom.

If there are any areas in your life that you have not fully surrendered to God yet, give them to Him now. There are times ahead when we will need to know that God loves us and is for us, no matter what. This will give us such a strong faith that we can overcome anything. If you haven't been allowing God to refine you and stretch you within your faith, let it begin now! Ask the Holy Spirit to reveal the things that you have been holding onto too tightly and have a deep fear of letting go. (This could be unforgiveness, or a loved one who is not saved, or someone who you know is not healthy for you). I promise you that God will always bring it back to you in greater measure than before if it is meant to be in your life. God is a God of true redemption and vindication! If something is taken from you by force, God will restore it with something better in mind. If God wants you to surrender something to Him, trust Him in this! He knows what is best for you. He loves you more than any other person in the World! Rest in His Love when difficult circumstances bring fear. Choose to rest and trust in the measure of faith that is within you that God talks about in Romans 12:3! God has your very best interest in mind, and always remember that when something is stripped from you, allow the Holy Spirit to strengthen you and show you a better way into something new.

Reflection:

1. Ask God to show you areas in your life where you have fear and write them down:

____

____

____

____

____

____

____

____

____

____

2. Now replace those fears with God's promises. Find Scriptures that counteract those fears. Write these down:

____

____

____

____

____

____

____

____

____

____

3. Say this out loud, "I repent for partnering with fear instead of God's truth. I come out of all agreement with fear and I reject any spirit of Fear." Then read the Scriptures from above out loud declaring God's promises over your fears daily until you conquer your unhealthy fears. I promise you that if you keep your heart soft and choose to trust God's protection over your life, it will begin to take root in your heart. You will begin to break free especially with all the other exercises I am giving you to do throughout this book.

4. I want you to begin challenging yourself to face your fears so you can practice overcoming them. Begin to take tiny steps forward. Remember, this is to break you free, not to put you back into fear. So take your time and be led by Holy Spirit. The main point of doing this is to encourage you that once you come out of agreement with your fears, you can overcome them with Jesus.

Declaration:

I believe the promises that my God has for me are good! I know He has plans to prosper me in every area of my life! I partner with faith from this day forward. I listen to my Lord and Savior, Jesus Christ, and I allow His powerful Holy Spirit to lead and comfort me. I am walking closer to my destiny every day and I will not back down. I am pushing towards the goals God had for me, which were born in eternity before I was even born. I am taking the proper steps to help me get there daily. I am an overcomer and I can do all things through Christ! I look at fear through the eyes of my heavenly Father knowing that no matter what, He will get me through every trial I come to because He knows what is inside of me! I choose His Love and faith over fear!

5 Fight, Flight, or Fire?

Over the years, I can now look back and recognize that I have been in the refiner's fire, and I know it will continue as I grow in the Lord. There has been a new intense trial that arises almost every year for my husband and me since we said yes to Jesus. I'm not going to sit here and lie to you that it has been easy to walk through because the refiner's fire does hurt. However, something amazing happens when we choose to continue to walk through the fire with Jesus. He begins to burn every unwanted desire, thought, and hurt from our hearts, all the while building strength like ones never known before.

You see when I said yes in complete surrender to Jesus Christ back in 2008, there was an onslaught of attacks. You have heard some of them thus far, but I can now say this with great joy, as Job 15:13 clearly states, because I have learned how to walk through hell and back and still trust My Jesus. I laugh sometimes when people look at Christianity as being weak because, in my walk, I've genuinely been trained as a warrior! Abiding with Jesus as a true believer is not for sissies! We are in constant training for war, but the best part is that He teaches us how to do this from a place of love and victory, which is the exact opposite of the way the world wars.

I am going to be bold and say this, hoping you won't take offense, but I invite you to open your hearts to receive correction if any is needed. I am a firm believer in iron sharpening iron and allowing correction to come in when a change is necessary. This is a wise thing to do. These warriors I am referring to are Christians who truly make Jesus Christ their Lord and dedicate their lives to Him on a daily basis. Not the ones who proclaim they love Jesus and then continue living for the enemy, never truly allowing God to refine them. Unfortunately, these types of "Christians" become hypocrites, giving all Christians out there a bad name. Honestly, it makes me wonder if they are true believers and followers of Christ.

Please know that I speak this in love. If there is any conviction happening in your heart, simply repent and start over because God wants you to live out your full potential. We do not serve a God who wants to leave us in our mess. He will begin to clean us up, teach us, strengthen us, and stretch us to keep growing. As Christians, we should always be increasing in our fruitfulness. This is especially true in the time we are now living on the Earth, where we are witnessing division firsthand. Christians must arise into who we are called to be. It is only through the refining fires that we become the light of the World, walking in His Truth and purity.

The Word of God says that whoever gives up their life will gain it. Matthew 16:25 clearly states, *"Whoever wants to hang onto their life, will lose it, but gives up his life for my sake, will find it."* The Bible also states in 2 Corinthians 5:17, *"Therefore if any man be in Christ; he is a new creature; old things have passed away and behold, all things become new."* This means that once you give your life to Christ, you become a new creation. You can no longer remain in the sin where you once were. The eyes of your heart become open to what is good for you and what is dangerous to you.

You become what you were always created to be before the foundations of the World. This doesn't happen overnight of course, but I can sit here while I write this today with complete conviction that I am no longer who I once was. I have allowed God to come in and refine everything that corrupted me from my childhood until I said yes to Jesus. I still allow Him to come in daily to correct me because I slip along the way. However, I have learned how to keep my heart open, stay humble, and allow God to burn off every bad fruit that still tries to fester.

I need to stay on the topic of "true Christians" for a moment because it is not a coincidence of all that is happening in the World right now. When I say "true Christians," I mean on-fire, born-again followers of Christ. Many Christians are lukewarm right now, and they are in perilous waters. If you have been spending time in the secret place with God, it is clear that God is sifting the tares from the wheat right now. In Matthew 7:16-20, it is stated that you will know a Christian by the fruits that are being produced in their life. "*You will know them by their fruits. Every tree that does not bear good fruit is cut down and thrown into the fire. Therefore, by their fruits you will know them.*" I believe we entered a pivotal time for this at the beginning of 2020. God is sifting the Church and shaking up the entire World to show His goodness to all who choose to see it.

God gave me a powerful vision in December 2019, just before the COVID-19 pandemic emerged. I mentioned this vision in another chapter. However, I'd like to delve a little deeper into this vision with you. It began with God taking me deep into the center of the earth, which I believe represented the deep places of our hearts. He then began shifting the tectonic plates, creating earthquakes that originated from within the entire earth and pierced to the surface, causing huge cracks all over the world. Then the heavens began to open up, and a waterfall from the skies poured down upon the earth, creating mighty rivers that ran through the broken quakes of the world, pushing all the mud, drudge, and debris out until the rivers became sparkling clean. Beautiful, fresh growth began to appear everywhere I looked, with flowers and trees, unlike anything I had ever seen before.

The clear water represented the Holy Spirit working in powerful ways through believers who choose to come into purity and holiness by willingly setting themselves apart from the world. Be aware of distractions that are coming in to get the Body of Christ off track. Be cautious of what you allow into your minds through the airwaves (TV, radio, social media). Ask the Holy Spirit for guidance, and allow Him to reveal the Truth and lead you where you need to go or what you need to be doing at this time. God is speaking with precise instructions to those who are listening right now.

God is wanting to purify His Bride at this time. He showed me that He is bringing all darkness into light! We need to be aware of this because great darkness is coming, and we will see much that has been hidden. However, this is our opportunity to shine brighter than ever before. This is our opportunity to reclaim the territory and all that the enemy has stolen from us. This includes school systems (our children's innocence), banks, hospitals, nursing homes, and other institutions. Everywhere the enemy has lured people into with the love of money, get ready because I believe we are taking it back, but in new ways. I encourage you to draw closer to Jesus than you ever have before right now because He is leading us into a revolutionary era.

God showed me that He has chosen specific people to do particular things during these times, but they are not rising to this calling due to fear that is overpowering them. Too many Christians have put their trust in things other than Him. God has amazing plans destined for you at this time! There are mighty gifts inside of you that He wants you to use. He wants you to break free from this worldly system. This includes your job if it owns you. (I'm not saying you shouldn't work; we must work. God tells us through several Scriptures that work is good for us and that no man deserves a good wage without working). However,

God wants us to be free in every area of our lives, and I see so many Christians walking around in this world, living as slaves to a worldly system instead of slaves to Jesus.

The Word tells us that we are to walk in freedom, that we are the head and not the tail, and that we are to be the lenders and not the borrowers! So, if this is convicting you or offending you in any way, let it! Seek God out on this matter. Proverbs 25:2 says to seek out answers. What is God telling you to do? I get so fired up on this particular subject because so many Christians do not want to come into the fire. We tend not to want to press into the hard things. But this is where we truly grow in the Lord. When we truly surrender our will for God's will, He will always lead us into Truth and goodness. He says He will never forsake us, so what are we afraid of?

The entire World is being tempted and tested, and I am giving you some prophetic insight into what is to come. God is sifting the body of Christ right now in powerful ways, and you do not want to miss Him or fail these tests. Satan is also testing the entire world with one of the biggest experiments we have ever seen done to humanity throughout history through these Covid vaccines, as well as all the different protests going on in the world. There are several tests taking place in the spiritual realm, and it is time to pay attention!

I encourage you to jump into the fire with God! What I mean is to fully jump in, freely abandoned, trusting Him with every single thing in your life. Because if you don't, the times ahead will become even more difficult for you. Please understand me; this is not a doom-and-gloom message. God will provide for His people just as He has always done throughout history. This is a fiery message to wake people up to all that is happening and to prepare us for what is to come. God will work powerfully in and through those who are surrendered to His will and who are willing to be His vessel in these end times.

Am I saying that Jesus is coming back this year, next year, or the year after? I'm not sure, but the Bible tells us that no one knows except the Father. However, it does say in Revelation 16:15 that we are to be ready every day as if He is coming like a thief in the night. It also says that Jesus will come back when times are just as it was in the days of Noah. Take some time to explore that revelation further. I will share just a glimpse of what God has been showing me, but I think as you seek Him on this matter, He will give you more profound revelation, and you will be wowed by all He wants to show you.

What does it mean in Luke 17:26? It says that when the son of man returns, it will be just as it was in the days of Noah. I want to provide some background information before I share what I'm about to discuss with you. While I was in prison, I had no one but the Holy Spirit to teach me His Word. God told me He was sending me into the prisons to set the captives free and that I, too, would be set free from chaos and disorder. While I was there, God began waking me up in the middle of the night, speaking to me in ways that I had never experienced before.

He would wake me up speaking Scriptures or telling me to write. The Holy Spirit would literally take over my hand as I yielded, and He would reveal things from heaven through my hands. One night in particular, he brought me back to the crazy days of Noah in a dream. Let me tell you, IT WAS WILD! There were characters similar to those in *"The Lion, the Witch, and the Wardrobe"* by C.S. Lewis. Some creatures were part human and part animal. I believe this is where mermaids and unicorns come from, too. What if all of the stories and myths that we've read about were actually real? That is a thought for you to ponder with the Lord, but this truly blew my mind. I had to seek more Truth out on this topic with Jesus.

The Bible talks about the start of this in Genesis, chapters 5-9, how God first created man, but then sometime after the fall of satan happened, his fallen angels began having relations with human women. Out of these relations came immortal, strong, and heavenly type beings. It talks about how wicked humankind had become, and it even says that God regretted ever making man! That is a powerful statement. It must have been so evil for God to have wanted to wipe out everyone except Noah and his family. The only reason he spared them was because the Bible says that Noah was the only righteous man and blameless in his generations before God. (Genesis 6:5-10).

There is a huge key right here that I am about to give you. During the days of Noah, people were no longer from the bloodline of God's original creation of man; they were no longer pure in the way God had made them. Their Godly DNA had been changed, and they wanted nothing to do with the God who made them. It states that there was only pure wickedness in their hearts, and God saw how corrupt the earth had become (Genesis 6:11-12). It also states in Genesis 7:15 that God only allowed creatures that had the breath of life in them to enter the ark. This is so powerful! God breathed into Adam when He created man. All God had to do was breathe into something, and it would come alive. In other words, this is stating that other creatures were obviously twisted into some other type of creation that wasn't by God.

This may be hard for some of you to swallow, especially if you have been deceived by all that has been going on in this World lately. However, the Bible states that Jesus will return just as it was in the days of Noah, and He says He's coming back for a ready Bride. Now, I think we still have a way to go because I can't even imagine the total evilness that must have been on the earth during Noah's time for God to have destroyed all of creation except eight people! However, I believe that we are entering a period that will be similar and it could happen faster than I think. We already saw a glimpse of all the evil God exposed during the early stages of the "pandemic." However, we are now experiencing a massive population of the World that is still taking something, the effects of which we have no idea will have on the human race down the road. I'm not intentionally trying to offend anyone here, especially if you are for the COVID-19 vaccines, but God showed me in early 2019, before COVID even came, that a massive experiment was coming to the World and to be very aware not to partake of it.

I'm not sure if you know this, but the Truth has finally begun coming out that the COVID vaccines have already taken several lives by death, but also by paralyzation and new diseases that Doctors cannot even explain nor cure. The bottom line is that none of the vaccines had fully been approved, and there is a reason vaccines take several years to develop. As I mentioned earlier, I believe this was, and still is, a massive human experiment taking place worldwide. I won't go into any rants here, but this experiment involved attempting to alter the DNA of God's original creation, and I believe it was just a setup for what's to come: the full alteration of God's creation when the mark of the beast does come. I don't believe this is a coincidence.

This experiment included individuals who received the real vaccine, those who received a placebo vaccine, and those who did not receive any vaccine. Now, for those of you who took it, I don't want you to partner with fear. I believe we serve a merciful and mighty God who has an amazing grace that will cover you. If you truly believe God told you to take it, then I think He blessed you by allowing you to receive a placebo, only by His grace. If you didn't pray about getting it, repent and ask Him to heal you if you have side effects, or thank Him immensely if you were one of the blessed protected ones to get a placebo without even knowing. I won't delve into the details of this either, but I do want to mention it because Jesus said to pay attention to the times and the seasons.

The Bible states that Jesus will return as it was in the days of Noah. So, how about the millions of people who are changing their bodies from male to female or from female to male? I have such a heart for these people because I know how real the demonic spirits are that are deceiving them. I, too, struggled with same-sex attraction and thought something was so wrong with me for years. These spirits can make a person truly feel that they are not what they were born to be and try to pervert their original design from God.

This is an agenda straight from the demonic pit, and it comes from a spirit that did these same things thousands of years ago to lure people away from the one true God. This spirit is all throughout the Bible. She has gone by many names over the years, but we know her by the name Asherah in the Holy Bible. If you'd like to find out more about this, read Jonathan Cahn's book called *The Return of the gods*, and you can dig deeper into your research. His book is an excellent read that offers amazing insights, providing a wealth of historical information with biblical confirmation. It was genuinely fascinating to see how spirits are always up to the same old tricks and how they move in patterns. Jesus is about to return, and Scripture tells us that the Kingdom of darkness will rise and rage against the Kingdom of God even harder in these End Times.

However, there is good news! We serve a loving God who does forgive, but we also serve a mighty and powerful God who hates evil. We must remember the sovereignty of God and that God will do whatever He needs to do to bring people to repentance because He does not want one to perish in the pits of hell. The God of the Holy Bible is a God of Love, order, power, abundance, war, and discipline. We must remember that there is always a perfect balance with God. We will become unbalanced if we only look at Him through the skewed lenses of our wounded hearts. We need revelation on all that is to come. We can only receive this by jumping into the fire, allowing Him to burn out every fear, wrong thought, wrong desire, and every bit of pride and confusion within us. God says He will give if you ask and that you will find if you seek.

Have you truly been seeking God with your whole heart? Have you been listening and then abiding? Please listen to my heart, for I believe the Father's heart is speaking through me. He loves you too much to allow you to miss what is coming. God is going to make a way for His people to thrive through all the evil that is coming. I believe there will be one of the greatest harvests into the Kingdom of God that the earth has ever seen. God is wooing the hearts of every human, but we have to be willing to come into the fire instead of running in fear or fighting in fear. It is time to face our fears and allow the Holy Spirit to heal us and purify us. People all over the world are yearning for a spiritual encounter, and it is our responsibility as followers of Christ to guide and disciple them when this happens. We must listen to the guidance of the Holy Spirit and study God's word daily, during these times, as many people will be deceived. The wolves in sheep's clothing that the Bible warns us about are already here.

Be very aware of everything going on around you and what you allow yourself to come into agreement with. Again, this is not to be in fear but to draw so incredibly close to God that you will allow Him to burn out of you everything that doesn't belong. Your burning for Him will then help burn off things from other people as well, just as it was in the fire with Meshach, Shadrach, and Abednego. This fire will not scorch you as long as you bring Jesus into the flames with you. You must have faith and trust God with all of your heart and soul. If we consistently come into the fires of life with Jesus, this will launch us into our destiny and protect us from all that is coming.

We have all heard of fight-or-flight responses, but neither of these helps us truly walk through our pain in a healthy way. God showed me there is another way. Coming into the fires of life with Jesus, allowing Him to burn out every desire to run or fight. This way enables God's love to reveal to you who you are in Him and the destiny that is before your life. Here, you will find where your power lies. You no longer have to carry the weight of whatever burden you may be facing. Here, you will learn how to rest during the raging fights that come against you. Here, you will learn to become a peaceful and mighty warrior of love! The choice is ours to either walk alongside God in these times or not. Dark forces are raging against us more than ever before, and it is time to wake up to all that God has in store for you. The time is now, my Brothers and Sisters in Christ, to come into the fire of God! He is waiting for you!

APPLYING WISDOM TO YOUR DAILY LIFE

Lord,

I ask You to forgive me for any unbelief that is in my heart. Help me to have the faith I need to believe that You will bring me through every trial I face in this life. Please give me the strength I need to come into your fire every time I want to fight or run from a particular person or situation. Help me to humble myself so that I can hear clearly from You and abide as You lead me through every situation that makes me angry or leaves me wanting to run away. Lord, I ask you to forgive me for not inviting You into every area of my life and my heart. I give you free rein to have access to every part of my being. Show me the places where I haven't fully let You in. I want You to be Lord over everything in my life and forgive me for not allowing You to be in the past. I love You, Lord! Thank You for loving me so incredibly much that You will never leave me nor forsake me. Thank you, Lord. In Jesus' Name, I pray. Amen

1 Corinthians 3:13-14: *"Each one's work will become clear; for the day will declare it, because it will be revealed by fire; and the fire will test each one's work, of what sort it is. If anyone's work which he has built on it endures, he will receive a reward."*

Psalm 139:23-24: *"Search me, Oh God, and know my heart; test me and know my thoughts. And see if there is any offensive way in me, and lead me in the way everlasting."*

Malachi 3:2-3: *"But who can endure the day of his coming? Who can stand when he appears? For he will be like a refiner's fire or a launderer's soap. 3 He will sit as a refiner and purifier of silver; he will purify the Levites and refine them like gold and silver. Then the Lord will have men who will bring offerings in righteousness."*

James 3:6: *"The tongue also is a fire, a world of evil among the parts of the body. It corrupts the whole body, sets the whole course of one's life on fire, and is itself set on fire by hell."*

Matthew 3:11-12: *"I baptize you with water for repentance. But after me comes one who is more powerful than I, whose sandals I am not worthy to carry. He will baptize you with the Holy Spirit and fire. His winnowing fork is in his hand, and he will clear his threshing floor, gathering his wheat into the barn and burning up the chaff with unquenchable fire."*

Exodus 3:2: *"There the angel of the LORD appeared to him in flames of fire from within a bush. Moses saw that though the bush was on fire it did not burn up."*

Daniel 3:19-17: *"Then Nebuchadnezzar was furious with Shadrach, Meshach and Abednego, and his attitude toward them changed. He ordered the furnace heated seven times hotter than usual and commanded some of the strongest soldiers in his army to tie up Shadrach, Meshach and Abednego and throw them into the blazing furnace. So these men, wearing their robes, trousers, turbans and other clothes, were bound and thrown into the blazing furnace. The king's command was so urgent and the furnace so hot that the flames of the fire killed the soldiers who took up Shadrach, Meshach* *and Abednego, and these three men, firmly tied, fell into the blazing furnace. Then King Nebuchadnezzar leaped to his feet in amazement and asked his advisers, "Weren't there three men that we tied up and threw into the fire?" They replied, "Certainly, Your Majesty."He said, "Look! I see four men walking around in the fire, unbound and unharmed, and the fourth looks like a son of the gods."Nebuchadnezzar then approached the opening of the blazing furnace and shouted, "Shadrach, Meshach and Abednego, servants of the Most High God, come out! Come here!" So Shadrach, Meshach and Abednego came out of the fire, and the satraps, prefects, governors and royal advisers crowded around them. They saw that the fire had not harmed their bodies, nor was a hair of their heads singed; their robes were not scorched, and there was no smell of fire on them."*

Deuteronomy 5:24: *"And you said, "The LORD our God has shown us his glory and his majesty, and we have heard his voice from the fire. Today we have seen that a person can live even if God speaks with them."*

Key #17: Come Into God's Fire Every Time You Want To Fight Or Flight

Reflection:

1. Every time you encounter a confrontation that makes you want to run away or get angry and fight, stop yourself. When you choose to do this, you are humbling your flesh and your soul. Then, when you have time later, spend time with God and allow the Holy Spirit to reveal the fears that have risen within you and write those down. This takes humility; be prepared.

2. Allow God to reveal to you things in your life, mind, and heart that you feel need to be burned out of you. Humble yourself and let him show you. This could be a multitude of things, from selfishness, addictions, lying, deceiving thoughts, and shame to unforgiveness and bitterness. Ask the Holy Spirit to show you areas that are holding you back in any way, and write these down on a piece of paper. Please understand that yielding to the fire of God is a profoundly influential act. It is a burning love from the Father that will consume anything and everything that is not from Him. He wants the absolute best for you! He knows all that you are meant to do, and He knows the things that have been holding you back. Journal these things on a separate piece of paper.

3. Once He shows you these specific areas in your life, choose to let it all go and allow Him to burn it out once and for all. There is tremendous power in this key. I have been doing this diligently ever since my powerful encounter after my 2nd miscarriage in Jan 2021. Doing this has radically changed my life. This will help you clear out the lies in your heart and see things in life more clearly, as well as hear God more clearly for all that is to come.

4. The final step I want you to take is to start a fire, gather the things you have written down from today's exercise, and burn them. Take time with God to watch everything that you wrote down burn in flames before you and ask the Holy Spirit to remind you of these things every time the enemy tries to use them against you in the future.

I am chosen! I am a child of the Most High God, and I will no longer live in fear. I will face things head-on from now with humility, patience, and grace. I have the Holy Spirit living within me, and I am allowing Him to work out my salvation daily. I am allowing Him to stretch me where I still need to produce good fruit. I will come into the fire with God every time I want to run away from a difficult situation and I will humble myself to no longer fight with people. I am a bond slave to Jesus Christ and I do what He leads me to do. I allow my rebellious flesh and soul to be burnt up in the fire with Jesus daily! I am being refined in Him.

4 Discerning the Voices

Today, I want to discuss how to discern in the spiritual realm, as I believe the Church often fails to give this topic sufficient attention. Paul clearly tells us in Ephesians 6:12 that we do not wrestle against flesh and blood, which means the fight is not with a person. We wrestle against the rulers, against the authorities, against the cosmic powers over this present darkness, against the spiritual forces in heavenly places. If we are to mature as Christians, we must learn about the power we possess as spirit beings once we are born again through the blood of Jesus. We must know how to recognize the voices that come into our minds.

I know some people may think it's crazy to hear voices, but the fact is that we all have voices in our minds. Our own thoughts are considered a voice, but this is why it is important to recognize these voices. I have met too many people who thought the evil thoughts plaguing them were their own. This is simply not the Truth. Jesus tells us in His Word that we have an adversary who waits like a roaring lion trying to kill, steal, and destroy us. So, don't you think we should be vigilant and learn how to discern and combat these spiritual entities?

There are four leading voices that we have to be aware of and learn how to discern. Number one is our voice. This voice will almost always seek to justify our selfish desires and usually originates from our fallen nature. Number two is the voice of our enemy, who is Satan and his demonic spirits. These voices will always lure you away from God. They will tempt you and can even deceive you that it is the Word of God, but their underlying deception will twist you against God's Word. This is why it is of the utmost importance that we read our Bible daily and have healthy accountability partners in Christ. And lastly, the voices of our enemies will eventually sound condemning, which will lead us into bondage.

Number three is the voice of God through His Holy Spirit. God's voice can sometimes sound like our voice within our head because we are used to hearing our own thoughts. However, His voice will always be loving, usually causing conviction to come into your heart. This voice will always confirm Himself with His Word (the Bible) and will always lead you into peace and freedom. The fourth voice to be aware of is the voice of other people. Even our Christian friends can miss God's leading, so we must allow the Holy Spirit to confirm the voices of others if it truly is from God. My question for you to ponder every day is, ***"What voice will you choose to submit to and partner with?"***

Deuteronomy 30:20 says this: *"And that you may love the Lord your God, listen to His voice, and hold fast to Him. And John 14:26 says the Holy Spirit, our advocate, will teach believers and remind them of what Jesus said."* It is essential to learn how to discern through the love of God. I will mention this first because I have learned firsthand how dangerous it can be when we are discerning from our wounded hearts or out of a religious spirit. In Jeremiah 17:9, Jesus tells us in His Word that the heart is deceitful above all things. I believe He says this because if we follow our hearts, we are likely guided by our feelings and emotions, which are often triggered by our past wounds and behavioral patterns. It is imperative to embrace God's love and experience His grace daily, which is what we have been focusing on for the past seven weeks. I hope you are now in a routine of meeting with God daily and hungering for more of Him.

Now, I want to discuss some aspects of religious spirits, so you can recognize if you are under the influence of one or if you are beginning to discern one. I have been under the bondage of a religious spirit before, and I know how to recognize it almost instantly now. Over the years, I have come to understand the characteristics of this spirit, which has enabled me to help others recognize it. It is a demonic spirit that smudges God's grace through the mud. A religious spirit will rage against the grace that is freely given to us by Jesus. A religious spirit can make you feel like you have to prove yourself to others and to God.

The Pharisees were a great example of operating under a religious spirit, and they are the ones who crucified Jesus! Think about that for a second. We must be aware of this spirit and its potential danger, as it can completely blind us. A religious spirit will always get in the way of our intimate relationship with Jesus because it will make you feel like you have to perform or work for it. This spirit will make you feel like you are not good enough to come into an intimate relationship with God. This is the same spirit that can operate in churches to crush the hopes and dreams of people, preventing them from reaching their full potential in everything Jesus is calling them to. It will try to put you in a box and keep you there. This is why it is so important to build an intimate relationship with God, so you can hear His voice clearly and know what your gifts and calling are.

You can freely have an intimate relationship with God because of what Jesus did on that cross. God now looks at you and me once we make Jesus Lord over our lives through the blood of Jesus! He is no longer looking at all of our disgusting sins. I encourage you to camp out in Romans chapters 1-6 and Ephesians 1 and 3 to gain a deeper understanding of this. This is how we can have righteousness. It is only through the blood of Jesus. We cannot work for our salvation, and we cannot work our way into righteousness. Righteousness was freely given to us by the pouring out of Jesus's blood. If we attempt to work for this, we will begin to birth self-righteousness and start operating in extreme levels of pride. This can open the door to allow a religious spirit to begin leading you astray. My biggest key to discerning whether people are truly operating from God's heart is by examining their fruit. The Fruits of the Spirit will continuously operate from the very first fruit, which is love!

It is from this place of knowing God's love that we can begin discerning out of love because we invite Jesus into every situation we face in life. There are several Scriptures that show us the character of God, as well as what God wants us to focus our minds on. Philippians 4:8, which I know I have referenced several times already, but this is one of my life Scriptures, and it will help you learn to discern from a place of love. I'm going to paraphrase Philippians 4:8 here: Finally, my brothers and sisters in Christ, we must focus our thoughts on these things: whatever is true, whatever is noble, whatever is right, whatever is pure, whatever is lovely, whatever is admirable, and anything that is excellent or worthy of praise.

I want to break down this verse when learning how to discern. The voice of God will always reflect these things. God is love. He is pure, and He is the ultimate Truth. He is worthy of all praise. He is just and is always right. He is noble, and every way that Jesus walked out His life here on earth is admirable! We should not only yearn to think about these things but also set a daily goal to be an example of God's love to both fellow believers and non-believers. We must learn how to live this out. This is of extreme importance because we all fall short, and we are far from being as perfect as Jesus. But we do have His Spirit living on the inside of us once we make Him Lord. This will help us to have grace and love for others, even if they are operating under a demonic spirit. What I mean by this is that when we learn how to discern from God's love, we can still love the person and hopefully love the "hell" right out of them.

What good are we if the Lord shows us some demonic spirit on someone and we just walk away doing nothing or, worse, gossiping about that person? God will reveal these demonic spirits to us for a reason. When we discern out of love, we can ask the Father, what is it that you want me to do with this, Lord? He will usually have you pray and intercede for that person or possibly have you speak into that person's life, planting a seed of God's love into them. This could result in a good conviction for that person, or it may just be a warning to you. But even if it is a warning, we, as believers in Christ, are called to pray for that person who is in bondage because they are probably blinded by the spirits operating within and around them due to deep wounds in their hearts.

The more I learn about the human heart's emotional wounds, the more grace I have come to have for other people. It draws me closer to the love of the Father, truly understanding that He does not want one human being to perish! So, what are we doing to be that example of God's love for others? What are we doing to invite them into an encounter with the one true answer that can bring them salvation? Are we operating from a place of love to truly be an example of Jesus' love? These are some intense questions, but I hope they prompt our hearts to start living this life from a place of God's love. Amen?

I emphasize learning to discern in love because this will help you gain authority over every voice that tries to plague your mind. If it is not from God, reject agreement with that thought or voice and then come into alignment with the Holy Spirit's leading. It is essential to recognize the voices that speak to us every day. There are various things in the world that can try to lure us, so it is essential to understand these things. If you find yourself constantly justifying your actions, even though you know it is rebelling against the Word of God, this is most likely due to your selfish flesh, which originates from your own voice. Our voice will almost always come from a place of selfishness. You must learn how to crucify your flesh daily; however, when it is compulsive, and you cannot control it, there may be an evil spirit attacking you.

The voice of the enemy and his evil spirits will usually antagonize you with thoughts that are not your own. Some examples of this could be lusting or doing something that you want more of than what you know is good for you. This is usually called an addiction, but most likely, you are being controlled by the influence of a demonic spirit. This is not to glorify the enemy in any way but to become aware that you are battling real spirits that are against God and the call of God over your life.

Evil spirits are conniving and can even try to sound a lot like God because, in 2 Corinthians 11:14, the Bible tells us that Satan masquerades as an angel of light and that we are to be aware of his schemes (2 Corinthians 2:11). Evil Spirits will always lure people into situations that seem promising but eventually make you feel guilty right after you engage with that situation. I will give you practical exercises on how to fight in the spiritual realm for your homework today, so please don't get discouraged. We must remember that if you are a born-again believer in Christ, you have authority over every demonic spirit. However, there are actions that we can take to shut the doors of access to these evil spirits. So be encouraged!

One more spirit I'd like to touch on that I just mentioned from 2 Corinthians 11:14 is the spirit of divination, also known as the angel of light. I need to address this because, unfortunately, I see it operating in the Christian Church today. I genuinely believe this is the spirit at work immensely in this end age. It is extremely deceptive. This is why I tell every Christian and new believer how imperative it is to begin working on your intimate relationship with Christ, learning His character and His Word as soon as you get saved. I have learned over the years that this is how the angel of light can deceive so many people. This spirit can look and feel exactly like the spirit of Jesus Christ, but it is a total counterfeit.

We must remember that Satan, his demonic angels, and spirits are created beings. They cannot create from nothing; they are not God. However, they can work through existing spiritual systems. I am going to reiterate that Satan is not God, nor is he the counterpart to God. The God of the Holy Bible, the God of Abraham, Isaac, and Jacob, is all-powerful and has all authority over everything He created, which is everything in this World. However, what Satan does have is thousands of years of learning how to twist and manipulate through mind control, divination, and witchcraft. This is deception at its best.

The easiest way I can describe divination is the ability to receive heavenly knowledge and power through demonic forces. However, most people who operate in this do not recognize that it is demonic because they have not given their lives to be awakened by Jesus. Satan's original name is Lucifer, which means angel of light or light bringer. He was one of the most alluring angels in all of Heaven. Beautiful from head to toe and adorned with dazzling jewels and musical instruments. You can find this written in Ezekiel 28:13. Satan is cunning and knows how to lure people away from the one true God. This is because he desires to be God. He wants to be worshiped whether a person admits to worshipping him or not. Satan is happy with the mere fact that he can keep people bound in whatever it is that is luring them away from God and His Word, which is Jesus. Jesus is the only way, the Truth, the life, and the light.

Do you remember the story of Pharaoh's magicians being able to mimic whatever Moses was doing? If not, then I encourage you to read the seventh chapter of Exodus. This is a great example to show us that the power of the spirit of light and divination can exemplify powers "like" those of God. These spirits, operating through Pharaoh's magicians, could turn staffs into snakes, rivers into blood, and bring frogs out of the waters. These spirits were mimicking what God was doing through Moses to deceive Pharaoh and his people into thinking that Pharaoh was still in control and that he had a say in whether or not to release God's people. My point is that if we do not have an intimate relationship learning how God speaks and leads, then the other voices that come in can deceive us. Additionally, others who perform signs, wonders, and miracles can also deceive us.

Be patient and have grace for yourself, and do not partner with any fear here. But encourage yourself to dig deeper into God's Truth through revelation in His Word! Our walks with God are progressive, and we learn and mature through time and obedience to His Holy Spirit. However, I encourage you, as you draw closer to Jesus daily, to ask Him to begin sharpening your gifts of Wisdom, Discernment of Spirits, and Words of Knowledge. Study these verses, and they will begin to reveal much wisdom on the things of the Holy Spirit: 1 John 4:1, Romans 12:2, Hebrews 5:14, and 1 Corinthians 12:7-11.

The most important thing is that we must use discernment from God's Holy Spirit and His Word (the Bible) to recognize demonic spirits and deception. As we grow in our relationship with God daily by spending time intimately with Him in worship, prayer, and His Word, we will begin to learn to discern from the place of His love. Love with Scriptures will always be your discerning factor if someone's spirit or word/prophecy is indeed from God. God will always confirm a Word with His word and two to three witnesses if it is from Him (2 Corinthians 13:1). Remember this because it will help you stay balanced in the midst of the prophetic and supernatural experiences you may encounter. The Word of God is your final deciding factor.

<u>APPLYING WISDOM TO YOUR DAILY LIFE</u>

Prayer for the day:

Father God, Jesus, and Holy Spirit,

I repent for not putting You first in every area of my life. I give You full permission to enter into every part of my heart, my body, and my soul. I want Your wisdom, Your truth, and Your guidance only. Help any unbelief that is within me, Lord. I trust You to help show me how to heal my heart and grow healthily in You, Lord. Teach me how to walk in your discerning ways and how to steward well the gift of discernment that You have freely given me. I ask that this gift be sharpened in my life during this season, Lord. Help me to be sensitive to recognize other spirits that rise against your Holy Spirit and Your Word.

Scriptures to meditate on:

1 Corinthians 12:7-11: *"Now to each one the manifestation of the Spirit is given for the common good. To one there is given through the Spirit a message of wisdom, to another a message of knowledge by means of the same Spirit, to another faith by the same Spirit, to another gifts of healing by that one Spirit, to another miraculous powers, to another prophecy, to another distinguishing between spirits, to another speaking in different kinds of tongues, and to still another the interpretation of tongues. All these are the work of one and the same Spirit, and he distributes them to each one, just as he determines."*

Hebrews 5:13-14: *"Anyone who lives on milk, being still an infant, is not acquainted with the teaching about righteousness. But solid food is for the mature, who by constant use have trained themselves to distinguish good from evil."*

1 John 4:1-8: *"Dear friends, do not believe every spirit, but test the spirits to see whether they are from God, because many false prophets have gone out into the world. This is how you can recognize the Spirit of God: Every spirit that acknowledges that Jesus Christ has come in the flesh is from God, but every spirit that does not acknowledge Jesus is not from God. This is the spirit of the antichrist, which you have heard is coming and even now is already in the world. You, dear children, are from God and have overcome them, because the one who is in you is greater than the one who is in the world. They are from the world and therefore speak from the viewpoint of the world, and the world listens to them. We are from God, and whoever knows God listens to us; but whoever is not from God does not listen to us. This is how we recognize the Spirit of truth and the spirit of falsehood."*

Romans 12:1-2: *"Therefore, I urge you, brothers and sisters, in view of God's mercy, to offer your bodies as a living sacrifice, holy and pleasing to God—this is your true and proper worship. Do not conform to the pattern of this world, but be transformed by the renewing of your mind. Then you will be able to test and approve what God's will is—his good, pleasing and perfect will."*

Psalm 25:4-5: *"Show me your ways, Lord, teach me your paths. Guide me in your truth and teach me, for you are God my savior, and my hope is in you all day long!"*

Acts 8:9-23: *(THIS IS A GREAT DEPICTION OF DIVINATION)* **Simon the Sorcerer:** *"Now for some time a man named Simon had practiced sorcery in the city and amazed all the people of Samaria. He boasted that he was someone great, and all the people, both high and low, gave him their attention and exclaimed, "This man is rightly called the Great Power of God." They followed him because he had amazed them for a long time with his sorcery. But when they believed Philip as he proclaimed the good news of the kingdom of God and the name of Jesus Christ, they were baptized, both men and women. Simon himself believed and was baptized. And he followed Philip everywhere, astonished by the great signs and miracles he saw. When the apostles in Jerusalem heard that Samaria had accepted the word of God, they sent Peter and John to Samaria. When they arrived, they prayed for the new believers there that they might receive the Holy Spirit, because the Holy Spirit had not yet come on any of them; they had simply been baptized in the name of the Lord Jesus. Then Peter and John placed their hands on them, and they received the Holy Spirit. When Simon saw that the Spirit was given at the laying on of the apostles' hands, he offered them money and said, "Give me also this ability so that everyone on whom I lay my hands may receive the Holy Spirit." Peter answered: "May your money perish with you, because you thought you could buy the gift of God with money! You have no part or share in this ministry, because your heart is not right before God. Repent of this wickedness and pray to the Lord in the hope that he may forgive you for having such a thought in your heart. For I see that you are full of bitterness and captive to sin."*

Ephesians 4:26: *"In your anger do not sin": Do not let the sun go down while you are still angry, and do not give the devil a foothold."*

Reflection:

This exercise is only for born again believers in Christ

Over the past 17 years, as I have walked closely with Jesus, I have come to learn that being in His Word and having an intimate relationship with Him truly brings deliverance. I used to suffer from demonic night terrors, as well as demonic attacks both within my mind and my body. I used to suffer from sexual and perverted thoughts as well as addictions. I suffered from self-hatred, suicidal thoughts, and even suicide attempts. I know firsthand that the deliverance that comes through knowing Jesus intimately is real! I am a firm believer in deliverance because Jesus says we, as His followers, will operate in deliverance and that He is our deliverer. Jesus mentions this in Mark, chapter 16:17-18, where He says, *"And these signs will follow those who believe: In My name, they will cast out demons; they will speak with new tongues; they will take up serpents; and if they drink anything deadly, it will by no means hurt them; they will lay hands on the sick, and they will recover."*

Now, I would like to say that I am not entirely sold out on all "deliverance ministries" out there. I was when I first came across deliverance in 2020 because I was blown away by all the supernatural things I witnessed. However, as I began studying this out Biblically, God started to reveal a lot about what was spiritually off about some of the ministries I was around. I am not saying this about all deliverance ministries, so please hear my heart. There may be many that are Biblically correct, and I also know that we are all still learning in this incredibly vast topic of deliverance. So, please know this has just been my observation. Over the past four years, I have observed a significant imbalance within the deliverance ministries I have been around. The two biggest red flags I found are these: #1 There tends to be no discipleship or follow-up with those who receive deliverance, to ensure they are being discipled and their deliverance is sustained. #2 I cannot stand it when Christians become overly demon-conscious or allow demons to take control over a deliverance session. It is essential to keep our focus on Jesus and the power that we have through Him.

My issue with the #1 flag is rooted in the Biblical principle of Matthew 12:43-45, which describes what happens when an unclean spirit is cast out: seven more can come in if they do not fill themselves with the Word of God and His Holy Spirit. My other issue is that we have been given all authority over the demonic through the blood of Jesus, so why act as if demons are more powerful than the blood of Jesus? This has rubbed me the wrong way and has sparked a fire in me to teach people more about the power that Christians have as believers in Christ. However, this power only comes through walking in intimate obedience to Jesus and His Word (Luke 10:17, James 4:7, Ephesians 6:11-12, Mark 16:17-18).

Please know that demons can manifest in many different ways and that they can be supernaturally strong but when you know your authority through Jesus Christ, we do have the supernatural power to tell them to shut up and cast them out. Jesus gives us several models of this in several scriptures. Here are some for you to research on your own: Luke 4:31-37, Mark 1:21-28, Luke 8:26-39, Luke 9:37-45, Matthew 17:14-18, Mark 9:14-29, Luke 4:40-41, Mark 1:34, Acts 8:7.

Now, I have personally been radically delivered from demons, including the spirits of fear, rebellion, perversion, abuse, lust, specific pains in my body, and generational curses while in sessions of inner healing. This is because inner healing reveals the roots of many things where demons can gain legal access. Once these roots become exposed and renounced by a person, along with the release of any unforgiveness, the demon usually loses its hold and has to leave. With my years of doing inner healing and deliverance, the legal access gained by the demonic is usually because specific parts of our life and/or our heart have not been fully surrendered to Jesus. There is a trust issue there, and therefore, it leaves a foothold for the enemy to gain access in the life of a believer.

I have personally helped other believers in Christ get delivered from demonic spirits oppressing and demonizing them. Therefore, I am in favor of Biblical Deliverance and inner healing. There are several spiritual and legal factors to consider when undergoing deliverance, and I have listed some of these below. However, we must keep in the forefront of our minds that Jesus is our deliverer. Deliverance from demonic strongholds and demons can naturally happen as we grow closer in our intimate relationship with Jesus by sanctifying ourselves to Him and His holiness.

You cannot stay where you are if you are truly walking with Jesus. He loves us too much to leave us stuck in our sinful ways. But we have a choice to allow this sanctification process to happen. I want you to have grace for yourself because, depending on how much trauma or manipulation you have been through in your past, this might take some time. To be honest, it has taken me several years. I personally do not know one person who has been delivered from every single thing from their past all at once. It usually takes time, and we are all in a process until we leave this earth.

I want to share some examples from my own life to offer you some encouragement. I didn't give my life back to Jesus until I was 22. This means that I had 22 years of building strongholds within my mind, and for me, there were many! This was due to all the molestation, abuse, and rejection that I went through from the age of 3-23, and even after I came to Jesus, there were still strongholds that the enemy held me bound in because the battle truly is within our soul realm (mind, will, and emotions). (Romans 12:2, Isaiah 26:3, 2 Corinthians 10:5, 1 Peter 5:8, Proverbs 20:27, Philippians 2:5 & 8). Our mind is the greatest place where our enemies can gain legal access. It has taken me years to break free from these, but freedom is ALWAYS possible with Jesus! So be encouraged!

Before I give you simple steps for you to walk through deliverance with Jesus, I want to provide some Scriptural background on how we, as Christians, can become "demonized" or demonically oppressed by legal agreements. Please know that I am barely scratching the surface here because deliverance is a vast topic that could take another book to explain fully. But one thing to take note of is that we can make legal agreements knowingly or unknowingly with spiritual enemies, and this is what gives them access to demonize people.

First, the Bible tells us that we do not wrestle against flesh and blood, so we know that our battles are against the spiritual realm (Ephesians 6:12). There is a reason why Paul and Proverbs constantly tell us to guard our hearts, ears, and eyes. They also share the importance of obedience, developing our identity in Christ, and taking every thought captive. Several scriptures tell us there is a battle going on for our physical lives, our eternal lives, our correct thinking, and it warns us about the open doors that can hand us over to demonic influence. I will list just a few here, but there are several more that you can search out. (2 Corinthians 10:4-5, 10:35, James 4:7, Proverbs 18, 1 Peter 5:8-9, Acts 5, Luke 13:11-16, 1 Corinthians 5:1-5, 1 Samuel 16:14-23; 18:10-11; 19:9-10, Romans 12:1-2, 2 Timothy 1:7, Isaiah 26:3, Philippians 4:6-8, John 8:32, 1 John 4:1-21, Hebrews 13:5, Proverbs 16:18, Proverbs 29:1-27).

I'm going to list a few more things that I want you to take note of. In Matthew 18:21-35, Jesus provides a powerful example of what can happen when we fail to forgive, illustrating how we can be turned over to our enemies. Unforgiveness is a substantial legal right for the enemy to demonize us. Then, in Numbers 21:4-9, Deuteronomy 17:16 & 28:68, Jeremiah 42:13-17 & 44:14, and Hosea 11:5, God warns us of the danger of hardening our hearts and slipping back into the yoke of slavery that bound us in the first place. This warning is confirmed again in the New Testament. Galatians 5:1 tells us that we can become bound again, even though Christ saved us. It is all up to the free will that God has given us and whether or not we are obeying these loving guidelines that He has graciously written out to us in His Word. These are just a few examples of how the enemy can gain legal access to attack our bodies, our minds, and our lives.

This is why continuing in obedience to the Holy Spirit and sanctification to Jesus is always essential. In 2 Corinthians 10:3-5, Paul tells us to demolish spiritual strongholds and I want you to read these two versions of this Scripture: *KJV~"For though we walk in the flesh, we do not war after the flesh: (For the weapons of our warfare are not carnal, but mighty through God to the pulling down of strong holds; casting down imaginations, and every high thing that exalteth itself against the knowledge of God, and bringing into captivity every thought to the obedience of Christ."* And in the NIV, it says, *"For though we live in the world, we do not wage war as the world does. The weapons we fight with are not the weapons of the world. On the contrary, they have divine power to demolish strongholds. We demolish arguments and every pretension that sets itself up against the knowledge of God, and we take captive every thought to make it obedient to Christ."*

This Scripture, right here, I have found to be one of the main things that opens the door for the enemy to get you to go back into slavery or that you possibly are not entirely free yet from the strongholds of your past. It takes time to renew our minds and get our hearts healed! Jesus tells us He will help us with this, but it is up to us to surrender our will to His, and then to learn to walk towards His Love in obedience, doing whatever He tells us to do. This will help you to tear down any demonic strongholds you may still have within your mind and heart.

I want to discuss spiritual strongholds for a moment so you understand what a spiritual stronghold is. I am going to put this into my own words from what I have learned about a spiritual stronghold after studying this in the Word. The simplest way I can explain this is that these are mental patterns that rise against God's Word. They have come from your past and have built strong protective walls around your heart, which, unfortunately, have helped shape you into who you are today. They are the defense mechanisms you have built within your mind and heart to keep you safe, but unfortunately, they have made you a prisoner in your own soul. You were trying to keep your enemies out, but now you have barricaded yourself from the outside in. This can block us from receiving God's truth. This is why God tells us to tear them down and that we have the power to do so once we are born again through the Blood of Jesus Christ. I am a strong advocate for new believers in Christ to begin washing their minds immediately with the Word and His presence. Why? Because the Word of God, who is Jesus, is the only one who can free us from these demonic strongholds. Encountering His presence daily is life-changing.

When we are living a life opposite to God's Word and His instructions, we can open doors for demonic oppression to come in. We allow these strongholds to remain in the places they have always been for years before we truly know Jesus. Once we come to know Jesus, we begin the process of becoming refined and learn how to connect to Him as our source of nutrients, enabling us to produce the fruit of His Holy Spirit. This takes time, but with obedience and sanctification, purification begins to happen, and this brings deliverance. You have been walking through the exercises in this book for almost seven weeks now, which contain a wealth of discipling literature and exercises within them. I hope you feel growth in your relationship with God and recognize some changes within your life.

> ### *Author's note:*

If you want to learn more about biblical deliverance, I highly recommend studying the works of the following individuals of great faith: Derek Prince, John Paul Jackson, and Kathryn Kuhlman. They each operated in deliverance in many different ways, but are all great examples of working through the intimacy of God's love to bring deliverance to people. Isaiah Saldivar is an amazing modern-day person to learn from. His testimony of how he got saved and how he came into the ministry of deliverance is powerful! God is truly AWESOME!

> ### *The next part of this reflection is only for born-again believers in Christ, who will be diligent to fill themselves back up with Jesus, (the Bible) and his Holy Spirit!*

Remember, the Bible warns us about delivering people who do not know Jesus, or who are not willing to come to Jesus, because once they get delivered, more demonic spirits can come back if they do not fill themselves up with the Holy Spirit. We must have complete reliance on Jesus and the Holy Spirit when we do this. It is only by the power of the blood and His Spirit that demonic oppression can leave us. Then, it is the Holy Spirit who fills us back up once we get delivered from whatever is oppressing us. If you are not a believer in Christ, but want to get born-again today, open your heart now, and say these words, "Jesus, forgive me of my sins. I'm sorry that I've been away from you for so long. I open my heart to you and give you full access into my heart, mind, and body. I give you my will and ask you to become Lord over every area of my life. In Jesus' Name I pray." If you said those words and truly meant them, it is that simple. Jesus says He receives anyone who calls on His name and accepts Him as Lord and Savior.

(Romans 10:13, John 1:12, John 6:37, Joel 2:32). However, I highly recommend that you find a Spirit filled believer in Christ who is plugged into a community of the Church to help you get discipled. This is essential in addition to what you are learning from this book. Remember, it is biblical to have accountability partners to help us understand more and grow throughout our journey with Christ. Ok, now it is time for simple steps of deliverance with Jesus.

1. Please select one full day when you can fast from food and drink, consuming only water. This is a day set aside for you to be alone with God. Fasting can help you overcome the desires of the flesh and become more sensitive to hearing from the Holy Spirit. The Bible also tells us that some spirits only come out through fasting and prayer (Mark 9:29 & Matthew 17:21). Now, this is not to get into any fear because we, as born-again believing Christians, have the Holy Spirit and He is more powerful than any demon trying to keep us oppressed. Jesus is our main answer; He is our deliverer. It is only through His Word, which is the only Truth that we can go by, that we can find deliverance, which is part of His ministry. This means that once we become born-again Believers in Christ and have Jesus living within us, we start to experience deliverance, and we are also called to deliver others. I say, "start to experience deliverance" because it is our spirits that become born again instantly, but we have a soul and body that still need deliverance. The Holy Spirit begins to bring about significant spiritual transformation in us as a whole, but we must walk this out and embrace this process. I have learned that oppression by demons can come in through legal agreements with the demonic realm, unknowingly. This could be from any form of abuse in your life, the use of drugs, having sex outside of marriage/creating soul ties with people, or participating in things of the occult. Generational curses that we have not broken from our family bloodlines are another way that we, as Christians, can be oppressed by demons. Lastly, this can happen by wounds from our past that cause deep unforgiveness and bitterness to take root. I need you to know that we have authority over every demonic entity that comes against us through the blood of Jesus! Demons can only gain authority if we give it to them. Know that every spirit that the Holy Spirit may bring up to you today can be easily let go of by simply renouncing all agreement with it out loud. Then take a deep breath out and release it!

2. During this time, I encourage you to start by putting on soaking music. This is instrumental Christian music, devoid of lyrics or specific melodies. This music always helps me to enter into God's presence. This is entirely optional, but I believe it will help calm your mind so you can begin to focus on one thing: God and His goodness. This will bring your focus to Him, opening your mind and heart to hear from Him. I recommend taking all authority over the atmosphere you are in. Speak this out loud, "I command every spirit that rises against Jesus Christ of Nazareth to get out. No spirit but the Holy Spirit can operate here. Thank you, Lord Jesus, for binding up every demonic spirit that may try to rise up against me and your word. Thank you, Jesus, for closing every demonic portal now and for covering this session with your blood! I ask you, Jesus, to bind every spirit of witchcraft from being able to operate here. In Jesus Name, I pray!" It is as simple as that. Demons must flee and obey the authority of Jesus Christ! Stand in your authority.

3. Once you feel connected to God and in His presence, I want you to ask Holy Spirit if there is anyone you need to forgive. I know we have done forgiveness exercises in the past, but holding onto any

unforgiveness can block us from getting free during a session like this. It is good to allow God to search your heart at this time. If anyone comes to mind, know that He is showing you that person for a reason. Be quick to repent for holding onto unforgiveness and any bitterness, then say out loud, I forgive (whoever He shows you):

____

____

____

____

____

____

____

____

____

Then write down and say out loud what you forgive them for, then release them:

____

____

____

____

____

____

____

____

____

____

4. Now, I want you to ask the Holy Spirit if there are any spiritual agreements you have entered into that are contrary to Jesus and His Word. The Holy Spirit is our helper. *"But the Helper, the Holy Spirit, whom the Father will send in my name, he will teach you all things and bring to your remembrance all that I have said to you" (John 14:26).* He may show you things that you have partnered with knowingly or unknowingly. Some things that you may hear in your spirit include fear, worry, anxiety, trauma, greed, gossip, malice, perversion, anger, murder, strife, lying, infirmity, jealousy, seduction, divination,

the occult,or witchcraft. There may be something else I'm not mentioning here; I just wanted to name a few so you know what to listen for. Trust whatever the Holy Spirit gives to you. Remember, this may not be specifically a result of you opening any doors; it could be due to generational curses or attacks coming against you. God will give you insight into where the enemy may still have legal access to attack you. Stay humble and just be obedient to whatever you hear in your spirit. Then, write down whatever you hear, feel, or see in your spirit:

____

____

____

____

____

____

____

____

____

____

____

____

5. After you have your list, this next step is simple. You repent to the Lord for partnering in agreement with every spirit that you listed, whether knowingly or unknowingly. Let this repentance come from a true deep place of your heart, knowing that these things have tried to separate you from God's love for you. If you need to wait, do so until you feel this deep in your heart. This is a crucial aspect of repentance. It needs to come from a deep place within our hearts, telling God how sorry we are for allowing anything to separate us from Him. After you truly repent, I want you to sever all ties with the enemies you have allowed yourself to partner with. You can sever ties by simply saying: "I reject all agreements with whatever spirit the Lord shows you." Ex: If it is a spirit of trauma, say out loud, " I reject all agreements with the spirit of trauma. Trauma is not my portion. It is something that happened to me, but it is not me. I am God's child, and my portion is His inheritance, which is healing, complete restoration, and wholeness by the blood of Jesus!"

6. Then you ask Jesus to cover every part of you with His blood and ask Holy Spirit to come and fill up any holes that may be left open now in your heart and soul. Ask Jesus to fill every wound with His Love and His acceptance. From here on out, ask God to give you a deeper revelation of His sensitivity to any spirits that do not align with His Holy Spirit and His Word. This will help you to become aware of what spirits come in to try and get you to partner with them in the future.

7. I know this may seem too simple, but the Gospel is simple, and we have the authority to cast out anything that doesn't belong once we become born-again Believers in Christ. Many times, we will be getting

delivered from demonic entities as we are coming closer to Jesus, and we may not fully know it at the time. But you will begin to realize that you are thinking differently or feeling differently about certain situations that used to upset you or that you are not craving what you used to be addicted to. This is because deliverance automatically happens when we become intimate with Jesus. These sessions are for addressing the deeper issues where you feel like you cannot achieve a breakthrough. It is about having daily encounters with your Lord, Jesus, becoming sensitive to hearing God's voice, and abiding in whatever it is He tells you to do.

Author's Note:

I want to share that I sometimes have to break agreements and cast off spirits of infirmity every day because this is where the enemy loves to attack me. He knows that if he can wear down my body, it can weaken my spirit, and he can then take some swings at me. Therefore, I have become more vigilant in this area. I know it can seem daunting at times, but I have learned how the enemy and his minions work. So, I simply obey if I hear the Holy Spirit tell me to do something. Again, we have to remember that the spiritual realm is more real than the physical. This can be challenging because most people cannot see through spiritual eyes, making it difficult to comprehend at times. But God will always lead His people into truth! So trust His Holy Spirit and His leadings.

Declaration:

I decree and declare that I am sensitive to God and His Holy Spirit's wisdom. I have a deep reverence for God and His Word! I will test every spirit with the Word of God, which is the truth, and the truth is Jesus. I give Jesus full reign to speak into my life whenever He wants to. I am learning how to walk in the gift of discerning spirits. I declare this by faith in Jesus' Name!

1 Does your brain need washing?

There are a few things I want to discuss this week, as they apply to every human being, but especially to followers of Jesus Christ. God tells us several times throughout His Word to guard our minds, our tongues, and our hearts. However, we have a powerful tool that God has given us, called our free will. Now, free will is fantastic; however, it can lead us in a direction that is not good for us if we haven't learned what God says is best for us. So, the first area I want to tackle is within your mind. This is considered part of our soul realm, which encompasses our mind, will, and emotions. Our belief system is essential. Wrong beliefs can deter us from our destiny and hinder our breakthroughs in life.

This chapter will require you to be open to the very real fact that your brain may need some rewashing. I use the word rewash because the word brainwashed is an accurate word for how most of us have been living our lives before we came to Christ. I still find myself allowing the Holy Spirit to guide me in this way frequently in my life. Unfortunately, we have been programmed from the very beginning of our lives. Suppose you weren't blessed to have been raised in a healthy home and learn about your true identity in Christ at a young age. In that case, you may have adopted some hindering belief systems.

If you are reading this book, it means that you want certain aspects of your life to change. I am a person who is constantly motivated by a process of continual improvement. If I hear someone speaking and it inspires, offends, or convicts me, I usually look deeper within myself. I constantly put a mirror in front of me and challenge myself to improve in areas where I'm weak. It's not that I live in a constant state of trying to measure up, but I allow myself room to always be willing to grow and learn along my journey.

One of the main tools I will have you walk through in this section of the workbook is writing down your belief systems and then identifying where you learned those belief systems. This will help you determine which belief systems are unhealthy for you. One huge topic that I want to address is religion. I have had so many people tell me throughout the last 18 years of my life once they hear me talk about God, that they are not religious at all, as if a wall automatically shoots up. I then laugh and say, "Thank God, because I am not either!" This is an excellent example because I think people have messed up the true gospel of Jesus Christ by taking the Word of God out of context and making up their own rules and regulations to put upon others to manipulate and gain some control or power. We should always be an instrument that draws people into wanting to know more about God by being God's Love in action.

I have also heard so many people say that the Bible is written by man, so why should I believe that this is a book from God? I was told this exact thing by someone of significant influence in my life while growing up, but this is an excellent question because I know many who struggle with this concept. When first starting your walk with God, many people become frustrated while reading the Bible, often feeling condemned or unworthy in some way. Let me share a great secret with you. You cannot read the Bible as if it were a regular book if you want to receive the power of your identity that is within it. We have an enemy that does not want us to receive the Truth! It is clearly stated in 2 Timothy 3:16 that *"All Scripture is breathed out by God and profitable for teaching, for reproof, for correction, and for training in righteousness."*

However, it is up to us to open our hearts to truly receive revelation within the Word by making Jesus our Lord and Savior, which means trusting God as our Father, Friend, Husband, and Counselor. This means giving Jesus complete control over your life and learning to be led by His Spirit, which is the Holy Spirit. It says in *Philippians 1:21, "For to me, to live is Christ and to die is gain."* This means I gave up the power of control and manipulation that I was using to steer my own life and decided to completely give my life over to the one who knows me better than anyone, my Creator. Once I did this, the Word of God truly began to come alive. As I began to read the Bible, I would ask the Holy Spirit to give me revelation on what this story or verse was written for. It was truly amazing how my understanding began to evolve in such profound ways.

To this day, 15 years after this encounter, I still get excited to read my Bible because God continues to choose to speak to us in many different ways through His Word. If you want to encounter a deeper relationship with Jesus, then it is key to begin reading the Bible. The entire Old Testament comprises numerous outstanding elements, including keys to our identity and prophecies that have already come to pass and are yet to come. It also shows us how badly we as humans needed a Savior, as well as the clear distinctions of good and evil. The entire New Testament consists of the freedom and power we get to live in through the blood of Jesus Christ, all the while keeping us in alignment with wisdom and Truth. I want to share with you the main differences between religion and what Jesus truly represents: love, freedom, and relationship.

I mentioned religion quite a bit in an earlier chapter. Still, it's essential to fully acknowledge and be aware of how to recognize a religious spirit. This spirit can block us from encountering a deeper understanding of who Jesus Christ truly is. Religion will always tell you that you are not good enough and that you are a sinner who has to constantly try harder to come to God and work for your freedom. Religion eventually makes God unapproachable and makes Him appear as a mean God. Religion will try to put you and God in a box. Religion can make you feel condemned, whereas having an authentic relationship with Jesus empowers you to embrace conviction and grow continually.

Conviction, which lovingly corrects you, will always bring you into freedom because you are no longer allowing sin to control you. A relationship with Jesus always leads you to freedom, whereas religion will keep you bound. The spirit of religion can operate out of control, leading to manipulation and often be extremely cunning. This was the exact spirit that crucified Jesus on the cross. We must be very aware of the differences between religion and relationship. True Christianity is all about relationships, and this relationship begins to bring us into a place of freedom where we can love ourselves and others so incredibly well without any strings attached. Religion brings division, whereas a relationship with Jesus will always bring unity and Love. I know many individuals, including myself, who were brought up under a spirit of religion and did not truly encounter a genuine relationship with Jesus. This fosters flawed understanding about God.

There are many incorrect belief systems that I want you to take the time to explore, because recognizing these will help you begin walking your life out in freedom. Please take some time to reflect on your childhood and consider the relationships that were modeled for you, as well as those you have had throughout your life. Are you living with any resemblances to these relations, or did you go the exact opposite direction due to fear? Some examples could be that you were raised in a religious home where

God was represented with control and manipulation. Or perhaps your parents just played the facade of "Christianity" but never fully walked out the Truth of who Jesus was. In turn, you decided you didn't want any part of any religion whatsoever, so you ran from Christianity altogether.

How about your parents? Did you grow up in a home where peace and Love were modeled for you, or was it chaotic with lies, manipulation, or even violence? What about sexual or physical abuse? Have you run from these things or to these things, allowing them to keep you imprisoned in your past? My story was that I ran into sexual relationships and allowed myself to be used and abused, as well as learned how to manipulate most of my intimate relationships by hardening my heart so I wouldn't feel the hurt that I knew would eventually come. You see, either way, I wasn't entirely free even though I had taught myself a belief system that I was happy where I was.

We all end up learning self-defense mechanisms that become belief systems, and this can be a very unfulfilling world to live in. We ultimately build up walls, placing our hearts inside different sections of prison through the unhealthy ways we learn to cope throughout life. We must look back into our past to grasp a deeper understanding why we think the way we do. What circumstances happened to make a particular belief take root in our hearts? We didn't just wake up one day and begin walking out the habits with the mindsets we have by coincidence.

Your mind has probably been programmed with years of wrong belief systems, just like mine was. However, the good news is that you have a choice to change your beliefs and your habits. ***You are the director of your own story, so why not begin choosing some healthy and robust directions with the guidance of the Holy Spirit?*** God is the perfect Creator and the author of our story. But it is when we come into alignment with Him that He somehow transforms our mess into a powerful message for others, bringing hope and beauty into their lives. It's time to renew our minds!

The time is now. I encourage you to write in this workbook and keep track of your daily mindsets, which stem from your belief systems. This will help you develop the habit of thinking correctly and be able to return to the place where your heart got hurt in the first place. It is so important to take time to release it and ask God to come in to heal those areas. Be patient with yourself. You may have to do this repeatedly until you begin to think differently. Still, as you continue, it will rewire your thought processes. We all have the power to change our thinking, allowing us to achieve the results we want to see. Still, it takes diligence, consistency, and humility.

APPLYING WISDOM TO YOUR DAILY LIFE

Lord,

Forgive me for not always partnering with Your truth. Help me rewire my thoughts and restore the parts of my brain that need to align with your truth. The truth of who I am in You! The truth that brings healing and wholeness. Show me how You think of me and all the restoration that You want for me. Help my faith to trust You for these breakthroughs within my mind. I know that you are a supernatural God. Lord, as I diligently do my part, I ask you to supernaturally begin rewiring my brain to come into alignment with Your Word. Heal me from all trauma and wrong belief systems. I trust You, Lord.

Romans 12:2: *"Do not conform to the pattern of this world, but be transformed by the renewing of your mind. Then you will be able to test and approve what God's will is—His good, pleasing and perfect will."*

2 Corinthians 10:5: *"We demolish arguments and every pretension that sets itself up against the knowledge of God, and we take captive every thought to make it obedient to Christ."*

Psalm 1:2: *"Instead, they find happiness in the Teaching of the Lord, and they think about it day and night."*

Philippians 4:8: *"Finally, brothers, whatever is true, whatever is honorable, whatever is just, whatever is pure, whatever is lovely, whatever is commendable, if there is any excellence, if there is anything worthy of praise, think about these things."*

1. As you begin to recognize the toxic belief systems within your mind, ask yourself, what message is being presented in and through me right now? Write these down here. This will help you recognize any patterns where the enemy is trying to keep you bound:

____

____

____

____

____

____

____

____

____

____

____

Then ask yourself, 'Is this something I want for my life?' ______________Will this help me grow towards my identity in Christ?______________ And on the other side when you experience something that brings energy and great joy to you, ask yourself how can I savor this and begin to create more energy from where this is coming from. Pay attention to the correct belief systems by checking to see if they align with the Word of God and your life's calling. Start implementing that into your life immediately. The bottom line is that we must quit doing the things that no longer serve us and be honest with ourselves. If you are on a track that isn't working, then why continue down that road. The truth is that these beliefs, which have taken root in our hearts throughout our lives, can cause actions that lead to destruction instead of building in a positive direction. This is why it is so powerful when we bring these roots to God, because He helps us process and release, and then He redeems by turning it all around for our good.

2. You will learn how to do some inner healing with God this week, so don't worry if you're feeling overwhelmed. Trust the process and allow things to come up to the surface. Make sure to write these down daily and weekly so you can begin fully addressing them and then break free.

Declaration:

I decree and declare that I have the mind of Christ! I can think like my Lord and Savior because I have made Him Lord over every area of my life! He lives in me and I abide in Him. My mind and heart are becoming healed and renewed daily as I trust the supernatural power of the Holy Spirit to do this in and through me. I read my Bible daily and receive all that it contains. I put a guard over my tongue, eyes, and my ears. I am coming into alignment with all that God has for me in Jesus Name.

2 Reset your mind

Often, our minds tend to operate within patterns formed by past experiences, particularly those with adverse outcomes. Isn't it interesting that most people tend to remember negative situations more often than positive ones? The primary reason is that we live in a fallen world, and most people have been conditioned to think more negatively than positively due to the way we process thoughts from our past experiences. Positive thinking begins with loving self-talk and training yourself to see things from a different perspective, which you have likely been learning over the past eight weeks. However, this does require time and diligence to consistently apply these new thoughts daily, creating healthy and productive belief systems for yourself. Remember to be kind and patient with yourself throughout this process.

The sole purpose of writing this book is to inspire people to truly come alive with joy and love, knowing that they have the power within them to change their mindset in any situation in their lives. One of the most powerful tools we have is our minds. When we finally take the time to slow down and be intentional with our thoughts, we can begin living the life we have always desired because it is what God has already put within us. We must trust in the Lord with all of our hearts, not relying on our understanding but allowing Him to guide us in all of our ways and acknowledge that He will direct our thoughts and our paths (Proverbs 3:3-6). The Bible goes on to say in Proverbs 3:7-8, *"Don't think for a moment that you know it all, for wisdom comes when you adore Him with undivided devotion and avoid everything that's evil. Then you will find the healing refreshment your body and spirit long for."* I know that I am paraphrasing here, but this verse is so good! The Bible should become your permanent guide in life if it isn't already.

The next belief system I want to challenge you on is how you look at mental and physical conditions within your body. This is a vast topic that many people struggle with. Could these conditions be spiritual, and if so, can we partner with the deliverance we need? Caroline Leaf, who is a believer in Christ, as well as a brain surgeon, says that 75% to 98% of mental and physical illnesses come from the thoughts that we are thinking. She also states that we can change these illnesses by using the Word of God to rewire our brains. I couldn't agree with her more!

I have personally witnessed incredible deliverance within my mind and body by speaking God's Word over my life, as well as undergoing inner healing with the Lord. I have also witnessed several people get delivered from physical ailments they have suffered for years once they undergo inner healing sessions. It is truly incredible. One of the major ones that I see is fibromyalgia. It is my personal belief that when we go through trauma, and we do not fully release wounds or bitterness, it gets lodged in certain parts of our bodies. This creates blocks in our body, as well as within our minds, which start misfiring. I am unable to explain it entirely, but I have personally witnessed the supernatural results that take place, so I agree entirely with Caroline Leaf. I know that the Word heals. Why? Because Jesus is the Word!

The Bible is full of Scriptures on how to renew our minds, as well as receive divine healing because Jesus took every sickness and disease on that cross thousands of years ago. We must trust that God has every key to break us out of any door that we have placed ourselves behind, whether knowingly or unknowingly. This is why we must begin living our lives in complete surrender, allowing the Holy Spirit to guide us into Godly belief systems through God's Word. Once you start doing this, you will be amazed to see how many things will completely turn around for the good in your life.

Jeremiah 29:11 clearly states that God has a good plan for every life He created, which is for every human being on this earth. However, it is up to us to begin partnering with His Truth and begin walking in that direction. I have faced numerous trials in my life, both physically and mentally, and I have trained myself by following the advice I am sharing with you in this book. These keys work, and you will begin to see the benefits in your own life as you apply them to your everyday life. The hardest part is allowing God to rewire our brains to the original creation within us because most of us have been living under years of flawed belief systems, thought patterns, and habits.

As new belief systems begin to take root in our hearts, it may seem difficult to heal, but with God, all things are possible. God tells us, above all else, to guard our hearts (Proverbs 4:23). I received a profound revelation about this Scripture three years ago. Jesus showed me how I was always striving to guard my heart. He lovingly corrected me one day and showed me how to do this. He gave me a vision of us hugging, and I just kept Him so close to my chest. I didn't want to let go of Him. He then said, 'This is how you guard your heart.'

You see? We must have daily intimacy with our King Jesus, always allowing Him to be right here next to our hearts. Allowing Him to convict, to heal, and to lead will change you. Living this way has radically changed my life! This Scripture in Proverbs 4:23 also relates to our minds. We must be vigilant about what enters our minds, as it then becomes a part of our inner selves and can take root in our hearts. God warns us about what we allow into our minds through many Scriptures. There is great wisdom in the Word. I encourage you to google scriptures on guarding your heart and mind.

I want to share some examples of wrong belief systems that I have had to work through and overcome so you can begin to challenge some of your own beliefs. A small yet powerful belief that I grew up with was this one: "Money doesn't grow on trees; hard work is the only thing that brings provision." I heard this phrase quite often while growing up. With this, I began working hard at the young age of eleven. I also wanted to be like my brother and my dad, so I worked hard in labor-intensive jobs, such as landscaping, roofing houses, and laying bricks. Now, don't get me wrong, I am incredibly thankful for part of this belief system because it has taught me a great work ethic, and even Scripture tells us that this is important. Proverbs 14:23-24 states that hard work always pays off, but mere talk puts no bread on the table. The wise accumulate wisdom, but fools get stupider by the day. (My paraphrase).

However, this little saying became a belief system that put me in a box, making me think that I would have to constantly work challenging jobs and not be able to do what I love to make money. This was also because I watched my parents not living out what they were truly meant to be doing but instead just working to put food on the table. They were both hard workers, and for that, I am thankful. For years, I pursued jobs that could simply earn me a living. Now, I am learning to pursue what I love and trust God to bring me the overflow of His abundance from the gifts He has put within me, and I genuinely love what I do. I get to help people break free from debilitating mindsets and trauma bonds through the council of the Holy Spirit, God's Word, and the blood of Jesus! I love it!

Another belief system that I have learned to overcome and replace with truth is that "I only deserve what has been given to me." From all the molestation and chaos I was raised in, I had roots in me that made me believe that I wasn't worth any more than drugs, alcohol, or sex. As I began my healing process, I started partnering with all that God says I am worth. It was then that I began attracting the right people into my life, as I finally learned how to discern through God's Word and set healthy boundaries with others. I finally started to honor and love who God made me to be. This began creating more powerful belief systems that aligned with all that God had designed for me in the first place.

Life has a way of throwing us crazy, unfair curveballs from generational curses and demonic agendas. Unfortunately, we often fall into the trap of believing lies from the enemy because he does not want anyone serving the one and only true God. His utmost goal is to try and deceive every human being of their true identity and lead them away from a true relationship with God. John 10:10 clearly states, *"The thief only comes to steal, kill, and destroy, but I have come to give you everything in abundance, more than you can imagine, life in its fullness until you overflow."*

We must be keenly aware of the enemy's tactics, never letting our guard down. This means living daily in our Word and having our minds renewed daily because there are too many things in this world that deceive people, especially within the body of Christ. My heart breaks for the ministers who have turned their backs on their belief in God or even those who are twisting the Word of God. The only thing I can think of is that perhaps they never had a genuine relationship with Christ, or they had deep wounds that they never allowed God to heal fully, which then opened the door to deception. I'm not entirely sure of this answer, but it deeply burdens my heart when I'm in intercessory prayer. All I know is that once I truly encountered God's love, there was no turning back.

This is precisely what I am talking about in today's chapter. People have allowed the enemy's lies and false belief systems to take root in their hearts for far too long, which has then hardened their hearts against the truth. I know this Christian walk is a struggle, but God will always bring us through powerfully when we depend solely on Him and live in obedience to Him. A real battle is currently underway for souls. This is not a time to be lukewarm! If this is where you are, I encourage you to seek out any unhealthy belief systems that are causing you to live with one foot in and one foot out of walking your Christian walk.

I am a firm believer that we are all on our own journey with the Lord, and I am not trying to condemn you in any way. I am just deeply convicted by God's love for the lost and the deceived. I may fail, but I do try to be led by the Holy Spirit and die to myself daily. Dying to ourselves helps us to hear from God clearly. We must pick up the Word of God daily and get our minds aligned with Heavenly belief systems. We must get eternally minded! God is the only one who can wash us white as snow and bring us into the true freedom we need within our minds and our hearts.

APPLYING WISDOM TO YOUR DAILY LIFE

Lord Jesus,

Thank you for being willing to go through all that You went through on Your day of crucifixion because this shows me that You are a faithful redeemer of all things. You know what it's like to suffer, and you did it all for me! You took all my sin, every wrong belief, and every wrongdoing upon that cross. Help me to believe in the power that I now possess, living within me, because I believe in You with all my heart. Help any unbelief that is within my heart and mind, Lord. Help me to humble myself when I need help and to come to You knowing that I cannot do this on my own. I ask You, Lord, to wash my mind with your precious blood, helping me to heal from the intense pain that I have gone through in my past. Please help me to be strong enough to consider all the pain I have gone through and will go through as pure joy because I know it is helping me mature into my destiny. Help me to be diligent in Your Word and believe Your truth. Help me to apply it to my life in every way, Lord. Lead me, Holy Spirit, in Your wisdom and help me to get rid of all of my pride. Help me to see myself as you see me, Lord, and as I do these exercises, be with me and guide me. I trust You in Jesus' Name, I pray, Amen.

Key # 18: Speak In Tongues Often

Speaking in tongues as often as I can has had a profoundly positive impact on my life! It has truly changed me for the better. Speaking in tongues instantly helps me to calm myself when I feel out of balance. It enables me to adopt the right thinking patterns, aligning me with God's truth. It has helped me gain heavenly knowledge and downloads from the Lord on many different occasions when I need guidance. It also convicts me to do God's will instead of my own.

It is always our free will to pray or not to pray, but here is the truth: praying in tongues changes things dramatically! If you do not speak in tongues, ask the Holy Spirit to activate it in you because if you are a born-again believer in Christ, you already possess this gift within you. God will bring it forth; ask Him and believe to receive! If you already have this gift operating, I encourage you to pray in tongues for at least an hour a day, but ideally, you should do it as much as possible. I have been praying in tongues for many hours a day for almost seven years, and I am seeing the abundant fruit from it.

Speaking in tongues was the first gift given to prove that Jesus left His Holy Spirit with His people. The Holy Spirit came upon the people after Jesus ascended to heaven (Acts 2:4). The Bible clearly states that when we pray in tongues, God's Spirit is praying for us. This means your spirit is in direct contact with God, praying out the will of God in your life and for others (1 Corinthians 14:14). Praying in the spirit, or "tongues," helps us to stay balanced in everything we do. God leads our prayers as we submit this gift to Him and allow Him to pray through us daily (Romans 8:26). Jude 1:20 specifically tells us that praying in the Holy Ghost builds our most holy faith! Lastly, James 3:8 and Proverbs 18:21 illustrate the power of our tongues and the importance of being careful with our words. Praying in tongues edifies us as believers in Christ, and when you interpret, it edifies the Body of Christ. This is a powerful weapon that I have learned to wield in my spiritual arsenal throughout my life, and it will be one for you, too, if you apply it to your daily life! You will begin to see an abundance of fruit! Get ready!

<u>Implement new belief systems:</u>

Remember the Word of God will cut through any lie! Trust God to show you every lie you have been believing and living. Let Him show you the truth!

1. I want you to write down any belief system that you have that you know is unhealthy for you, so you can reject all agreement with them:

____

____

____

____

____

____

____

____

____

____

2. Now, I want you to write down some belief systems that you feel you have that are good:

____

____

____

____

____

____

____

____

____

____

3. Now, I want you to look up Scriptures to confirm or disprove your "good" belief system. What I mean is that you need to look up what God says about the belief system you have chosen for your life. Sometimes, what we think is good is not from God. Look up whatever belief system you are partnering with in the Bible. This will help you see what God says about your particular belief system that you think is good. Let me give you an example: Perhaps one of your belief systems is that you justify holding onto unforgiveness because you believe it is keeping you safe. You would then look up what God says in the Bible about unforgiveness. God always has the final say. His word will cut through bone and marrow and any lie we want to keep believing. We must humble ourselves and choose to partner with His Word. We can try to argue with God all day long, but this will only bring double-mindedness and confusion into our lives. When we choose to partner with His Word, it helps us bring balance to our minds, allowing us to begin embracing the correct and truthful belief systems God has for us. Then, ask the Holy Spirit to continue to show you any belief systems that you no longer need to hold onto throughout the entirety of reading this book.

4. As God leads you, take the time to renounce any wrong "good" belief that you have been partnering with as your truth. Break agreement with it by repenting, and then decree and declare what belief systems you will begin partnering with and back it with God's Word. Write down these new belief systems and begin speaking them over your life all day long if that's what it takes:

____

____

____

____

____

____

____

____

____

____

____

____

____

____

____

I think you will be amazed by all God shows you. He is still helping me overcome wrong beliefs to this day, which is 17 years after I fully started walking with Him. We are all a work in progress, but the key is staying humble. Be open to correction and keep your clay (heart) soft so the Father can continue molding you into all that He has created you to be. I hope that by incorporating this into your mind and heart, it will become a habit in your everyday life, and you will live with the mindset of being open to continuous improvement at all times, until we leave this earth.

5. As you begin doing these exercises this week, be very aware of the things that will try to pull you back into old patterns and incorrect belief systems. Ask the Holy Spirit to help you discern things and recognize any familiar spirits that will try to come back around to place seeds back into your mind after you have been delivered. We must remember that we have an enemy who sits and waits to devour us. 1 Peter 5:8 says, *"Your enemy the devil is prowling around outside like a roaring lion, just waiting and hoping for the chance to devour someone."* But God! You must remember that you have the power to overcome him through the blood of Jesus Christ! Do not let him overpower you!

Declaration:

The power of "I Am":

With every wrong belief that you have believed about yourself, I want you to replace it with a Godly "I Am" statement. These will be your declarations for today. By the end of this book, you should have a comprehensive list of 'I Am' statements. I want you to begin speaking these affirmations out loud daily, as well as the other things you have already been saying. I encourage my clients to record themselves with relaxing instrumental music in the background while speaking their I Am statements. Something powerful begins to happen when you listen to your voice speaking over yourself. You are a fantastic creation, and you possess the power of Christ living within you because we were all created in God's image (Genesis 1:26-27). You have the power within you to change your life radically.

Here are a couple of examples:

I used to struggle with a poverty mindset as well as a "works" mentality. This is now my "I Am" declaration over these struggles:

I am blessed beyond measure with heavenly riches that overflow my life, giving me the ability to bless others. I am the lender and not the borrower. I am a child of God, which means I have direct access to my heavenly inheritance here on Earth. My Father in Heaven has an abundance of riches, which means I do as well. I am becoming more eternally minded each day, which means I am building the Kingdom of God and not pursuing my own wealth. I decree and declare that I will live on 20% of my income and give 80% to help build God's kingdom here on Earth! I walk in God's abundance in every area of my life! I am deeply loved by my Heavenly Father, and this is all I need to move forward in whatever it is that He is calling me into!

If you struggle with self image, here is a great affirmation to declare:

I am beautiful both inside and out. My body is perfectly and wonderfully made in every area internally and externally! I am working towards my goals that I will reach with the help from the precious Holy Spirit. I love who God has created me to be.

3 Inner Healing

As I mentioned on the first day of this week, there is great power in the gift of our free will, but we must be aware of how we are using this gift. Are we feeding our flesh more than our spirit? Feeding our flesh will always keep us in bondage because there is no fruit there. It allows us to stay wounded and will eventually enable our "old man" to dominate. This should not happen since that old man was supposed to die once we became born again and were water-baptized. However, the Word does tell us to crucify our flesh daily so that old man does not resurrect.

It is a process to crucify our flesh, as we talked about last week and have been learning. This is a process we will have to continually engage in until we leave this earth, but it is here where most doors of access are opened for the enemy to come in. I have learned and witnessed throughout my life that woundedness often leads to rebellion and pride. Woundedness keeps us in the dark and blinds us to stubborn pride, which always leads to destruction. Untended wounds in our hearts will keep us in bondage and usually end up creating even more bondage.

So, the very first thing I want to talk about is the incredible power of love and humility; these will always bring deliverance. This may sound so cliche, but we have to grasp this. We all have the ability to choose love over fear, which is the first tangible act that you can begin doing for inner healing. Over the years that I have walked in my relationship with Jesus, I have learned more about inner healing. This is a process that allows the Holy Spirit to lead us into overcoming deep wounds within our hearts. Still, we must first acknowledge that we need healing. Everyone has faced hardships in life, which can create deep wounds that we are not even aware of. Inner healings are intentional sessions with God, often facilitated through fasting and prayer, and sometimes with the help of trusted individuals who can guide you into the encounters you may need for deliverance.

Inner healing with Jesus brings deliverance

I want to make it clear once again that Jesus is our Deliverer! He can deliver you just by spending intimate time with Him, by worshiping and reading His Word, and by the process of sanctifying yourself to Him. This is how much of my deliverance has happened throughout my early years of coming to Christ. However, over the past few years, the Lord has shown me some interesting ways to go deeper into healing my heart and staying steady in this arena.

The first revelation God began to share with me was about the power of humility and vulnerability. However, these two things are challenging for most people to act out, even as a believer in Christ, who has the Holy Spirit's conviction. Humility and vulnerability can be difficult because many people have been wounded, so they are hesitant to fully trust people and often end up building walls around their hearts. Most will say that their situation is between them and God. Now, this may be true, but are you allowing yourself to grow and mature within that fully? If so, great, but if you still feel bound in any way... Stay tuned.

You do have free will in this. God will not push you to do anything, but He will gently nudge you because He wants you whole and free. Wholeness and freedom is what Jesus died for! However, the lies you believe about your wounds are the exact areas where the enemy can keep you in bondage if you do not let God fully in. When we allow the Holy Spirit to lead our lives completely, we will be challenged to begin walking in this freedom. I am a firm believer that we should let people with good fruit into our lives to help us grow and be sharpened. It is essential to remain incredibly humble and have accountability partners with whom we can be open and vulnerable. This will help us avoid being deceived by our own self-righteous beliefs and pride. This is the biggest tactic of the enemy, and this is what he is still using to this day to cause such enmity within the church. We must stop this!

Humility and vulnerability are power keys in the kingdom of God. God revealed to me a few critical aspects of this. One of them is the importance of having accountability partners. For me, this includes my husband and a couple of true brothers and sisters in Christ with whom I can be completely honest. Being able to be vulnerable with someone is so important. This helps us expose any lies where the enemy is trying to hold us back or trying to make us partner with bondage from our pasts or possible deception. When we are able to expose the exact thing that we feel the need to hide, it breaks the enemy's power over us.

Again, we all have the free will to stay where we are, but God wants to stretch, grow, and mature His children, just as a good father should. He is calling us deeper and telling us to stop allowing the wounds of this life to deceive us further. We can experience wholeness in Him, but most people need others to help them get there. This chapter is crucial to absorb. Please be open to receiving a more profound revelation today, as there can be great freedom when you undergo deliverance and Inner Healing. However, you must be led by the Holy Spirit. From my perspective, I'd like to explain what inner healing is and share some testimonies of how it has benefited me.

2008-2012 were my first four years coming to Jesus; I began to have intense flashbacks and nightmares from my past. As I was going through these tormenting things, the Holy Spirit began speaking to me to learn how to rest in Him, which was both new and very scary for me because I didn't like silence or "rest." But during these "resting" times, I would lie on the living room floor and earnestly listen for his voice. This took some practice and time. However, as I became diligent in this, by reading His Word for hours a day and learning to be still with Him, He began to bring me into encounters with Him. He would give me scriptures, and I would literally imagine the Scriptures coming into my mind and into my body, trusting that there was power in His Word, that there was power in His blood.

I began to partner my imagination with His Truth, and something powerful began to happen. God began leading me into deeper encounters. He would start to bring up difficult memories from my past, and I would have to face them even though I did not want to relive them, but I trusted God as He led me through these visions. As I trusted Him, He showed me where Jesus was in the exact room I was in when I was younger, where my abuse was taking place. He was there weeping and interceding on my behalf, speaking life and declarations over me. Experiencing this began to radically change my life because I actually saw Jesus there with me while all my abuse was happening.

It helped me to release the lie that God was a "mean God" to allow this, and it also helped me to see that I was never alone and I am not alone now. This enabled me to start tapping into the belief that God was for me, even though that was the biggest truth that the enemy had fought me on since my childhood. I had believed the lie that God was against me until two years ago when I finally broke free! This lie tormented me for 35 years, but God is faithful to deliver us, and He used all those years to teach me how to heal with Him. He truly turns all things around for our good if we continue to trust His amazing love.

Fast forward to 2021, when I was going through a very difficult season in life, and a friend recommended a ministry for me to undergo inner healing and deliverance. Now, I had only heard of deliverance because I had been studying Derek Prince's teachings for the past two years. Still, the title "Inner Healing" was new to me. However, I prayed about it and felt the Holy Spirit tell me to go, so I went. Let me tell you, this three-hour session completely changed the direction of my life!

The power that came from sitting in that room with three mighty women who lavished me with the Father's love is hard to describe. It began with me telling them all that I was facing at that time. Then they had me close my eyes and told me to picture myself with one of the Trinity. Jesus showed up first, and then it was truly miraculous to watch how effortlessly we flowed together with the Holy Spirit to reveal deep wounds from my past that still needed healing, the roots of unforgiveness, and any curses that had come against my life.

This may sound unusual to some of you. Still, we serve a supernatural God, and He reveals deep secrets through the supernatural. This one session freed me from so much that the enemy still had me bound in. Then, I attended two more sessions and began training with this ministry, learning how to start walking in freedom. I truly began stepping into my destiny! I suffered almost my entire life from being attacked by demonic forces. Literally, from the time I was three years old until I was 39. Thirty-six years, I allowed the enemy to torment me both in my mind and physically in my body. However, after these sessions, I can boldly say that I am no longer afraid of the dark or the demonic.

You see, the enemy will always try to bind you in the exact area where God calls you. God gave me a mandate in my life in 2012. He told me that I carry an Isaiah 61:1 anointing. I had never heard this verse before He gave it to me, but then He confirmed it the next three days from three different people! Isaiah 61:1 states, *"The Spirit of the Lord GOD is upon me, because the LORD has anointed me to bring good news to the afflicted, to bind up the brokenhearted, to proclaim liberty to the captives, and release to the prisoners."*

I was destined to help people break free from the bondage of the enemy since before I was in my mother's womb. This is why the enemy attacked me so hard in all of these areas. He tried to put deep fear of him and his demons in me because he knew God would use me as a deliverer. The enemy wanted to wound me so deeply through abuse and molestation because I was actually destined for purity and to help bring healing to others. I'm here to tell you that the exact areas where you have been attacked are the exact areas where you will carry the power to deliver!

Overall, I highly recommend to every believer in Christ I come across to learn how to go through inner healing with God or attend a well-trusted inner healing ministry. We live in a fallen world where hurts are trying to come at us all day long, but we must keep our hearts right. When we choose to do these inner healings with the Lord, allowing ourselves to be vulnerable and humble, it exposes deep things within our hearts and delivers us! This is especially important for people in full-time ministry, as we must ensure that we are discerning out of love and not making poor judgments from our wounded hearts.

Inner healing sessions have helped me to go deeper into the layers of wounds from my childhood, where I unknowingly saw that the enemy still had a hold over my life. You see, I do allow the Lord to examine my heart daily, but I have found it extremely helpful to have others who are seasoned in the Lord help me process and then repent in front of them, exposing anything that needs to be addressed. Something powerful happens when we humble ourselves and repent in front of another person, and then we are held accountable. As I mentioned earlier, it exposes anything hidden and helps us break free from it.

Being vulnerable also gives these other people an opportunity to intercede with us and for us. We truly need each other within the Body of Christ, and this is a great way to keep us connected in the spirit. I still have people whom I have done sessions with years ago that come to my mind, and I lift them in my prayers whenever I think of them. Sometimes, I reach out as the Holy Spirit leads, and I get to pray with them as well. We need each other!

I recommend doing inner healing at least twice a year, but I prefer to do it every four months. This means I get together with a couple of sisters in Christ who are intercessors, and we dig deep to reveal anything that needs to be released from me. This helps me not only become aware of any areas that still need healing but also reveals anything that I may have inadvertently opened the door to. We live in a fallen world, and especially in my ministry, I need to ensure that I keep my heart right. Staying humble and being consistent in doing these helps me recognize how cunning the enemy truly is.

Every time I have undergone inner healing, I have become aware of things that gave the enemy access to my life. Inner healing has helped me walk out Galatians 5:1, keeping me conscious of not moving back into slavery! It also helps immensely when we have accountability partners to help us identify the blind spots that tend to hold us back in life. Proverbs 27:17 tells us the importance of having other like-minded believers to help sharpen us. Jesus brought me through many of these "inner healings" when I was first saved and for the last 14 years of my walk with Him. However, I didn't know that these things had actual titles or that ministries even existed to do these types of sessions.

As I was fully surrendering my life to Jesus, I was being delivered and fully healed internally. I now understand the importance of allowing my heart to be vulnerable and letting Him into every part of me so that nothing is hidden from Him. However, as humans, we tend to become prideful at times and do not always take the time to let Him tend to the surgeries that need to be done within our hearts. The main reason these particular deliverances with other experienced individuals are so powerful is that God often highlights simple yet profound things that we sometimes cannot see on our own.

He has revealed to me that it is usually our free will that holds us back within our minds and our bodies. Please stay with me here, because there is a great deal of freedom in this. In my first inner healing session, I saw two roots in my heart, and I knew I had to choose to forgive once and for all so that bitterness would not continue to take root. Meaning that every time this offense tries to come back, I remind the devil and myself that I have forgiven. It is done. Then, I search the Scriptures to begin declaring this truth until I feel a total release. Unforgiveness is a vast open door for the enemy to gain access into our lives, and it is our free will to forgive someone. Forgiveness is not a feeling; it is a choice. We must continue to choose to partner with that choice every time the enemy tries to bring that pain up again.

It was truly amazing to see how much freedom I finally had in my heart after those two roots were exposed. I was able to fully begin walking myself through even more deliverance as the Holy Spirit led, and now I can walk in love with this person. I look at them through the eyes of Jesus, and I even have respect for them, which I didn't have before. It's been so refreshing because this particular individual is close to me, and I have yearned for this for a long time.

Then, in my 2nd deliverance/inner healing session, I realized how many things came into my life that I had no control over, like being sexually molested when I was three. However, there were generational curses that I had to break and more unforgiveness that I had to release, even though I didn't realize I was still holding on to any. Then, it was as if a light bulb went off in my mind, telling me, "It is not your fault, Kristin!" None of this has been my fault. I had to identify the areas of my mind where the enemy gained legal access. This is where the enemy holds so many people in bondage.

If we do not humble ourselves to truly seek God and ask Him for revelation in the areas where we are being attacked, then it is on us. However, when we seek these things out with Jesus, and He reveals the bondage, and then we walk out in obedience to what He shows us, it is then up to Him to deliver us. As much as I would love to admit that we will all be fully delivered after these sessions, I cannot. What I can tell you is that you will come up higher in whom God is calling you to be, and you will gain authority in the areas where you have overcome torment from the enemy.

Inner healing allows God to fully search our hearts and it helps us recognize that God truly turns all things around for our good. It guides us through a process with the Holy Spirit to show us that God never leaves us or forsakes us. It then helps us heal and gives us power over the exact things that tried to destroy us. God is good, and Romans 8:27-28 is true, but we must be willing to accept and trust God's Word. These verses say, "*And he who searches our hearts knows the mind of the Spirit, because the Spirit intercedes for God's people in accordance with the will of God. And we know that in all things God works for the good of those who love him, who have been called according to his purpose.*" Trust God, Holy Spirit, and Jesus in this! I know He will give you great breakthrough in your mind and heart when you go through inner healing sessions.

<u>APPLYING WISDOM TO YOUR DAILY LIFE</u>

Prayer for the day:

Abba Father, Holy Spirit, and Jesus,

I ask that You help me as I embark on this journey of learning how to fully heal with You. Father God, I ask you to come in and be the father to me where my father may have lacked in truly loving me the way a father should. I ask for You to show me and fully allow me to both feel and experience Your love, Your goodness, Your security, and Your protection. Holy Spirit, I ask You to come in and be the true comforter of my heart and soul. I ask You to fill every area where my mother may have lacked in this arena of fully being there for me to comfort me and help me to feel safe and process through difficult times. I ask that You soften my heart so I can be sensitive to Your leading and guiding me. I permit You to come into every area where my heart needs healing. Jesus, I ask You to come in and let me experience you as the friend who will never leave me. I ask You to be the loving husband that I have never experienced before. I want to tangibly experience You, Lord. As I fully surrender my will to Yours, I want to fully experience who You all are in each of your functions and as fully being one. Help any unbelief that there may be inside my mind and my heart. Help me to clear these blocks out as I begin to heal with You. I love You! Thank You for loving me and for never giving up on me. In Jesus' name I pray!

Scriptures to meditate on:

Proverbs 20:5: *"The purposes of a person's heart are deep waters, but one who has insight draws them out.*

Psalm 68:5-6: *"Sing to God, praise his name; exalt the rider of the clouds. Rejoice before him whose name is the Lord. Father of the fatherless, defender of widows – God in his holy abode."*

James 1:16-18: *"Do not be deceived, my beloved brothers: all good giving and every perfect gift is from above, coming down from the Father of lights, with whom there is no alteration or shadow caused by change. He willed to give us birth by the word of truth that we may be a kind of firstfruits of his creatures."*

Luke 12:32: *"Do not be afraid, little flock, for it is your Father's good pleasure to give you the kingdom."*

2 Corinthians 6:16-18: *"What agreement is there between the temple of God and idols? For we are the temple of the living God. As God has said:"I will live in them and walk among them, and I will be their God, and they shall be my people… and I will be your father, and you shall be my sons and daughters, says the Lord Almighty."*

2 Corinthians 1:3-4: *"Blessed be the God and Father of our Lord Jesus Christ, the Father of mercies and God of all comfort, who comforts us in all our affliction, so that we may be able to comfort those who are in any affliction, with the comfort with which we ourselves are comforted by God."*

John 14:16-17: *"And I will ask the Father, and he will give you another Helper, to be with you forever, even the Spirit of truth, whom the world cannot receive, because it neither sees him nor knows him. You know him, for he dwells with you and will be in you."*

Isaiah 54:5: *"For your Maker is your husband, the Lord of hosts is his name; and the Holy One of Israel is your Redeemer, the God of the whole earth he is called."*

Hosea 2:19: *"And I will betroth you to me forever. I will betroth you to me in righteousness and in justice, in steadfast love and in mercy."*

Hosea 2:14-17: *"Therefore, behold, I will allure her, and bring her into the wilderness, and speak tenderly to her. And there I will give her her vineyards and make the Valley of Achor a door of hope. And there she shall answer as in the days of her youth, as at the time when she came out of the land of Egypt. "And in that day, declares the Lord, you will call me 'My Husband,' and no longer will you call me 'My Baal.' For I will remove the names of the Baals from her mouth, and they shall be remembered by name no more."*

Revelation 19:7-9: *"Let us rejoice and exult and give him the glory, for the marriage of the Lamb has come, and his Bride has made herself ready; it was granted her to clothe herself with fine linen, bright and pure"— for the fine linen is the righteous deeds of the saints. And the angel said to me, "Write this: Blessed are those who are invited to the marriage supper of the Lamb." And he said to me, "These are the true words of God."*

Key #19: Choose Love Always

1 Corinthians 13:13: *"So now faith, hope, and love abide, these three; but the greatest of these is love."*

1 Corinthians 16:14: *"Let all that you do be done in love."*

Colossians 3:14: *"And above all these put on love, which binds everything together in perfect harmony."*

1 John 4:8: *"Anyone who does not love does not know God, because God is love."*

When you begin to look at yourself, your life, and other people through the eyes of Jesus, you will gain wisdom that surpasses your own understanding. Jesus always operates from a place of love. It says that God is a God of war and a God of Love. This is a powerful statement: even in war, God operates from love. Perfect love casts out all fear (1 John 4:18). This key will help you overcome every obstacle in life by choosing to love and seeing things from a loving God's perspective. When we operate from a place of fear instead of love, it can block the way God wants to flow through us. This is why our free will to choose love is so important! Faith will always operate out of a place of love, and this is what moves the Father's heart; it is also what moves mountains. Without faith, it is impossible to please God (Hebrews 11:6). When you choose to begin looking at life through the lenses of His love, you will be amazed by all God begins to show you. You will begin to see people as He sees them, and He will trust you with Words of Knowledge to release to others. Allowing God's love to flow through you is what heals people. We must get this revelation. We must first receive His love and then operate out of this love at all times. Through God's love, He will reveal His power to you. Everything He created was out of love. Even where the seas stop and the earth begins, it was created with love. Love has healthy boundaries. Love is powerful beyond anything else in the world (John 3:16). This key is essential to apply to your life to experience true freedom.

Reflection:

I am going to give you some simple steps to bring yourself through inner healing with the Holy Spirit anytime you feel stuck in life or if you feel like the enemy is antagonizing you. I have found that if I cannot move forward, I need to fully immerse myself in Jesus, and His Word to gain a deeper perspective and understanding of His love. He always brings up deep places in my heart that still need tending to as well. Our hearts are like an onion. Many layers need to be peeled back, and this is a process that continues until we leave this earth. Learning how to dive deep with God brings so much freedom and truly helps us to walk in His love instead of our wounded justifications.

There are amazing inner healing resources available that can help you with your inner healing and deliverance process. I will list a couple of those places here as resources for you, as I know they will conduct Zoom meetings. I trained and worked with Truhope Ministries in 2022, and underwent inner healing sessions with Cross Counsel in 2023. As a result, I can attest to the character and biblical principles of both these ministries: https://mytruhope.com and https://www.crosscounsel.com. Heart Sync is another amazing resource for you to learn more about Inner Healing. You can find their ministry here: https://heartsynchealing.org. I am another resource for you as well if you have difficulty pressing in to finding breakthrough and can be reached at www.kristinlynneataylor.com

I am a firm believer that if you are a born-again believer in Christ, you can experience inner healing on your own, because you have the Holy Spirit living within you. However, I do recommend that you share with a brother or sister in Christ what you've been going through to expose anything hidden so you can have accountability partners to help you through. They can also be praying for you and with you when needed.

Inner healing steps to do on your own with the Lord:

1. Set aside 1-2 hours where you can be alone with just you and God, without any disruptions. *(The more you do this, the more comfortable you will become with having this special intimate time with God).* Put on instrumental soaking music and simply rest with him, allowing yourself to enter a state of peace. This may take 5-20 minutes to allow your mind to relax. Be patient and focus on God's goodness and mercy.

2. God created every human being with an incredible mind that has a fantastic imagination. It is powerful to remember this when you enter into intimate times with God because He can reveal things within your mind. I want you to ask God to meet you in a vision. Meaning this: I want you to picture yourself with God and have faith that you will hear from Him and sense His presence. This is no different from when someone says to picture an apple in your mind, and you can then see what an apple looks like within your imagination. This is the same thing, but what will begin to happen is that you will start to have intimate communication with God. There are numerous supernatural encounters throughout the entire Bible, but a simple example of this is found in 1 Samuel 3. Eli tells Samuel to go to the Lord in his quiet time, to seek God, and to tell God that his servant is listening. I want you to enter this with the faith that you are coming into an intimate time with God, and all you are doing is asking God to speak to you because you are listening. He may give you a vision, a daydream, or some picture that comes to mind. Or He may speak to you about what He wants you to see or hear so you can align your imagination with what you hear. I

want you to just try to picture yourself meeting with one of the Triune God. This could be the Father, the Holy Spirit, or Jesus. I have even had all three show up to be with me at one time during an inner healing session, so be open to whatever God shows you or speaks to you.

3. Once you have this picture or words come into your mind, ask whoever shows up *(Jesus, Father God, or Holy Spirit)* how to deal with the issue you are having. This could be wanting to let go of an intense fear you are battling, or some sort of addiction, or something you just can't let go of, or someone you can't seem to forgive. Once you ask, be patient and listen for an answer. God is good, and He will answer you.

4. His answer may look different than you think it should be. Be open to what you see or hear in your spirit. He may show you something where you are in the vision with Him, or He may give you a different vision of a memory that He wants you to revisit from your childhood, or He may give you a scripture to look up, or a word to look up the biblical meaning of. Be open to whatever He shows you.

5. Then, with whatever it is that He shows you, ask the Holy Spirit, "What do you want me to do with this?" Again, this could look like you going back into that difficult memory and having the Lord show you where He was in that very traumatic situation that you felt like you had to face alone. (*This is powerful because when you fully open your heart to receive, God can show you where He was during your trauma and this can replace the horrible memory with an encouraging one, knowing that God was always with you. Ask Him for this if you need to*)! Or, perhaps He brings up a picture or a name of someone you need to forgive. Unforgiveness is a significant barrier that hinders us from reaching our full potential and experiencing intimacy with God on a daily basis. Perhaps He gently tells you that you need to break bloodline covenants with your parents and their ancestors or renounce agreement with things and/or spirits that you have partnered with willingly or unknowingly. Whatever it is, be open and then be obedient to whatever the Holy Spirit leads you to do.

6. Once you have gone through one thing, ask the Lord if there is anything else you need to let go of, and then you can continue through this process with the guidance of the Holy Spirit. Again, this can look different every time you do this. We serve a mighty supernatural God who wants to break us out of our little minute box thinking minds, so be open to what He has for you!

7. Lastly, if you release anything deep or feel that you still have any gaping holes, ask the Holy Spirit to fill in any area that still feels wounded. Ask Him to fill you with His love, peace, and perseverance so that you can fully walk out your healing in the times ahead. Be patient with yourself because healing is a process. Sometimes, you will feel instant relief and total deliverance from a situation, while other things may take some more time. The key is to stay humble and be patient. We are all in a process until we leave this earth but getting into the practice of doing these inner healing sessions with God will radically change your life.

8. Remember, consistency is key. This should not be done out of a place of work or performance, but this is done out of wanting to meet with your Heavenly King to seek out the answers that only He can give you.

I want you to be patient if you don't feel like you hear much the first couple of times of doing this, especially if you are new to hearing God's voice or partnering with Him in your imagination. For some people, this can take time. Suppose you cannot hear anything after doing this a few times. In that case, you may need to reach out to me or the ministries listed above for help with your first inner healing, to achieve a breakthrough and/or deliverance. This doesn't mean there's something wrong with you. You may just need a little help from a brother or sister in Christ who is experienced with inner healing. God loves you and He is for you! Know that you are breaking free!

Declaration:

My spirit is healed and whole by the blood of Jesus, and my body and soul are coming into divine alignment with this healing. I can do all things through Christ, who gives me strength, and I will be mightily used by God. I am worthy and deserving to hear my Father's voice because I am His child! He is for me and not against me! He leads me through this life, and I follow Him. I am a supernatural being because I am a born-again believer in Christ. I have surrendered my life and my will to Jesus. Therefore, I allow Him to operate in me and through me!

4 Humility brings clarity

Our free will is such a powerful key to our freedom! God is not a controlling or manipulative God. He gave us free will on purpose to enable us to make our own choices. We must get this revelation because it brings freedom! We have a choice: to love, to forgive, to be happy, to be depressed, to be successful, or to be miserable. I hope you get my point,, and if this is irritating you in any way, ask God to reveal the roots in your heart that may be causing the irritation. I have learned that whenever I become irritated or offended, it is usually something within me that I need to let go of. Most of the time, it ends up being pride.

We need to humble ourselves by letting go of our pride and realize that it is always our free will that holds us back from living in God's abundance. Try your hardest not to fall into condemnation here, because this is actually very powerful; however, the enemy would love to use it against us. Let me give you an example. I have been battling a type of sickness off and on in my body since I was a child. Now, this type of sickness is very common among women, and every health professional I have been to told me that some women are just more susceptible. Then, I went the healthy route by doing cleanses to reset my gut, all the while praying for God to reveal the truth to me.

The Bible tells us that Jesus came over 2000 years ago to heal us! I have often found myself wrestling with this throughout my Christian walk, as I'm sure many other Christians have. I began to fast and pray, seeking answers with the help of the Holy Spirit. He revealed to me that the only way sickness can come upon us once we are born again is by some door that has been open for the enemy to have access and then bring harm upon us. This door is not always opened by us; it can come from curses. This is why being led by the Spirit is so crucial. I also want to ensure that you understand I am not suggesting we can heal ourselves.

It is only by the Blood of Jesus and the deep revelation of deliverance He brings us. We cannot work for our deliverance, but we can stand in faith and trust God until the deliverance comes. It is our free will to partner with this mindset! God revealed to me that I had bitterness in my heart, as well as witchcraft that had been coming against me for years. Once I was aware of this and was obedient to do what he showed me to do, I haven't had this particular health issue ever since he gave me this revelation!

One of my greatest inspirations of all time is the story of John G. Lake, who was involved in the response to the bubonic plague outbreak in the early 1900s. This man walked in such faith that the plague never affected him, even while he was carrying out dead bodies to bury them. There was proof under a microscope showing that the disease began to die as soon as it came in contact with his skin. If this worked for him, why isn't this working for us? I believe the main reason was not only because of this man's faith but also because of the deep intimacy he had with God. He knew how important it was to keep his soul (mind, will, & emotions) and his body (flesh) in submission to Jesus.

He had a mighty call upon his life, and he knew that God would protect him. It takes true humility to fully trust God and His plan for your life. He was fully convinced by who God said He was and the power that was within him. If you are unfamiliar with this story, I encourage you to look it up, as it will deepen your faith. I also encourage you to research mighty men and women of God, such as Kathryn Kuhlman, Derek Prince, or Smith Wigglesworth, among others. I believe it will stir something deep within you, helping your faith to arise. If we believe God's word is true, then why are most Christians not operating in the power that His word says we should be operating in? Let me show you a powerful scripture that I want you to meditate on this week:

John 14:11-31 says, *"Believe me when I say that I am in the Father and the Father is in me; or at least believe in the evidence of the works themselves. Very truly I tell you, whoever believes in me will do the works I have been doing, and they will do even greater things than these, because I am going to the Father. And I will do whatever you ask in my name, so that the Father may be glorified in the Son. You may ask me for anything in my name, and I will do it. "If you love me, keep my commands. And I will ask the Father, and he will give you another advocate to help you and be with you forever—the Spirit of truth. The world cannot accept him, because it neither sees him nor knows him. But you know him, for he lives with you and will be in you. I will not leave you as orphans; I will come to you. Before long, the world will not see me anymore, but you will see me. Because I live, you also will live. On that day you will realize that I am in my Father, and you are in me, and I am in you. Whoever has my commands and keeps them is the one who loves me. The one who loves me will be loved by my Father, and I too will love them and show myself to them." Then Judas (not Judas Iscariot) said, "But, Lord, why do you intend to show yourself to us and not to the world?" Jesus replied, "Anyone who loves me will obey my teaching. My Father will love them, and we will come to them and make our home with them. Anyone who does not love me will not obey my teaching. These words you hear are not my own; they belong to the Father who sent me. "All this I have spoken while still with you. But the Advocate, the Holy Spirit, whom the Father will send in my name, will teach you all things and will remind you of everything I have said to you. Peace I leave with you; my peace I give you. I do not give to you as the world gives. Do not let your hearts be troubled and do not be afraid. "You heard me say, 'I am going away and I am coming back to you.' If you loved me, you would be glad that I am going to the Father, for the Father is greater than I. I have told you now before it happens, so that when it does happen you will believe. I will not say much more to you, for the prince of this world is coming. He has no hold over me, but he comes so that the world may learn that I love the Father and do exactly what my Father has commanded me."*

Jesus clearly says it all right here in John! This chapter is a powerful one to implement in our daily lives. There's so much revelation in this one chapter that will truly set us free if we choose to obey and trust what Jesus says here. We may not get healed instantly, but we can become free in our minds. One thing I want to highlight is John 14:12-14, which says, 'Whoever believes...' Go back and reread this verse and meditate here until it gets so deep into your soul and your heart that nothing else can take its place. It is here, when we truly believe in who God is and who lives on the inside of us, that we think we can be free from all sickness and disease. However, it is within the perfect timing of God. I do not believe that God brings this upon us in any way, but it tells us to consider all suffering as joy because God will use it for our good if we continue to love Him no matter what.

Another Chapter that has radically changed my life is Ephesians 1. I also want you to meditate on this chapter in Ephesians this week, as well, because I will believe with you that you will begin to see the power of Jesus living within you. It is my prayer that everyone who reads this book will encounter the love and truth of Jesus so mightily that it changes you from the inside out and that you begin walking out your destiny! Power comes when we humbly place our lives in the hands of Jesus. We become His vessel, and we begin working out our salvation as well as discovering our identity in Christ through fear and trembling. We must learn to walk in humility having true reverence for God, allowing Him to work through us continually.

Ephesians 1:3-22 says, *"Every spiritual blessing in the heavenly realm has already been lavished upon us as a love gift from our wonderful heavenly Father, the Father of our Lord Jesus—all because he sees us wrapped into Christ. This is why we celebrate him with all our hearts! And in love he chose us before he laid the foundation of the universe! Because of his great love, he ordained us, so that we would be seen as holy in his eyes with an unstained innocence. For it was always in his perfect plan to adopt us as his delightful children, through our union with Jesus, the Anointed One, so that his tremendous love that cascades over us would glorify his grace—for the same love he has for the Beloved, Jesus, he has for us. And this unfolding plan brings him great pleasure! Since we are now joined to Christ, we have been given the treasures of redemption by his blood—the total cancellation of our sins—all because of the cascading riches of his grace. This superabundant grace is already powerfully working in us, releasing all forms of wisdom and practical understanding. And through the revelation of the Anointed One, he unveiled his secret desires to us—the hidden mystery of his long-range plan, which he was delighted to implement from the very beginning of time. And because of God's unfailing purpose, this detailed plan will reign supreme through every period of time until the fulfillment of all the ages finally reaches its climax—when God makes all things new in all of heaven and earth through Jesus Christ. Through our union with Christ we too have been claimed by God as his own inheritance. Before we were even born, he gave us our destiny; that we would fulfill the plan of God who always accomplishes every purpose and plan in his heart. God's purpose was that we Jews, who were the first to long for the messianic hope, would be the first to believe in the Anointed One and bring great praise and glory to God! And because of him, when you who are not Jews heard the revelation of truth, you believed in the wonderful news of salvation. Now we have been stamped with the seal of the promised Holy Spirit. He is given to us like an engagement ring, as the first installment of what's coming! He is our hope-promise of a future inheritance which seals us until we have all of redemption's promises and experience complete freedom—all for the supreme glory and honor of God. Because of this, since I first heard about your strong faith in the Lord Jesus Christ and your tender love toward all his devoted ones, my heart is always full and overflowing with thanks to God for you as I constantly remember you in my prayers. I pray that the Father of glory, the God of our Lord Jesus Christ, would impart to you the riches of the Spirit of wisdom and the Spirit of revelation to know him through your deepening intimacy with him. I pray that the light of God will illuminate the eyes of your imagination, flooding you with light, until you experience the full revelation of the hope of his calling—that is, the wealth of God's glorious inheritances that he finds in us, his holy ones! I pray that you will continually experience the immeasurable greatness of God's power made available to you through faith. Then your lives will be an advertisement of this immense power as it works through you! This is the mighty power that was released when God raised Christ from the dead and exalted him to the place of highest honor and supreme authority in the heavenly realm! And now he is exalted as first above every ruler, authority, government, and realm of power in existence! He is gloriously enthroned over every name that is ever praised, not only in this age, but in the age that is coming! And he alone is the leader and source of everything needed in the church. God has put everything beneath the authority of Jesus Christ and has given him the highest rank above all others. And now we, his church, are his body on the earth and that which fills him who is being filled by it!"*

We must learn to abide in Jesus, just as Jesus walked in close fellowship with the Father. He said I do nothing unless my Father tells me to. Jesus walked in a level of humility that few will ever experience, but it was because of His humility that He fully trusted and only did what the Father told Him to do. Jesus had free will and possessed the same power as God in Heaven to do things His way, but He chose to abide in His Father. Jesus was a perfect example of how we need to live our lives and all that is possible through Him. This means we should operate with power and love that conquer every lie and every sin. We can read about something all day long, but it's only when we actually learn and experience it firsthand that we genuinely believe it.

It is beneficial to embrace suffering while trusting in Jesus, as you will grow significantly in your faith. I have endured a great deal of suffering, and I still do, even as I finish this book. However, we must grasp the fact that God is for us. He will turn all things around for our good, and He will deliver us in His timing once we learn all that we were supposed to during that particular season. Sometimes, this learning process is simply to draw closer to Jesus because when we suffer, it brings us into a deeper place of relatability with Him. It also brings us into a deep intimacy with Him and He longs to come so incredibly close to us if we will allow Him to.

So, I will repeat it: your free will is powerful! Your choice to believe what the Word of God says and to choose to trust the power of God living inside of you can radically change your life! We must humble ourselves and ask God what we are missing. Ask Him what doors have been opened and why the enemy has access to steal your portion. God will show you if you are willing to see and then be obedient to close the doors and walk out what He is telling you to do. Be kind to yourself and patient if you still have to wait. We are always in a process but God will use every single detail of our lives if we allow Him to.

This is a huge key to getting free! God has put every single thing that we need to live out our destiny within us (*His divine power has given us everything we need for a godly life through our knowledge of him who called us by his own glory and goodness. 2 Peter 1:3*). Allow God to come in to strip you of all that needs to leave and then sharpen you into how to reign with His power. The choice is always ours and has always been since Jesus did what He did on the cross. We serve a good Father who wants us to live in freedom, walking in His love and His power. He gave that back to us when he sent us his son!

APPLYING WISDOM TO YOUR DAILY LIFE

My Precious heavenly Father,

Thank You for loving me so much that You will never leave me nor forsake me. Help me to trust You like Jesus trusts You. Help me to know that no matter what comes against me, You are with me. Thank You for using me as your vessel. I yield everything within me and my will to You. Show me any area where I have not surrendered my will. Forgive me for any pride and fear that I may still harbor towards You and/or the plans You have for my life. Help me daily to surrender my will for Yours. I ask for a deep sensitivity to Your Holy Spirit's leading. Show me Your ways and the paths You have for me, Lord. Thank You. In Jesus' Name, I pray.

Scriptures to meditate on:

1 Peter 5:6-7: *"Humble yourselves, therefore, under God's mighty hand, that he may lift you up in due time. Cast all your anxiety on him because he cares for you."*

Ephesians 4:2-3: *"Be completely humble and gentle; be patient, bearing with one another in love. Make every effort to keep the unity of the Spirit through the bond of peace."*

2 Chronicles 7:14: *"If my people, who are called by my name, will humble themselves and pray and seek my face and turn from their wicked ways, then I will hear from heaven, and I will forgive their sin and will heal their land."*

Reflection:

True humility will begin to birth your identity in Christ!

1. Every time you feel an offense rise within you, ask the Holy Spirit to reveal to you what needs to be worked on within your heart. When we learn to humble ourselves and start looking inward instead of blaming or staying in a victim or prideful mindset, everything changes. You will begin to see clearly. You will begin to see things from God's heart and love for others rather than through your own judgment.

2. Start paying attention to patterns in your life. Do you realize the same issues keep happening in your life? For example, do you and your husband keep arguing about the same things but haven't truly worked it out by going to counseling or digging deep to find the roots that keep causing the issues? Or, how about you keep ending up in the same financial pit every time you work yourself out of debt? What about talking about where you want to be but never taking action steps to get there? When these things come up, I want you to write them down and spend time with the Lord in prayer. Ask God what is inside your heart that you need to work on, and then walk out in obedience, whatever He tells you to do. This humility will lead to an admission of wrong, followed by obedience and, ultimately, some victory.

3. We can no longer say the whole clichéd saying, "Oh, Jesus has it, I know He'll provide!" I used to do this, but I have learned that this type of thinking is a cop-out, avoiding the work that God is asking you to do so you can grow through whatever pattern keeps coming up in your life. You must humble yourself to work on whatever God is leading and asking you to do. Let us take a look at the Israelites when they left Egypt and finally got their freedom. According to biblical interpretations, they could have entered the Promised Land in as little as eleven days, but it took them forty years. This is wild to think about but also very eye-opening to me in areas where I could have been further along in life if I hadn't rebelled. This was due to their pride and rebellion, as they thought they knew better than God. They partnered with pride, fear, and selfishness and chose to run to other gods for answers instead of allowing God to work out their salvation in Him! Let us not be like the Israelites anymore! Amen? I'm preaching to myself here, too! We must receive this and humble ourselves to truly recognize where God wants to take us and allow Him to lead us there. This takes humility and faith.

4. Begin spending time with God daily, asking Him what He says about you and what your calling and giftings are. True humility comes when we finally start believing in all that God has put within us. Why? Because we no longer have to prove ourselves to man. We start loving who we are! Now, this may sound contradicting because this could be perceived as prideful from a worldly view, but with God, we should be excited about how He created us. We should go after all that He has put inside of us, trusting that He is a good Father and that He knew what He was doing when He made us! God tells us to love Him with all our heart and soul and then to love ourselves so we can love our neighbors well. I'm telling you, this is a great nugget to get a hold of!

Declaration:

I can overcome every obstacle in my life through Christ! I am a surrendered vessel willing to do whatever it is that God asks me to do. My heavenly Father leads me, and I follow through with all that He tells me to do because He knows all that I am destined for! I am learning to humble myself daily by asking Him these questions throughout the day. How do you see this situation, God? How do You want me to proceed? How do You see this person, Lord? How can I pray for them instead of being offended by them? What is it in me that still needs healing in order for me to love them like You do Jesus?

5 Tossed to and fro

Another topic related to our free will that I would like us to explore is the importance of being aware of double-mindedness. We tend to become double-minded when we want our way instead of God's way. It is usually a telltale sign of pride, which stems from the root of fear. God warns us of this in James 1, and He provides us with powerful wisdom to apply to our lives throughout the entire book of James. I'm not going to lie to you and act as if I have it all figured out. Everything I am telling you in this book comes from places I have walked through and learned from, but I am still being molded into His image.

I have overcome numerous attacks, but I must stay vigilant and continue to persevere with all that I have learned when new trials come. As much as I love Jesus, I have become double-minded at times in my walk with Him, and we must be vigilant in this area. I am finally beginning to see the pattern that the enemy uses to try and trigger this thinking pattern in me. Being double-minded in life, especially when it comes to matters of God, is a perilous place to be. Every time I find myself in this headspace, it's like an open season for the enemy to attack me in every area of my life.

James 1:2 *"Consider it pure joy, my brothers and sisters, whenever you face trials of many kinds, because you know that the testing of your faith produces perseverance. Let perseverance finish its work so that you may be mature and complete, not lacking anything. If any of you lacks wisdom, you should ask God, who gives generously to all without finding fault, and it will be given to you. But when you ask, you must believe and not doubt, because the one who doubts is like a wave of the sea, blown and tossed by the wind. That person should not expect to receive anything from the Lord. Such a person is double-minded and unstable in all they do."*

These Scriptures can sound very intense, but the wisdom they convey is quite powerful. Imagine if you kept the mindset that when every trial came, you were determined to stay joyful and praise God throughout your trial, knowing that He would turn it around for good, no matter what. Imagine facing each trial with a warrior mindset, saying, "OK, trial, here I am, and I am ready to be tested because I am going to learn so much from you, and I will overcome you with my God!" This can take time to reach this place because, just as Scripture tells us, we must persevere, and with that perseverance comes maturity and faith. Even for myself, I think, well, I should be a professional at walking through trials by now, but I can still become a little shaky when the big ones come.

However, it may only take me one or two days now to get off of my pity pot and begin declaring and believing all the good things that will come from that particular trial. It used to take me months at first, and then it became weeks. I'm thankful that it's now only days. I am currently learning why it is even taking me days. I have figured out that it's because I am still allowing hurt to come in and take root. I also still wrestle with the fact that this life is not my own, and I find myself becoming weary at times. This weariness usually occurs when trials come one after another, like waves of the sea, not giving me much time to breathe. But God! He is allowing things to become stronger and more fierce because He is training me for more. This is why James and Paul talk so much about considering it all joy when trials do come because God has chosen you for a great and mighty purpose. We will be used mightily for His Kingdom here on this Earth if we choose to be.

Every time I recognize myself becoming double-minded in my life, I check my heart with the Holy Spirit to see where I got off track. It is usually due to me being too busy and not spending enough time with God. I become weary and realize how quickly I am not thinking correctly and how unwise my decision-making has become. We must have balance in life. I know that for me to feel balanced, I need time with God, time for myself, time with my family, and time for fulfilling work of some sort. This should be part of my daily routine. It is essential to take note when you begin to feel double-minded in your life. Becoming double-minded is a tool the enemy uses to get us off track and to be tossed as the waves of the sea, so we must be aware. A couple of the main reasons I have found for becoming double-minded are getting into fear or rebelling against the instructions God has already given us to follow. Be cautious here, humble yourself, and allow God to check your heart, to see where the double-mindedness is coming from.

Double-mindedness and rebellion against God usually come from a deep place of fear. It is crucial to allow God to begin healing that area of bondage within you. You have learned how to go into inner healing and a simple deliverance session with Him. It is all about being obedient and coming into intimate places with Jesus daily until you feel yourself free from this double-mindedness. I believe God has shown me a special grace for the Body of Christ at this time. This grace is for those who genuinely want to be in His will but have struggled for so long to break free. As you are diligent in coming to Him, He will break you free more quickly than you think.

What I mean by this is that what took me 15 years to heal from, I see individuals being born again and getting miraculously delivered in a short time. I have witnessed this personally with a few dear clients of mine already. It's happening, and it's wonderful to watch! I want to point out another scripture for you to meditate on this week, as it contains powerful keys that you need to receive. Please take time in your daily routine to meditate on the entire chapter of Psalm 24.

Psalm 24 in the NIV says, *"The earth is the Lord's, and everything in it, the world, and all who live in it; for he founded it on the seas and established it on the waters. Who may ascend the mountain of the Lord? Who may stand in his holy place? The one who has clean hands and a pure heart, who does not trust in an idol or swear by a false god. They will receive blessings from the Lord and vindication from God their Savior. Such is the generation of those who seek him, who seek your face, God of Jacob. Lift up your heads, O you gates; be lifted up, you ancient doors, that the King of glory may come in. Who is this King of glory? The LORD strong and mighty, the LORD mighty in battle. Lift up your heads, O you gates; lift them up, you ancient doors, that the King of glory may come in. Who is he, this King of glory? The LORD Almighty-- he is the King of glory. Selah."*

God has been speaking to me about the hearts of men through this Psalm. In the Passion Translation, verse 7 says, *"Wake up, you living gateways, lift up your heads, you doorways of eternity!"* This is a powerful translation: the time is now to wake up. You and I are the living gateways that this Psalm is talking about! For us to live this life full of His power, walking out our destiny, we must allow our hearts to swing wide open! Allow God in and allow Him to have His way in you! God is always going after the hearts of all humanity. God connects with us through the openness of our hearts. So, I am pleading with you to open your heart to God even more. Open it wider than you have allowed it to in the past. Allow God to show you the things you need to release at this time because He wants you to walk out Psalm 24, Ephesians 1, and chapters 14-17 in John confidently.

He is the one who will prepare you, making you armed and ready for battle. He will make ways for you that no man can stop! He will steady your mind and your heart as you seek Him and allow Him to purify all that needs to be released so He can use you how He pleases! We are in a special time right now, where God is calling us into deeper intimacy with Him, because He wants you to know your identity in Him and how much access you actually have! When we abide in Christ, the access that we get to participate in is mind-blowing!

God is doing a quick and radical work because He needs influential people to lead the way for all that is coming in these end times. Whether or not we will see Jesus return, it is our job to prepare the next generation to lead well! He is appointing leaders now, and if you feel a tug on your heart to lead, then please don't miss this opportunity. God showed me that there are many people He has chosen for a time as this, but they keep running from the call that is upon their lives. Do not shy away! Run into God and give Him everything you have because once you do, He will give you back more than you can even think or imagine!

The fact is, you do have free will, and God will not force you to do what He has called you to do. But, I am here being a mouthpiece for God. He is speaking through me to you! I know this because I feel it with every fiber of my being as I type these words. Some of you need to get right with God and answer the call that is upon your life! Allow Him to come in and wreck your heart for all that wrecks Him. He wants every bit of you, and He will lead you powerfully! He will not fail you!

This means that as you surrender your will for His, you cannot fail. Failing is not an option when you are in Christ. You will never fail when you walk by the leading of the Holy Spirit because God is for you. He always makes a way even when we can't see it as long as we keep our hearts right towards Him. Romans and Philippians promise us this, as well as many other Scriptures throughout God's word. One huge truth that the body of Christ needs to grasp is that we were bought with a price. You and I were purchased with the precious Blood of Jesus, and your life is not your own, neither is mine (1 Corinthians 6:19-20).

So why do many Christians tend to seem so incredibly broken and selfish? Free will enables us to choose how we want to live our lives and what we want to do with them. This will cause double-mindedness because if we are not living out the life that God has for us, we will never feel fulfilled. I am here to tell you, choose to live and abide in Christ because abundance in every area flows from here! I am learning to live in God's abundant flow because I have given my life entirely over to Him (Philippians 1:21). It is a lie from the enemy that once we surrender everything, we will then be without or that God won't provide for us. This is what fear tells us, and it is the furthest thing from the truth. Once we surrender all and allow God to birth out of us what he put inside, true abundance begins to overflow through us! There is a process of stripping, but it is for our good!

God has given me a great deal of revelation on this topic, and I will write a future book on the abundant life, as this is how God intended for us to live. He always intended for us to live and walk through His power. We must remember that God's ways are higher than our own. His power can look like total brokenness, meekness, and gentleness. It can look very different from the world's view of abundance and power. We must remember that God calls us the head and not the tail. He says we are above and not beneath (Deuteronomy 28:13)! Jesus told us that we will do greater works than He did (John 14:12)! He says that we are to be the lender and not the borrower (Deuteronomy 15:6, 28:12)! God calls us to conquer all things through Him (Romans 8:37)!

There are many truths in the Bible for us to discover, receive revelation from, and then live out. God gave us His Word because it is a lamp unto our feet in this dark world! It is the anchor for our souls when the raging waves of double-mindedness come. We must read His Word with the revelation from the Holy Spirit daily! Then, we must speak and declare His word over our lives and the lives of others daily. God is always talking to His children. However, most Christians are too busy to listen and too busy to be diligent to speak His promises daily. I am the first to admit that I have to be cautious of this, too, but it is essential. The time is now for the Bride to arise into every bit of who God is calling her to be! All of creation is groaning for you to arise (Romans 8:19-23)! Do not allow the enemy to toss you to and fro any longer. Find your anchor in Christ, and let Him raise you up! Arise, dear one! Arise into your destiny!

APPLYING WISDOM TO YOUR DAILY LIFE

Jesus,

Forgive me for holding onto my ways instead of yours. Help me to humble myself and die to my flesh daily so I can hear clearly from Your precious Holy Spirit. I want to abide in You, Jesus, as You did here on this earth with our Father. Help heal every part of my heart that is trying to keep me from doing this. I surrender my life to You, Lord. Have Your way in me and through me. Lead me every second of every day and especially when trials come, Lord. Help me to stay strong in faith, trusting that You will turn every single thing around for my good and the good of Your people. Help me to recognize the enemy and stay steadfast, knowing that You have allowed certain situations to befall me for my good. Sustain my hope and my faith when these trials arise. Holy Spirit, I give You full permission to convict me every time I become double-minded, and I ask You to increase the sensitivity in my heart and my mind as I abide in You more. God, it says in Psalm 115:16 that You rule over the universe, but that the earth has been given to man. So, help me to lead well and subdue the earth, Lord. Have Your way in and through me. I know I have free will, but I submit my will to Yours. I give You permission to remind me daily that I was bought with a price and help me to walk out Your will for my life humbly. I want my life to be a representation of You, Lord Jesus! I pray all of this in Jesus' name! Amen.

Proverbs 18:21: *"The tongue has the power of life and death, and those who love it will eat its fruit."*

James 3:3-10: *"When we put bits into the mouths of horses to make them obey us, we can turn the whole animal. Or take ships as an example. Although they are so large and are driven by strong winds, they are steered by a very small rudder wherever the pilot wants to go. Likewise, the tongue is a small part of the body, but it makes great boasts. Consider what a great forest is set on fire by a small spark. The tongue also is a fire, a world of evil among the parts of the body. It corrupts the whole body, sets the whole course of one's life on fire, and is itself set on fire by hell. All kinds of animals, birds, reptiles and sea creatures are being tamed and have been tamed by mankind, but no human being can tame the tongue. It is a restless evil, full of deadly poison. With the tongue we praise our Lord and Father, and with it we curse human beings, who have been made in God's likeness. Out of the same mouth come praise and cursing. My brothers and sisters, this should not be."*

Psalm 141:3: *"Set a guard over my mouth, LORD; keep watch over the door of my lips."*

1 Peter 3:10: *"Whoever would love life and see good days must keep their tongue from evil and their lips from deceitful speech."*

Colossians 3:8: *"But now ye also put off all these; anger, wrath, malice, blasphemy, filthy communication out of your mouth."*

Colossians 4:6: *"Let your conversation be always full of grace, seasoned with salt, so that you may know how to answer everyone."*

Ephesians 4:29: *"Do not let any unwholesome talk come out of your mouths, but only what is helpful for building others up according to their needs, that it may benefit those who listen."*

Proverbs 15:28: *"The heart of the righteous weighs its answers, but the mouth of the wicked gushes evil."*

Proverbs 17:9: *"Whoever would foster love covers over an offense, but whoever repeats the matter separates close friends."*

Proverbs 21:23: *"Those who guard their mouths and their tongues keep themselves from calamity."*

Psalm 34:13: *"Keep your tongue from evil and your lips from telling lies."*

Proverbs 17:27-28: *"The one who has knowledge uses words with restraint, and whoever has understanding is even-tempered. Even fools are thought wise if they keep silent, and discerning if they hold their tongues."*

Proverbs 18:6-7: *"The lips of fools bring them strife, and their mouths invite a beating. The mouths of fools are their undoing, and their lips are a snare to their very lives."*

Key #20: Guard Your Tongue!

When I first came to the Lord, I'll never forget a little book that was given to me by my pastor, and I remember getting offended. It just shows you how immature I was in the Lord, but that pastor did me a huge favor! That book was by Derek Prince, and it was called, "Does your tongue need healing? Well, guess what? My tongue required some healing, and that little book, along with a daily partnership with the Holy Spirit, helps me guard my tongue. The tongue may be little, but it is mighty and can guide our lives, so we better be aware of what is coming out of our mouths.

James 3:4-5: *"Look at the ships also: though they are so large and are driven by strong winds, they are guided by a very small rudder wherever the will of the pilot directs. So also the tongue is a small member, yet it boasts of great things. How great a forest is set ablaze by such a small fire!"*

The very first thing God did when He created was speak, and the Bible says the Holy Spirit waited for God's instruction to bring it into creation. Genesis 1:1-3 says, *"In the beginning, God created the heavens and the earth. Now the earth was formless and empty, darkness was over the surface of the deep, and the Spirit of God was hovering over the waters." And God said, "Let there be light," and there was light.* If God made man in His image, aren't we supposed to pay attention to how God does things as well as wait to listen to His instructions? Several scriptures remind us of the importance of guarding our tongues, and I want to list them in today's scripture readings because they are particularly convicting. I hope that they will resonate with you on how you speak in your everyday life and how you speak about others. These Scriptures convict me greatly because we all have our bad days. I think it's a good idea to process if you need to verbally, but then get into agreement with what God says about the situation you're facing. I am learning that as I abide by the Word, the Holy Spirit helps guide me and helps me guard my tongue.

Reflection:

1. Take a moment after reading these Scriptures to ask the Holy Spirit where you may need help with your "tongue." Write these down, then work on being mindful of changing the way you speak on a daily basis. Remember, we are all a work in progress. Stay humble, repent, and work on changing your direction to walk in the Spirit of Jesus rather than in the flesh.

____

____

____

____

____

____

____

____

____

2. Every time you feel yourself getting entangled with a double-minded spirit. Please look up whatever it is that you are feeling double-minded about. If you feel like you cannot let go of control, look up what the Bible says about double-mindedness and control. If it is fear, pride, stubbornness, lust, perversion, whatever it may be, look up what God says about that thing you are struggling with.

Then humble yourself to whatever it is that He says and pray into that. Allow the Holy Spirit to bring up a wound if there is something there. Otherwise, it is up to you whether you want to continue rebelling or choose to obey God's Word as He instructs you. I have learned over the years that every time I feel tossed to and fro, it is usually because I am not in obedience to the instructions the Lord has given me.

Once we become born again, this means that we are in Him, and He is in us! When we get out of alignment with Him, it can make us feel tossed to and fro, and that never ends well if we rebel. Believe me, I have learned the hard way. My best advice to you is to humble yourself and get back into alignment with God. He knows what's best for us, and He always wants what is best for us.

Declaration:

I am sensitive to the Holy Spirit's leading, and I think before I speak. I pause when someone or something upsets me, and I ask the Lord to guard my tongue. I am slow to anger, slow to speak, and slow to respond. I am learning to abide in my Heavenly Father's ways through His Spirit. I am learning to humble myself daily and walk in total obedience to my Lord because His path is straight, and His lamp guides my feet. Therefore, I follow Him.

WEEK 9

～∞～

The Sovereignty Of God Is Returning

1 Become His Vessel

God told me boldly in 2019 that His sovereignty is coming back to the Church! Now, does this mean that God's sovereignty is gone, or was it gone when I heard these words? Of Course not! But what He was showing me is that people have taken the sovereignty of God out of the Church and out of their lives, which has unfortunately led them astray. The Sovereignty of God goes hand in hand with the Fear of the Lord. However, this has become such a negative connotation. If we say that we love the Lord, then the fear and reverence of God should genuinely pour out of us as Believers in Christ.

When we understand the sovereignty and the fear of God, we will honor Him and genuinely want to do what He directs us to do. His Spirit, the Holy Spirit will always lead us in the right direction. Ecclesiastes 12:13-14 tells us: *"Now all has been heard; here is the conclusion of the matter; Fear God and keep his commandments, for this is the duty of all mankind. For God will bring every deed into judgment, including every hidden thing, whether it is good or evil."*

It is unfortunate though, that most Christians live a double-minded life, thinking they can please God as well as the desires of their flesh. When we do this, people begin to become their own God because they have not had a true reverent fear of the Lord's supremacy or authority in their lives. I have personally witnessed this happening all over the world, but especially within the United States. I believe it has been since the 1960's when we took the Bible out of our schools. There is now an entirely different level of chaos within America because when the reverence for God almighty is taken out, the sinful nature of man begins to rule and spread quickly. This ultimately leads people away from God.

Overall, we have taken God as well as the Bible out of schools and homes, and now the governments are trying to take it out of Nations as well. I won't delve into the politics of all this, but I will hit the nail on the head to convey a key point to you: The sovereignty of God will become essential in every Christian's life during these End times. The bottom line is that if we claim to love God, we should wholeheartedly embrace every aspect of His Sovereignty and His Word. Knowing that He is God and we are not. There will be no room for justification, as the level of deception present and expected to increase is dangerous. God tells us in Matthew 24:37-39 that Jesus will return when it is as in the days of Noah. Many similarities are occurring right now that align with the specific days Jesus refers to in Scripture. One of the main points I want to highlight is that Noah preached for 120 years. He preached on the Sovereignty of God, calling people to repentance to receive eternal life, but not one came. It was only Noah and his family that got saved. We need to be paying attention here.

Sovereignty means the supreme power or authority. I want to ask you, as a Believer in Christ, is God the main power and authority over your life? I know we have discussed this throughout the entire journey of this book, but here we are in our last week together, and I must reiterate this. Have you truly made Jesus Lord over every area in your life? Have you chosen to surrender your control in order to trust Him with everything you have and everywhere you go? Do you ask Him questions before you make big decisions? Or, even with the simple ones, such as, can I watch this or will it harm my spirit? Do you want me to go there? What do you say about this situation or person, Lord? If He told you to give something up or not to do something, would you? Lastly, are you beginning to believe that God is good, no matter what the circumstances you may face in your life or those of others may look like?

Now, some of you may be asking, does God actually answer? The answer is yes, but you must seek the answers out for yourself by delving into the Word of God. The Bible has every answer to our questions, but we must take the time to seek the answers within the Word and take time to pray. If you have a question, look up what the Bible says about that question. This has been an incredible learning experience for me, and it has had a profoundly positive impact on my life over the past few years. I no longer trust what I think or feel because the Bible tells me in Jeremiah 17:9, *"that our hearts are deceitful above all things."* Nor do I automatically trust what other people say because God says in Proverbs 3:5-6 that it is foolishness. I now look up in the Bible the things that I have questions about in life. As in literally asking, "What does God say about?"... you fill in the blank.

This may sound intense and could even come across as legalistic or religious to some, but I'm telling you, this is the furthest thing from that. Once you truly understand how much God loves you, you begin to trust His Word above all else. This will bring a great deal of freedom because you begin to understand why God is telling you no. I have learned that God is always protecting us in some way or another. God is calling His Bride to come into a place of sanctification. This will help her burn with pure love and to arise into her identity in Christ. To reach this point, we must reestablish our agreement with the fact that God is Sovereign.

We must experience the awe and reverence of God! He is mighty and He knows what is best for us. He sees the end from the beginning and has everything figured out for us, but he wants us to partner with Him to accomplish His plans and purposes here on Earth. Did you hear that? God, as in the God of the universe, wants to partner with us, you and me, to accomplish His plans here on Earth! This is why establishing your identity in Christ and reorienting yourself with God's sovereignty is crucial.

APPLYING WISDOM TO YOUR DAILY LIFE

Prayer for the day:

Father God,

I repent for not truly making you Lord over every area of my life. Help me, Lord, and show me how to do this. I want to trust You with every single thing in my life! I give You full permission to expose any area of my heart that has become blind with pride. I ask that You remove this hardened shell and soften my heart so that I may see clearly and love as You love, Lord.

Scriptures to meditate on:

1 Corinthians 13:4-8: *"Love is patient, love is kind. It does not envy, it does not boast, it is not proud. It does not dishonor others, it is not self-seeking, it is not easily angered, it keeps no record of wrongs. Love does not delight in evil but rejoices with the truth. It always protects, always trusts, always hopes, always perseveres."*

1 Peter 5:6-7: *"Humble yourselves, therefore, under God's mighty hand, that he may lift you up in due time. Cast all your anxiety on him because he cares for you."*

Philippians 2:12-13: *"Therefore, my beloved, as you have always obeyed, not as in my presence only, but now much more in my absence, work out your own salvation with fear and trembling; for it is God who works in you both to will and to do for His good pleasure."*

2 Corinthians 4:13-15: *"We have the same Spirit of faith that is described in the scriptures when it says, "First I believed, then I spoke in faith." So we also first believe then speak in faith. We do this because we are convinced that he who raised Jesus will raise us up with him, and together we will all be brought into his presence. Yes, all things work for your enrichment so that more of God's marvelous grace will spread to more and more people, resulting in an even greater increase of praise to God, bringing him even more glory!"*

Key #21: Walk In Humility

I know we discussed humility last week, but when you begin to approach every situation in your life with humility, you will grow immensely. We must choose to be humble. Pride is our biggest downfall, and it creates a breeding ground for all the evil seeds that the enemy tries to sow in us. Getting into pride can open the door for seeds to take root in us that will always lead us astray from God's ultimate will for our lives. Pride will block our ability to be fully used as God's vessel. Pride stems from the root of fear, but when we stay rooted in God's love, knowing that He is for us and that He will bring us through whatever we are facing, we can then walk in true humility. Humility keeps us in a place of trusting His will over our own, trusting His justice over our own, and trusting His love over the hate that may be coming against us.

Choosing to walk in humility is a beautiful key that helps us hear God's voice clearly and walk in His love. Constantly remind yourself to stay humble and crucify your flesh that wants to rise, demanding justice. Remember always to ask God if you need to argue or stand up boldly for whatever it may be.

Listen for His voice and be led by Him. Most of the time, we do things on our own initiative instead of waiting patiently and listening for His guidance and wisdom. He knows what is best for us and others, even if they aren't saved. He loves and His ultimate will is to love.

1. What areas in your life do you feel you may still be prideful in? It is essential to acknowledge this because it reveals the places where we still harbor fear and are hesitant to trust God fully. Most of the time, rebellion will expose pride. Humble yourself to allow God to show you any areas where you may still be operating in pride. Write these down:

____

____

____

____

____

____

____

____

2. Now, take some time to allow the Holy Spirit to search your heart and reveal the roots of fear you may still be battling against. These will likely come from past memories; allowing them to surface is extremely important here, so be patient, wait, and listen. Write these down:

____

____

____

____

____

____

____

____

3. Now, spend some time with God, allowing your heart to come into a place of deep repentance and forgiveness if needed. Remember this is the only way to truly start changing the direction for your life. Repentance is a crucial step in your growth with Christ. It helps you to walk away from the thing that is holding you in bondage. Please take time here until you feel it from deep within. Don't do this just because I am telling you to. True freedom comes from exposing the lies and then repenting when necessary. Trust God to bring you into His divine alignment. Write down anything you need to repent of here:

____

____

____

____

____

____

____

____

____

____

4. When you finally feel free from repenting to God for any area where you may not be fully trusting Him, allow Him to start building your trust in that specific area. I have learned that once I walk through something with God, He will then give me an opportunity to prove to myself that I have actually been freed from that thing that once held me back. Trust Him to provide you with wisdom for the next time a situation arises that tests your trust in Him. Be sure to journal this process when these things arise, as it will help build your faith. You will see that you are indeed growing in Him! For now, I want you to write down the promises of God over the areas that you have surrendered to Him. Find Scriptures over everything you released to Him today and declare these out loud:

____

____

____

____

____

____

____

____

Declaration:

I declare that I am God's vessel. I will allow Him to soften my heart daily and be used in any way that He deems necessary. I trust God and the plans that He has for my life! I know that every opposition that comes against me gives me an opportunity to trust God to bring me through it powerfully. I declare this by faith in Jesus' name!

2 Seek it out

God calls His sons and daughters royalty, and we, as Christians, become joint heirs with Christ once we are born again. The Bible also tells us in Proverbs 25:2, *"that it is the glory of God to conceal things but the glory of kings to search these things out."* As Christians, we should always seek answers from the Lord. What I mean by this is that when we read His Word and do not understand something, we should dig deeper and study it out. Or how about when other people give us prophetic words? Or when we have visions and dreams? We need to examine these things to ensure they are indeed from God. We can do this by seeking out Scriptures to substantiate what we see, hear, or think we receive from the Holy Spirit.

We must develop the habit of seeking out answers in the Bible daily; otherwise, pride can enter and begin to sear our hearts. Then, deception will follow. Let me mention some particular frustrations that can sometimes come from this. If you cannot seem to find an answer or fully understand something that God has given you right away, be patient. Have grace for yourself and put it on your "spiritual shelf." I have learned, through patience and perseverance, that God will reveal the purpose of a particular word, vision, or dream at His perfect timing. Stay humble and continue to trust His Sovereignty and His goodness.

We must seek out answers when trials come into our lives, asking the correct questions not of why this is happening, but rather, is there anything that you want me to learn from this, Lord? I hope you have already been applying this to your daily life habits from all of the chapters you have read. If you haven't been paying much attention to how God speaks over these past eight weeks, I encourage you to ask Him again to open your heart, mind, ears, and eyes. Then, become diligent in seeking Him more daily. When we go through trials, it is always for a bigger purpose. This is why it is imperative to seek out the wisdom of God, knowing that He is truly sovereign and His ways are higher than ours.

Even now, as I am writing this chapter, I am going through a trial, but I am grateful. I have had to be on bed rest for almost a month. I broke four of my ribs, having one of them break into three different pieces, meaning bedrest is crucial so I do not puncture a lung. If you have broken a rib, you know the debilitating pain. I find it ironic, though, that it has taken me almost a year to write this chapter because the Sovereignty of God can be such a touchy topic. Yet, here I am, again, trusting His Sovereignty. My positive outlook on being grateful is that this time of rest gives me hours to study and finish writing this book.

We must always keep in mind the truth that "God is for us" at the forefront of our thoughts. I know you have been learning this over the past nine weeks, but it is imperative to be able to fight against our adversary. We must be able to recognize and reject the defeating thoughts that come when trials arise. Especially physical trials that can try to take us out. Here I am lying in bed, and yes, I did have a few days over the past two weeks where I began to feel defeated, but I persevered and trusted God. Now, here I am, getting a download from Jesus to finally write this chapter!

God is good, and He only allows things to happen for our good! But it takes a true warrior to humble ourselves and choose to trust that God is good even when all hell is breaking loose in our lives. These warriors are arising now, and I encourage you to be willing to jump into the fire and allow Jesus to purify your soul (mind, will, and emotions) so that you can hear Him clearly in the times that are upon us. This is not meant to make you feel bad in any way, but if you do feel an offense rising, check your heart here because we are living in the end times, and deception is already present.

Jesus clearly told us in Luke 12:51 that the truth of Him and His Word will bring offense but that this is to separate His followers from the world. You should study this Scripture because it gave me a deeper understanding of why there is and will be so much division here on Earth. We, as believers and followers of Christ, are to look differently than the world. We are to sanctify ourselves to the Sovereignty of God. This is why it is of the utmost importance to seek out who God is, what his character is, and whether we truly know Him. Are we studying His Word daily so that we can discern quickly from other false doctrines that come in looking similar to His Word?

This will help us stay steadfast in Him when a greater division comes upon the Earth. When we do this, we can remain at peace and in faith, linking arms with true brothers and sisters in Christ when all hell breaks loose in the End Times. In Matthew 24:10-12 it says, *"And then many will be offended, will betray one another, and will hate one another. Then, many false prophets will rise up and deceive many. And because lawlessness will abound, the love of many will grow cold."* We must be prepared for this. How do we do this? By getting as close to Jesus as possible every day.

I don't know about you, but I have read this Scripture many times throughout my life. However, when I read it now, it resonates deeply with me. Why? Because I believe that we are in the beginning stages of Matthew 24. It is happening right before our eyes, and if you do not feel this, I implore you to meditate on Matthew 24 with the guidance of the Holy Spirit. I am not sharing this to instill fear in you at all! I am sharing this because when we truly learn to seek every answer through prayer and the guidance of the Holy Spirit in the Bible, we will have peace. We will have clarity and confidence to move forward with faith, no matter what comes our way. Why? Because we have learned to fear God more than we fear anything else in this life! This is the most powerful place to be.

A scripture passage in Matthew 24 that I want to focus on is in verse 5. Jesus warns us that many will be deceived because many will come in His name, claiming to be Christ. I don't know if you're aware of this, but it has been happening for many decades already. There are several "Christian" cults out there that look very similar to Christianity. They even use our Holy Bible to twist people into their beliefs. Again, I am not telling you this to try to get you to partner with a spirit of fear. However, I am sharing this in the hope of inspiring you to cultivate a holy, reverent fear of God and begin seeking His Truth.

I don't know about you, but the closer I come into a deep, loving, intimate relationship with God, the more I long to do His will. I want to please Him. I want to be used as His vessel, willing to do whatever He calls me to do. I long to get to know Him more so that I can understand the revelations within His Word. I have a mighty call to help others become aware of this deception that Jesus tells us about. And guess what? If you are a born-again Believer, then you have this call too! We are all called to be His disciples. So, are we going to walk this out?

In Christianity, a Disciple of Christ is considered to be a devoted and dedicated follower of Jesus. We should be hungering to get to know Jesus on such an intimate level that we begin to emulate His Character. We are to be committed to living out anything that God tells us to do. When you look at Jesus in John 5:19, He said that He did nothing of His own accord but did only what He saw the Father doing. Can you imagine the level of obedience that Jesus had to walk in? The restraint He had to steward? We are referring to God Almighty, incarnated in flesh, here on Earth. He could have taken someone out with one look or one breath if He wanted to. He had all the power that God had because He is God. However, He walked in total obedience to His Father's Voice. Only doing the will of His Father. Why? Because He knew the intimate Love He had with His Father, and He knew His Father's will. He knew what He had to do on that cross. He knew He had to lay down His life, even though He didn't want to, as God tells us in Matthew 26:39.

When we understand God's Sovereignty, we can comprehend more of His ways and recognize that He always acts out of Love. When we truly understand this, it brings us to a place of deep humility, trusting God over our own will. Most people think this would be the opposite, but look at what I just wrote in the last paragraph. God gave up His only Son. God gave up His power to give it back to us by the shedding of His blood. He allowed Himself to be humiliated time and time again and then to be brutally murdered. He did this so He could give us His Helper, the Holy Spirit, and have the chance to spend all of eternity with us! I say "to have a chance" because it is our own free will to choose Jesus or not.

<u>APPLYING WISDOM TO YOUR DAILY LIFE</u>

Prayer for the day:

Lord,

Help me to humble myself so I can see clearly. Help me to see any area within my heart and my life that I do not want to fully surrender to Your will. Help me to believe in Your goodness and that You are always for me no matter what comes into my life. I want to fully trust You, God, in every area of my life. I give You full permission to convict my heart and open my eyes to see. Help me to be diligent in Your Word daily. Help me to seek out deeper revelations so I can understand You and Your Word more. I want to walk in Your Ways, Lord, not my own. In Jesus' Name, I pray.

Scriptures to meditate on:

Proverbs 25:2: *"It is the glory of God to conceal things, but the glory of kings is to search things out."*

Matthew 26:39: *"And after going a little farther, He fell face down and prayed saying, "My Father, if it is possible (that is, consistent with Your will), let this cup pass from me; yet not as I will, but as You will."*

Deuteronomy 4:29-31: *"But if from there you seek the Lord your God, you will find him if you seek him with all your heart and with all your soul. When you are in distress and all these things have happened to you, then in later days you will return to the Lord your God and obey him. For the Lord your God is a merciful God; he will not abandon or destroy you or forget the covenant with your ancestors, which he confirmed to them by oath."*

Luke 12:50-53: *"But I have a baptism to be baptized with, and how distressed I am till it is accomplished! Do you suppose that I came to give peace on earth? I tell you, not at all, but rather division. For from now on five in one house will be divided: three against two, and two against three. Father will be divided against son and son against father, mother against daughter and daughter against mother, mother-in-law against her daughter-in-law and daughter-in-law against her mother-in-law."* (When you study this out, Jesus is saying that not everyone will believe and follow Him, so this will cause division amongst families and people. There will always be people that want to live their selfish and prideful ways. God gives us free will, but there is such power when we choose to follow after and honor His Sovereignty).

Reflection:

1. Do you know who you are in Christ? Do you know who God says you are? Write some things down that you feel coming up in your heart and mind when you read these questions:

____

____

2. I will provide you with the Scriptures below, along with their relevant context, to help you better understand your identity in Christ. However, your homework for today is to seek out each Scripture and meditate on it until it becomes deeply ingrained in your heart. I highly recommend writing these Scriptures out and speaking them out loud over yourself daily as declarations. This may take some time, but continue to do so until you start to believe in every bit of who God says you are! We must believe that God is for us and that He loves us! This will then help you trust God more and surrender to His sovereignty.

Declaration:

**I WANT YOU TO DECLARE EVERY ONE OF THE SCRIPTURES BELOW
OVER YOURSELF OUT LOUD DAILY:**

ROMANS 15:7 ~ I ACCEPTED & I BELONG

1 JOHN 1:9 ~ I AM FORGIVEN WHEN I CONFESS MY SINS

GALATIANS 4:7 ~ I AM NO LONGER A SLAVE, I AM FREE

JOHN 15:16 ~ I AM CHOSEN

1 CORINTHIANS 3:23 ~ I BELONG TO JESUS

JOHN 1:12 ~ I AM A CHILD OF GOD

GENESIS 1:27 ~ I AM MADE IN GOD'S IMAGE

2 CORINTHIANS 5:17 ~ I AM A NEW PERSON

ROMANS 6:4 ~ JESUS OFFERS ME A NEW LIFE, IT'S TIME TO BURY MY OLD ONE

PHILIPPIANS 3:20 ~ I AM A CITIZEN OF HEAVEN

1 CORINTHIANS 12:27 ~ I AM PART OF SOMETHING IMPORTANT

1 PETER 1:5 ~ I AM PROTECTED BY GOD

ROMANS 8:38 ~ GOD LOVES ME NO MATTER WHAT TRIES TO SEPARATE ME

PSALM 139:13-16 ~ I AM GOD'S SPECIAL CREATION, HE KNOWS ME

ZEPHANIAH 3:17 ~ GOD IS ALWAYS WITH ME

EPHESIANS 2:19 ~ I AM PART OF GOD'S FAMILY

ROMANS 8:17 ~ I AM AN HEIR OF GOD

JEREMIAH 29:11 ~ GOD HAS A GOOD PLAN FOR MY LIFE

GALATIANS 3:13 ~ I AM RESCUED & REDEEMED

ISAIAH 43:4 ~ I AM PRECIOUS TO GOD

PSALM 23:1-3 ~ GOD IS TAKING CARE OF ME

1 JOHN 5:14-15 ~ GOD LISTENS TO ME

ROMANS 10:13 ~ I AM SAVED

PHILIPPIANS 4:13 ~ GOD GIVES ME STRENGTH TO OVERCOME

1 CORINTHIANS 6:19 ~ THE HOLY SPIRIT LIVES IN ME

JOHN 15:11 ~ JESUS GIVES ME TRUE JOY

EPHESIANS 1:3 ~ I AM BLESSED

EXODUS 19:5 ~ I AM TREASURED BY GOD

PSALM 139:1 ~ GOD UNDERSTANDS EVERY PART OF ME

GALATIANS 2:20 ~ JESUS DIED FOR ME

COLOSSIANS 2:10 ~ I AM COMPLETE IN CHRIST

3 Lay Down your Life

In today's chapter, I am going to reiterate what's been on my heart for the time and season that is now upon us. Once again, I am going to be bold, hoping you do not take offense to this but open your hearts to receive correction if any conviction needs to happen here. I'm sure you have received this by now, but I'm a firm believer in iron sharpening iron and allowing correction to come in when a change is needed (Proverbs 27:17). God is calling us to be incredible love warriors in these End Times. These warriors are the Christians who truly make Jesus Christ Lord over every area in their lives and walk daily in complete surrender to His Voice. These people are not perfect, and they may fail daily, but they understand the Sovereignty of God. They truly abide in God's Love and leadings by His Word and His Holy Spirit.

We must be cautious of the spirit of this age, which has covered the world with complete selfishness. One would have to be completely blind not to see this, even if they are not fully opening their hearts to this conviction. But take a look around at all the people obsessed with themselves. We have people taking selfies constantly. People parading the streets with their selfish agendas, rising fully against God. Self-proclaiming prophets, false prophets of the media, and everyone seems to think they are right about everything. They don't seem to need, nor do they want Jesus because they are too busy feeding their selfish desires.

It is sad to watch this, but 2 Timothy 3:2 and Isaiah 5:20 are playing out before our very eyes. 2 Timothy 3:2 says, "*For People will love only themselves and their money. They will be boastful and proud, scoffing at God, disobedient to their parents, and ungrateful. They will consider nothing sacred.*" Isaiah 5:20 states that everything will be contradictory, saying what is right is wrong and what is wrong is right. These are the times in which we live. Now, on the other hand, we have people who proclaim they love Jesus, but they do not have any fruit of the Holy Spirit. They continue in their same old ways, still looking like the world, never allowing God to entirely change them into the new creation He always planned for them. These people end up becoming hypocrites, which then gives all Christians a bad name. The Bible tells us in 1 Corinthians 13:11 that we are to put away our selfish, childish ways and begin to grow in the Lord.

Please know that I speak this in love and out of deep concern for people who are living in this way. If any conviction is happening in your heart due to living this way, simply repent. Choose to start over with Jesus and begin living for Him today. God wants us to live at our full potential as on-fire, born-again, humble, and loving warriors for Him. There is a mighty purpose upon your life for these End Times! Again, You are living in this time for a reason!

I am convicted at least once a month because I know that I can always be doing more for the Lord, and I truly hunger to know Him more. We are all in a process, but becoming aware of this hypocritical living will help us to walk out God's love in humility. We must allow God to come into every area of our lives. It is crucial, especially in the times we are living in now, where we are witnessing grave evil and division firsthand. Christians must arise into who we are called to be. It is through the refining fires that we become the light of the world, walking in His truth, His pure love, and His power.

The Word of the Lord says whoever gives up their life gains it. We must grasp what it truly means to have reverence and a holy fear of God. To reach this place, we must first acknowledge God's sovereignty. Mathew 16:25 clearly states, *"Whoever wants to hang onto their life will lose it, but whoever gives up his life for my sake will find it."* The Bible also states in 2 Corinthians 5:17, *"Therefore if any man be in Christ; he is a new creature; old things have passed away and behold, all things become new."* This means that once you fully give your life to Christ, you become a new creation. You no longer have to remain a slave to sin but now carry the power of Christ within you to overcome sin. God does not want to leave us where He found us. He is all about advancing His Kingdom, and once we say yes to Jesus, we become a part of His Kingdom.

When you give your life to Jesus, the eyes of your heart suddenly become open to what is good for you and dangerous to you. The things in the world you used to have a taste for should now become a disgust within your spirit. This can take some time, but the more you press into Jesus, the desires of your flesh and the world begin to die. The Lord loves you too much to let you stay where you are when you come to Him. Once you make Him Lord, He will lead you out from the bondage that you were in, and He will begin training you in His ways so you come up higher and leave the muck and mire that kept you stuck for so long. God is a good Father. He doesn't want you to stay bound where He found you, so He will begin to convict you and help you grow.

When you choose His will, you will end up growing into who you were always created to be before the foundations of the world. This doesn't happen overnight, of course, but I can sit here while I write this today with complete conviction that I am no longer who I once was. I have allowed God to come in and refine everything that corrupted me from my childhood until I said yes to Jesus. And I continue to do this as I walk daily with Him. Yes, I may slip along the way, but I continually keep my heart open to correction, and I allow God to remove every bad root so that He can constantly grow and strengthen me. He humbles me often, but I receive it because I know it is only for my good. Once I finally grasped the revelation of God's sovereignty, I learned the importance of humility and laying down my life for His will.

If you haven't done so already, it is time to lay down your life fully. Choose to lay down your will and choose God's will. As you begin to do this, you will start to see the goodness of God and how much He truly works all things out for your good. It's all about taking those baby steps of faith, but I promise you this. You will begin to encounter God's love in a whole new way. You will see how much He is truly for you and feel honored when you go through any suffering. This is because you begin to recognize the mighty call that God has chosen you to do here upon this Earth. This life is rarely about us. It is for the one. Jesus says He will leave the 99 and go back for the one. Never despise what God is doing in and through you. It is a true honor to die to ourselves and live for God.

APPLYING WISDOM TO YOUR LIFE DAILY

Lord,

Help me to live a fully surrendered life with You. I give You my life, Lord. I surrender every single thing that I have been holding on to too tightly, and I give it all to You! Help me to honor Your Sovereignty and recognize its importance. Show me, Lord, when I honor You in this way, how powerful You can be by shining through me as Your vessel. Help me to get out of myself and my limited thinking so You can use me mightily. Show me Your love and Your truth as I study the meaning of sovereignty in Your Word. Reveal to me any areas in my heart where I need to forgive You and repent for holding any anger towards You. Help me understand the importance of fully accepting that You are sovereign and that You are good. Help me, Holy Spirit, to know when a sermon is just tickling my ears to feed my desires from this world instead of my spirit. Lord, I humbly ask You to put a high level of discernment on the inside of me so I can hear Your voice clearly. I want to abide in your love, Lord. I give You Lordship over every area of my life. I trust You, God. Help me to recognize the importance of Your Sovereignty and how I can be a vessel to witness this in your church. Thank you, Lord, in Jesus' Name I pray!

Psalm 139:23-24: *"Search me of God, and know my heart; test me and know my anxious thoughts. Point out anything in me that offends you, and lead me along the path of everlasting life."*

Philippians 2:3-4: *"Don't be selfish; don't live to make a good impression on others. Be humble, thinking of others as better than yourself. Don't just think about your own affairs, but be interested in others, too, and in what they are doing."*

Isaiah 5:20: *TLV: "They say that what is right is wrong and what is wrong is right; that black is white and white is black; bitter is sweet and sweet is bitter." NIV: "Woe to those who call evil good and good evil, who put darkness for light and light for darkness, who put bitter for sweet and sweet for bitter."*

1 Corinthians 13:11: *"It's like this: when I was a child I spoke and thought and reasoned as a child does. But when I became a man my thoughts grew far beyond those of my childhood, and now I have put away the childish things."*

God's Word has the final say and always will! It will cut through every lie, and it will always bring freedom. Why? Because the Word is Jesus, and Jesus is the Word! Jesus is Love. Jesus is Truth. Jesus is light, life, and the only way into eternity. When we receive a revelation of how much God loves us, it becomes much easier to live a surrendered life to Him and to do whatever He asks of us.

When we live a surrendered life to Jesus, this helps us exude His mercy, grace, forgiveness, humility, righteousness, gentleness, servitude, patience, and love. It truly is miraculous all that He will do through us when we posture our hearts in the way of complete surrender. It is time to put God's sovereignty first in our lives. If something happens, know that God has allowed it for a reason and surrender your will for His. As difficult as this is to accept, we must remember that this life is no longer our own, and everything we have belongs to God first.

I like to think of God as the owner of my life, and I am just blessed that He allows me to manage it. However, in order to manage our finances, children, and lives effectively, I need to follow my owner's instructions. He can see the future, and He knows my life better than anyone. So, I choose to trust God to bring me through, no matter what I may face. There is a purpose behind it all! When we believe that God is good, trusting Him becomes much easier. However, we must also remember that God did not promise this life would be easy, but He did say He would always be with us.

Invite God into every situation in your life. Let Him take the reins and help guide you. He loves to partner with us if we will allow Him to. When the next stressful situation comes, pause for a minute to take a deep breath. Breathe in the sweet presence of the Holy Spirit and say, "I trust you, God. I surrender this situation completely to you. Guide me and show me how I am supposed to move forward." Know that we may not hear clearly all the time, but follow after peace. Every time I don't have peace about something, I pray and wait on God until I have peace, and then I move forward. Remember, the enemy always pushes, and the Holy Spirit gently persuades with Truth. Living in complete surrender to Jesus has radically transformed my life, and I am confident it will do the same for you.

Every time we are not fully surrendered, whether we realize it or not, we are not walking in God's rest or His Love. Which means we are not living the best life that God has chosen for us. God tells us that His love bears no burdens, so why do we take on life's burdens? God promises to give us rest. So, when we walk a surrendered life, we will have peace and rest. When we find ourselves stirring in worry or anger, we must take authority over every fiery dart and choose to seek out answers until we enter into His rest. This is our portion as becoming followers of Jesus Christ. Choose to be single-minded, trusting that God is good! Jesus paid it all upon that cross, and His blood carries the most power over every situation and every demonic entity! Remember your authority through the blood of Yeshua because God is the ultimate authority and has supremacy over it all!

Reflection:

1. What areas in your life have you not fully surrendered to God? I know you worked on pride in your heart 2 days ago, but today, I want you to dig a little deeper into where you may still have fears. You will usually find the unsurrendered parts of your life in the areas where you still have fear in your heart about something. We all have areas where we can improve, so humble yourself here. Allow the Holy Spirit to search your heart and reveal any area that needs to be exposed. Remember that God's perfect Love casts out fear. Allow His Spirit to reveal any fears within you. List what you know you need to surrender here:

____

____

____

2. **Now, how will you surrender these things? What is your plan?** (Example: Maybe you have been hurt by the "Church." So, you don't want to go to church anymore because you are fearful of getting hurt again. However, you feel God pressing it upon your heart to go because He wants to heal you, and He knows how important it is to be around other believers in Christ. So your plan of action may be to start researching churches and then going until you find the right fit for you and your family). **These exercises that you write down will cause you to step out in faith. I want to encourage you that it is ok to do this "afraid." It is better to take a leap of faith with a little fear than to never step out and stay bound by a spirit of fear. Remember, we must fear God more than anything else in this world. This will bring freedom! Know that God loves you, and He is revealing these things because He wants you to be free. Be obedient to whatever it is that the Holy Spirit shows you. List your action steps here to help you surrender to His will:**

Declaration:

I declare that my heart is always soft towards God's love, His Sovereignty, and His Word. I am learning how to abide in Christ Jesus! I choose to embrace God's love daily, believing that He wants the absolute best for me. His Word says that He knows what is best for me, so I believe it! I believe in His Word over whatever circumstance I may be facing. I surrender all of my fears to Him daily, and I trust in God's goodness over my life and the lives of others. I am learning to surrender my will and walk in obedience to God's love every day.

4 Be Prepared

God gave me a powerful vision in November 2019, just before COVID-19 hit the World, and I now know it is time to share this in detail. It is essential to discuss the significance of dreams and visions and why we need to connect the dots right now. God has been showing me visions that He gave me ten years ago, which finally hold deep meaning for this point in time. I believe He is doing this with the entire remnant of the Body of Christ at this very moment. If you have old dreams and visions, pull them out and ask the Holy Spirit to help you see if they relate to what is happening. As I have begun doing this, it has brought me great confirmation and excitement for all that God is doing on Earth right now. Ask God to confirm your vision or dream with Scripture, and watch Him enlighten your mind! The time is upon us now to arise!

If you are a faithful follower of Christ, then you are grafted into the bloodline of Jesus. This makes you a daughter or a son of the most high God. This makes you Royalty! The time is now to rise into your Royal calling and begin living His Kingdom way here on this Earth. This doesn't necessarily mean full-time ministry. This means whatever God has put inside of you. Find it, dig deep, and allow God to stretch you and mold you into all you were created for! Let Him use you powerfully on this Earth by being His vessel to work in and through you.

My vision from 2019 started out with God taking me deep into the center of the Earth. I believe this represents the deep places of our hearts, as well as the people who have been hidden for such a time as this and for times to come. Going deep into the foundation also represents *Ephesians 1:4, "God chose us before the foundation of the world, that we should be holy and without blame before Him in love."* (This is a call into purity). He then began to show me that he was shifting tectonic plates deep within the Earth, which created earthquakes that originated from within the entire Earth and pierced out to the surface of the globe. This represents a few things. The first is in *Acts 4:31, "When they had prayed, the place where they assembled together was shaken, and they were all filled with the Holy Spirit and spoke the Word of God with boldness."* This is a call for the Bride of Christ to intercede and allow anything that needs to be shaken out of us to go! Pray like never before and also begin coming together in unity to pray together as one.

I would like to take a moment to address the topic of "True Christians," as it is not a coincidence that all the current events in the World are related to it. As I've said before, if you have been spending time in the secret place, then you know that God is sifting the tares from the wheat. He is shaking us and the entire World. Matthew 7:16-20 tells all people that you will know a Christian by the fruits that are being produced in their life. *"You will know them by their fruits. Every tree that does not bear good fruit is cut down and thrown into the fire. Therefore by their fruits you will know them."* I believe we are in this time right now and will continue until Jesus returns. This earthquake is only the beginning of the shaking, but when a tree is shaken, the rotten fruit will fall off. However, the good, healthy fruit will stay attached to the vine. Is your life deeply rooted in Christ that you are ready to be shaken this way?

I believe that God is sifting the Church and shaking up the entire World to show His goodness to all who choose to see it and His wrath to those who still choose not to see. Wrath has such a harsh connotation, but I've come to view it in a different light. It is only to bring divine order and to ultimately save us from the destruction of living an eternity in Hell. Even a good earthly father will do everything in his power to stop his children from enduring significant harm. It is better to administer "tough love" than to not prepare a child at all. This realization has come to me after many years of going through severe trials. If it weren't for these trials, I wouldn't be the person I am today, and I wouldn't have come to know the true character of God.

God is calling Christians to arise into their unique callings right now. The remnant saved for this time is going to begin emerging from hidden places with God's Power and Truth like never before, and more will rise up with this shaking. Another verse God showed me for this vision was in *Isaiah 14:16, "Those who see you will gaze at you, they will ponder over you, saying, is this the man who made the earth tremble, who shook the kingdoms?"* This not only represents the recognition of God's Sovereignty but also the shaking and sifting that God is doing in the entire Church Body right now. It also represents the "called" non-believers who are finally going to awaken to the only Truth. Who is Jesus Christ! They will rise into their rightful place because God has chosen them!

In this vision, the heavens began to open up, and a waterfall from the sky poured down upon the Earth, creating mighty rivers that ran through the broken quakes of the Earth, pushing all the dark mud, sludge, and debris out until the rivers became sparkling clean and crystal clear. The Scripture God gave me for when the heavens opened up was *Hebrews 12:25-27, "See that you do not refuse Him who speaks. For if they did not escape who refused Him who spoke on earth, much more shall we not escape if we turn away from Him who speaks from heaven," whose voice then shook the Earth but now He has promised, saying, "Yet once more I shake not only the earth but also the heaven." Now this, "Yet once more, indicates the removal of those things that are being shaken, as of the things that were made, that the things which cannot be shaken may remain."* This represents the shaking that is going to come upon everyone, both His Body and the world.

Whether people want to believe it or not, this is happening. Be of good courage, though, because those who serve and love God will begin to heal in deeper ways and come into even more purification. We are living in a powerful time of awakening and preparation. It is time to pray and walk in the identity God is calling us to be. We must be mindful of the times and seasons in which we are living.

God wants to break down any idols that we have chosen to worship over Him, especially in America. I believe this is why everything unfolded as it did in the last two elections. Daniel 2:21 clearly states that God changes times and periods of history as well as appoints Kings and removes them. Regardless of what we think happened with the 2020 election, the bottom line is that God allowed it. I also believe it is because the Church allowed it. America is in the position she is in right now because the Church, as a whole, has not known her identity in Christ, nor has she truly revered the Lord. I believe we are entering a time when the Church is beginning to awaken to her identity in Christ.

The other relevant part of this vision, as mentioned in this verse, refers to the heavens being shaken as well as the Earth. God is shaking up the demonic realm right now, so we are going to begin seeing even crazier things than we have been. One can clearly see the demonic being bold and playing their hands at large. I don't think I can remember a time in my life when people were blatantly worshiping the demonic and having no shame about it like we are witnessing now. Be prepared and take up your shield of faith because those who are in Christ will not be shaken!

There are two other verses that God wanted me to share with you about this vision. The darkness of the mud and all the debris in the rivers becoming clear was significant for the Body of Christ in these verses of Isaiah 60:1-7. *"Arise and Shine, for your light has come! And the glory of the Lord is risen upon you. For behold, the darkness shall cover the Earth and deep darkness over the people, But the Lord will arise over you, and His glory will be seen upon you. The Gentiles shall come to your light and Kings to the brightness of your rising. Lift up your eyes all around and see they all gather together, they come to you, your sons shall come from afar, and your daughters shall be nursed at your side, then you shall see and become radiant, and your heart shall swell with joy; because the abundance of the sea shall be turned to you, the wealth of the Gentiles shall come to you; the multitude of camels shall cover your land, the dromedaries of Midian and Ephah; All those from Sheba shall come; they shall bring gold and incense, And they shall proclaim the praises of the Lord! All the flocks of Kedar shall be gathered together to you, the rams of Nebaioth shall minister to you; they shall ascend with acceptance on My altar, and I will glorify the house of MY GLORY!"*

There are several aspects I want to break down for you in this verse so you have a better understanding of what's to come. I am writing this in 2024, and I believe the Lord has shown me that this will be happening over the next 11 years, marking only the beginning of what is to come. A deep darkness is coming, but we are called to have joy and hold onto our faith during this time. Those who do will shine brighter with His light and His glory like never before! Signs, miracles, and wonders are about to pour out, just as they did in the Old Testament, the days of Jesus, and the Book of Acts. This is a time when the Body of Christ needs to be readying herself in the refining fire, allowing God to burn out every unclean thing inside of her. This way, she can be His willing vessel in this time to come! We do not want to miss this time or season.

God goes on to discuss the transfer of wealth from the wicked to the righteous. He says the abundance of the sea shall be turned to you, and the wealth of those not serving Me are coming to you. Let me highlight some specific aspects here. The fact that God chooses to mention the Gentiles and the sons of Ishmael is very significant. I believe there will be more than just the righteous ones whom this transfer of wealth will bless. I believe God is prophesying here that the enemies of God, who come from the bloodline of Ishmael as well as the Gentiles, will come to the one and only true God, who is Jesus Christ.

I believe these people will be awakened to Jesus and will come with their millions of dollars, including riches, wealth, and land and businesses. They will be radically transformed by the love of God and finally begin to fund the right kingdom in these times because God says He will accept their offerings on His altar, and they will glorify the house of God. Get ready to see these verses come to pass; I believe we are entering into these times now, and it is only the beginning of 2025 as I am finishing the last two days of this book.

However, please understand me. The abundant wealth I'm talking about is not only about finances, which is extremely important to bring Heaven to Hell within this earthly system. But it is also the glory that Christians will fully walk in during these End Times because we are allowing ourselves to be refined daily for new revelatory wine to flow out of us. I encourage you to draw closer to the Father, draw closer to Jesus, and draw closer to the Holy Spirit like never before. God Almighty is opening doors and giving very strategic plans right now for His Bride to rise in unity, glory, and power. Get ready to see restoration and recompense on a whole new level in your life when you surrender all of it to Him.

APPLYING WISDOM TO YOUR DAILY LIFE

Lord,

I give You permission to shake anything and everything out of me that needs to be shaken. Burn everything out of me that tries to keep me from Your presence! I do not want to miss all that you have for me to do in these last days. Prepare my heart and soul for what is to come, Lord. I want You more than I want anything else in this world. Help me to become so rooted in You that I fear nothing else when the shaking comes. Help me crucify my flesh and align my soul to be so focused on You that I do not miss Your leading. Help me to keep my heart soft towards You, so I will keep my heart soft towards others. I know this will help me to not be deceived in these times. I love You, Lord, and I know that You love me. Forgive me for putting anything before You. I am Yours, Lord. Have your way in my life. I pray this in Jesus' Name!

Scriptures to meditate on:

Isaiah 60:1-7: *"Arise and Shine, for your light has come! And the glory of the Lord is risen upon you. For behold, the darkness shall cover the earth and deep darkness over the people, But the Lord will arise over you and His glory will be seen upon you. The Gentiles shall come to your light and Kings to the brightness of your rising. Lift up your eyes all around and see they all gather together, they come to you, your sons shall come from afar, and your daughters shall be nursed at your side, then you shall see and become radiant, and your heart shall swell with joy; because the abundance of the sea shall be turned to you, the wealth of the Gentiles shall come to you; the multitude of camels shall cover your land, the dromedaries of Midian and Ephah; All those from Sheba shall come; they shall bring gold and incense, And they shall proclaim the praises of the Lord! All the flocks of Kedar shall be gathered together to you, the rams of Nebaioth shall minister to you; they shall ascend with acceptance on My altar and I will glorify the house of my glory!"*

Daniel 2:21: *"World events are under his control. He removes kings and sets others on their thrones. He gives wise men their wisdom and scholars their intelligence."*

Daniel 4:35: *"God controls all that happens on earth and in heaven, and no one can stop him."*

Acts 16:14: *"God opens the hearts of sinners and draws them to himself."*

John 6:44: *"No one can come to me unless the Father who sent me draws him. And I will raise him up on the last day."*

John 6:37: *"All that the Father gives me will come to me and whoever comes to me I will never cast out."*

Psalm 145:18: *"The Lord is near to all who call on him, to all who call on him in truth."*

Hebrews 10:19-25: *"Therefore, brothers, since we have confidence to enter the holy places by the blood of Jesus, by the new and living way that he opened for us through the curtain that is, through his flesh, and since we have a great priest over the house of God, let us draw near with a true heart* *in full assurance of faith, with our hearts sprinkled clean from an evil conscience and our bodies washed with pure water. Let us hold fast the confession of our hope without wavering, for he who promised is faithful.*

Ephesians 1:3-14: *"Praise be to the God and Father of our Lord Jesus Christ, who has blessed us in the heavenly realms with every spiritual blessing in Christ. For he chose us in Him before the creation of the world to be holy and blameless in His sight. In love, He predestined us for adoption to sonship, through Jesus Christ, in accordance with His pleasure and will to the praise of His glorious grace, which He has freely given us in the One he loves. In Him we have redemption through His blood, the forgiveness of sins, in accordance with the riches of God's grace that He lavished on us. With all wisdom and understanding, He made known to us the mystery of His will according to His good pleasure, which He purposed in Christ, to be put into effect when the times reach their fulfillment—to bring unity to all things in heaven and on earth under Christ. In Him we were also chosen, having been predestined according to the plan of Him who works out everything in conformity with the purpose of His will, in order that we, who were the first to put our hope in Christ, might be for the praise of his glory. And you also were included in Christ when you heard the message of truth, the gospel of your salvation. When you believed, you were marked in Him with a seal, the promised Holy Spirit, who is a deposit guaranteeing our inheritance until the redemption of those who are God's possession—to the praise of His glory."*

Reflection:

Your homework today is to continue allowing the Holy Spirit to search your heart, building upon yesterday's reflection. Allow yourself to reflect on the situations and circumstances in your life and how you handled them. Are you still trying to control due to your fears? Or are you allowing God to lead? Keep digging deep with the Lord. This is not about having to work for something but resting in His goodness. Knowing that He wants the absolute best for you. He doesn't want you to be bound to anything but Him. He is where our freedom is. So keep running to Him and resting in Him.

Declaration:

I am preparing myself by crucifying my flesh daily. I am preparing for the times and seasons that are upon us by feeding my Spirit more than my flesh daily. I worship daily. I pray daily. I read and study my Bible daily. I meet with other strong believers in Christ every week to strengthen my walk with God. I am softening my heart throughout the day by repenting when needed and forgiving when needed. I release all control and give it to God.

5 Obedience out of Love

Faithful obedience comes willingly in a relationship when you know that you are loved and when you love in return. It is here where the power lies. I want you to think of a healthy relationship that you are in. This could be with your husband or wife or a best friend. When you think about that relationship, do you find yourself wanting to rebel when things are going well in that relationship? What I mean is that rebellion usually rears its ugly head when the reality of not getting our way, or when we feel threatened within that relationship, hits. The old spirit man, our flesh, and our soul want to rise against the Holy Spirit who exudes the Love of God. Our old fallen spirit man intends to insist on having his own way. However, when we remember how much we love that person and how much they love us, we can have grace and patience for them. We do not have to rebel. We trust that they have our best interests at heart.

This is the same way it should be with our relationship with God. However, it is a more profound love than anything we will ever have with a human being. God's Love will never fail us. He created us, and He knows what is best for us no matter what we may face. His love never leaves us. Once we get the revelation of how much God loves us and is for us, we will then surrender our lives fully to Him. When we begin to experience the depth of God's love, we start to fall in love with God and all His ways. This begins to fortify our trust in Him, and everything in life as we know it changes for our good! This is when obedience to Him becomes more important than anything. A deep longing will begin to stir in your heart to please God with everything in your life, and this is a powerful place to start living.

When I reflect on every instance in my life where I have rebelled, it has always stemmed from a place of fear. When I research the lives of people in the Bible who rebelled, I find that they, too, operated from a root of fear. Remember the revelation I shared about the two places from which we operate: either Love or Fear. When we rebel, it comes from a place where our hearts have roots of fear. When we do not allow the Holy Spirit to convict us quickly, pride can begin building in our hearts. We start to think that we are right and have the right to do what we want. Living a life of rebellion is a dangerous place to stay because God tells us that obedience is better than sacrifice and that rebellion is as dangerous as the sin of witchcraft (1 Samuel 15:22-23).

Please refrain from partnering with any kind of condemnation here. This should convict our hearts deeply to want to honor God's Sovereignty and be obedient to Him. When I discuss this scripture in 1 Samuel, please note that God is referring to deliberately disobeying His words. I want you to humble your heart when you read this next part to see if you have been deliberately disobeying anything in God's Word or what His Spirit may have been telling you lately. We must remember that conviction brings us to a wonderful place of growth. There is no shame here. Shame stems from pride and rebellion, which are rooted in fear and insecurity. Choose to shift your mind right now into a place of love and God's goodness. God wants us to be free, and He always has the best in mind for us.

Please take some time to read the entire chapter of 1st Samuel. This will give you a better understanding of the context presented in 1 Samuel 15:22-23. However, I will paraphrase for you. Samuel gave specific instructions from God to King Saul to wait for the appointed time to offer the burnt offering to God before a battle, but Saul made the offering without Samuel. He grew impatient and began to feel anxious while waiting. He decided to sacrifice on his own accord. God was still gracious to Saul and His army at this point, though, because God is good. One important key here is to be patient and not rebel by taking matters into your own hands when you do not feel God moving quickly enough for you. If God gives you instructions for something, then it is essential to do whatever He tells you to do, and then wait upon the Lord, trusting Him until He moves.

The next battle in 1 Samuel is against the Amalekites. God tells Saul to kill every last one of them, including women, children, and their livestock. He said, do not leave one alive. Now, this may sound intense, but you have to remember these people were extremely wicked and entirely against God, wreaking havoc against God's people. They chose evil over the goodness of God. However, Saul was not obedient to this explicit instruction. He decided to keep the Amalekite King Agag alive as a prisoner and kept the best of their livestock to sacrifice. They also kept the plunder. This was deliberate disobedience to God on Saul's part.

In 1 Samuel 15:22-23, it says this: Then *Samuel said, "Does the Lord take pleasure in burnt offerings and sacrifices as much as in obeying the Lord? Look: to obey is better than the fat of rams. For rebellion is like the sin of divination, and defiance is like wickedness and idolatry. Because you have rejected the Word of the Lord, he has rejected you as king."* Wicked in Hebrew means guilty and ungodly. As soon as we choose to disobey God, the enemy will instantly bring guilt and shame. We may not readily accept that right away due to pride, but this is how the enemy traps and holds people in bondage. The enemy loves to get us to rebel because he loves to try to ensnare us with the trap of shame. He also loves to entice us with sin because it separates us from God.

We must maintain a tender heart towards God. We also need to spend time with God daily, getting to know His character and His love, so we can recognize wickedness as soon as it tries to enter. I wanted to share this Scripture because it offers a valuable lesson for us to learn as God's children. When we deliberately disobey or rebel against God's Word, we open the door to witchcraft, divination, and idolatry. Remember, I am not talking about not knowing what you are doing. God has amazing grace when we do not understand what we are doing. However, when we choose to disobey, fully aware of what God has told us, this is what opens the door to wickedness.

I would like to clarify the meanings of witchcraft and divination so you can gain a better understanding of these concepts. It is of vital importance that you understand this because I am observing these two things operating within the Church Body today. We must be aware of this so we are not deceived in these End Times. Witchcraft has to do with sorcery, magical arts with power and skill, and speaking with demons or the dead. Divination is the belief that spirits inhabit various elements of life. These can include idols, crystals, rocks, and other similar items. These spirits are able to impart heavenly knowledge of the future to a person, including a myriad of different techniques to help them communicate with the supernatural. This gives them insight into heavenly wisdom, but this is not from God. This is from fallen angels, fallen spirits, and demons.

When you look up the root word for both witchcraft and divination in the Greek, you'll find the word "pharmakeia." Pharmakeia translates to sorcery or magic and is often associated with potions, spells, and idolatry, as well as spiritual manipulation. I am sharing this with you because any and all drugs can open a door to the demonic. We must learn to study God's Word and the warnings He gives to us, then be obedient to all He is saying. His Word truly is a lamp unto our feet to lead us and guide us in this crazy fallen world.

When we are not rooted in knowing God's Word, knowing His Character, and learning the Bible daily, we can open the door to being misled by other spirits. We must remember that the Angel of Light does not come as a frightening, demonic presence. He comes in looking like a "good" light bringing a twisting of God's Word. As I mentioned earlier in a previous chapter, this is indeed dangerous! Why? Because I have witnessed a lot of Christians think they are communing with the Holy Spirit, but instead, they are entertaining demons through the Angel of Light. Deliberate disobedience to God's Word will sear our hearts with pride, and this can blind us. Be very aware of this.

Now, I want to touch base on the other part of this Scripture where God says, "Obedience is better than sacrifice." What does He mean here? I always thought sacrifice was pleasing to God. Well, sacrifice is good, but obedience is better. Psalm 51:16-17, David tells us that *"God doesn't delight in sacrifices or burnt offerings, but instead desires a broken spirit, and a contrite heart, which God will not despise."* This is about reaching a point of utter desperation for God. It is a place of complete surrender and obedience out of love, fully trusting God and His plan for your life. Laying down your will and your ways. We must come to this place if we truly want to allow God to accomplish His will through us.

Mark 12:33 tells us, *"To love God with all your heart and with all your understanding and with all your strength and to love your neighbor as yourself. This is more important than all the burnt offerings and sacrifice."* Jesus is telling us to discard the "works" mentality that tries to earn God's love and instead simply embrace God's love. Trust His Word! Trust that God was willing to die for you, and He gave His only Son to die for you! This is the ultimate picture of Love. Once we fully embrace this Truth, we will love God, want to obey God and be able to love other people as we love ourselves. We then begin operating from a place of God's Love and not our own ways in which we think love is.

I want to mention one more Scripture on this topic. Hebrews 10:5-9 says, *"Therefore, when Christ came into the world, He said: "Sacrifice and offering You did not desire, but a body You prepared for me. In burnt offerings and sin offerings You took no delight. Then I said, 'Here I am, it is written about Me in the scroll: I have come to do your will, O God.' First he said, "Sacrifices and offerings, burnt offerings and sin offerings you did not desire, nor were you pleased with them" -though they were offered in accordance with the law. Then he said, "Here I am, I have come to do your will." He sets aside the first to establish the second."*

The Old Covenant is still necessary, but it is here that we must remember that Jesus came to fulfill the Law. He is the ultimate sacrifice. Our job is to love God and embrace His love for us. This will motivate us to do whatever God tells us to do. Jesus was the ultimate example for us to live by. He was obedient even unto His death. This life is no longer our own once we say yes to Christ. However, once we come to Him, God is so good that we will begin to feel fulfilled because He knows the destiny He has put within us. When we learn to walk in obedience to God out of Love, we will come to the fulfillment of our destiny.

Doors of destiny will begin opening for you when you are obedient to do whatever it is that God is calling you into. Take this book for example. I have tried writing this book since 2018, but when I finally heard in my spirit, "Now is the time to write," in 2020, I was obedient. I wrote the first few chapters of this book in two weeks! Then He took me through a few more seasons of intense lessons over the past few years, finally prompting me to write in this book again. I thought I finished this book in 2022. However, I heard

God say that this book is not done yet. I was patient until I got a more profound revelation of what that meant exactly.

I have been working over the past two years to rewrite and organize this book into daily readings with homework to apply to your lives each day. Did I want to do this? Not really, because it has been a lot of extra work for me. However, I know the importance of being obedient to my Lord and Savior. I know His ways are always higher, so I choose to submit to them. Now, after rewriting this book, I also see the importance of doing this. I see how applying what you learn daily can help you change your mind and your life. To bring about change requires diligent practice to begin applying what we have learned. Knowledge is only knowledge, but once we use it and start living it out, this brings wisdom.

There is power that comes from being in alignment with God's timing and stepping out in faith when He leads. I encourage you to look at God's Sovereignty as a powerful and mighty force to be reckoned with. Know that God's timing is absolutely perfect and that He will bring you through every trial, every heartache, and every debilitating defeat powerfully if you stay humble, trust Him, and follow His lead. We must remember that we are not God. He has a plan in the crazy chaos on this Earth, and that plan is good! He makes a way even through our past mistakes. God is that good! He is for you, and He is for me! We must stay in faith, filling our minds and hearts with His promises because He will never lead us astray!

He sees the end from the beginning. Nothing gets through the hand of God without Him knowing. He knows every trial that will bring us to our knees to raise us back up into our destiny through Him. He also knows the journeys that we must embark upon to reach the souls that no one else could reach. You are a key component in God's plan. He thought of you before you were formed in your mother's womb, and He will complete the work that He began in you if you will allow Him to, as He tells us in Philippians 1:6. Be encouraged, my beloved sisters and brothers in Christ! We will make it through mightily in this life and into Eternity!

I am praying for each of you, and I believe in you. Most importantly, we have Jesus interceding for all of us at the right hand of God. If God is for us, who can be against us? Stand firm and trust in the Sovereignty of God. He only allows things for a greater purpose, and we must remember that He can see things that we can not. We may not fully understand why such horrible things happen, but we must remember that this life here is only temporary. It is time for us to truly become eternally minded, knowing that all will be restored in Heaven.

Every tear and sadness will be wiped away, for there is no evil or pain in Heaven. It is hard to imagine, given all that we have been through here on Earth, but God tells us that a thousand years is as one day to Him. We must remember that He knows all that we have been through, all that we are going through and all that we will get through. Trust in the goodness of God. Know that He will bring you through powerfully in this life if you follow His lead and walk in faithful obedience, knowing He loves you! He will never forsake you. Trust His plan and purposes upon your life.

<u>APPLYING WISDOM TO YOUR DAILY LIFE</u>

Prayer for the day:

Father God, Holy Spirit, & Jesus, I ask You to reveal any deep roots that are still in my heart where I do not fully trust You. Please help me to release any pride, anger, and bitterness within me. Take any scales from my eyes, Lord. Please help me to die to myself and the desires of my flesh. Help me to heal any and all wounds and keep me from wickedness. I want to recover healthily with You only. I want to be sensitive to Your Holy Spirit and Your Word. I ask You, Lord, to open my eyes, ears, and heart to hear You clearly. I repent for staying in my selfish ways. Please help me to surrender all. I want Your ways for my life. I know that You are the one and only True God, so I am laying down my will today. I am Your Vessel Lord. Use me for Your Glory. I pray this in Jesus' Name.

Scriptures to meditate on:

Romans 1:28: *"And since they did not see fit to acknowledge God, God gave them up to a debased mind to do what ought not to be done."* (It is always someone's choice to come to God or not. He has the absolute best for us but when people do not choose Him, they are unknowingly choosing Satan. This opens many demonic doors to keep their minds in bondage to this fallen world).

Proverbs 19:8: *"The one who gets wisdom, loves life; the one who cherishes understanding will soon prosper."* (There is danger when we rely too much on our own knowledge and abilities and ignore God's Word/ Godly wisdom).

1 Corinthians 13:4: *"Love is patient, love is kind. It does not envy, it does not boast, it is not proud. It does not dishonor others, it is not self-seeking, it is not easily angered, it keeps no record of wrongs."*

1 Peter 1:13: *"Therefore, preparing your minds for action, and being sober-minded, set your hope fully on the grace that will be brought to you at the revelation of Jesus Christ."*

Proverbs 27:17 *"Iron sharpens iron, and one man sharpens another."*

Romans 12:2: *"Do not be conformed to this world, but be transformed by the renewal of your mind, that by testing you may discern what is the will of God, what is good and acceptable and perfect."*

2 Corinthians 3:14: *"But their minds were hardened. For to this day, when they read the old covenant, that same veil remains unlifted, because only through Christ is it taken away."*

Matthew 5:6-10: *"Blessed are those who hunger and thirst for righteousness, for they will be filled. Blessed are the merciful, for they will be shown mercy. Blessed are the pure in heart, for they will see God. Blessed are the peacemakers, for they will be called children of God. Blessed are those who are persecuted because of righteousness, for theirs is the kingdom of heaven."*

1. Do you have any areas in your heart where you still question whether God loves you? We must find any remaining roots so that we can forgive, release, and receive God's love. It is time to put away our selfish, childish ways of holding onto wrongs that have been done against us. We must choose to forgive and then allow the Holy Spirit to come and fill up any wounds that are blocking us from receiving God's Love. Make a list of any area in your life where you are still questioning if God loves you. (This includes any area you know that you are not being obedient in as well) One example might be the "Why would God allow this?" type of questioning. This can make us rebel against Him and not trust Him. List any lies or areas of rebellion you are still battling here:

____

____

____

____

____

____

____

____

____

____

____

2. I want you to go through the "WHY" exercise again for any items you have listed above for question one. This will help you find the root cause of why you are not fully trusting God. You may have to release some more and forgive some more, but that's okay! Remember, the lies that come in about God usually come from hurts from other people that cause our hearts to put up barriers against God. These hurts come from people closest to us, whom we were supposed to be able to trust. When you discover these roots, they can help you recognize where the lie originated and begin to repent of any pride, release any bitterness, and fully surrender to God. Do some WHY exercises here with any situation the Holy Spirit reveals to you that you may still have blocks:

____

____

____

____

____

3. Once you find these roots, I want you to renounce agreement with every lie that comes into your mind about you and God. Write these down here and declare these things out loud:

4. Now, I want you to find scriptures to speak God's truth over you, over Him, and over any situation where you have partnered with lies. Write these down and declare them out loud over your life daily until you begin to believe them. These declarations should consist of God's love for you:

____

____

____

____

____

____

____

Declaration:

I am a Child of the Most High God. God loves me, and He has a mighty plan and purpose for my life. He created me with everything I need to do His will here on this Earth. I am dying to my selfish desires daily. I am learning to walk in God's ways and His will for my life. I know this life is not just about me but about the other people whom God wants to save through me. I have the mind of Christ because I have given my life over to Christ. I read and study my Bible daily. I am growing in Christ, and I can do all things through Him. I am learning how much God loves me and how much He is for me! I am obedient to Him and His Word because I know He is God. I know that He knows what is best for me, so I choose to follow Him.

It has been a great honor to go through this
healing journey with you!
May God bless each and every one of you!
I pray God's abundant blessings upon you!
I hope this book will be a "go-to" for you throughout
the many different seasons of your life.
We must remember that we are constantly growing,
and it can't hurt to revisit something again and again to remind us
how to navigate through challenging times.
The principles and keys within this book have helped me to
break free in several different ways, and still help me to this day.
I hope you have already begun seeing the fruit of them working in your own life.
The goodness of our Heavenly Father overwhelms me each
and every day when I think of all that He has delivered me from.
Trust Him; He is our deliverer!
God loves you so much!

ENJOY YOUR *22 Keys* TO
FREEDOM
THAT UNLOCK YOUR DESTINY WITHIN

God can always bring beauty from dead things if we let Him . . . .

Kristin Taylor

References

The New King James Version of the Bible

The English Standard Version of the Bible

The New Living Translation of the Bible

The New International Version of the Bible

The Passion Translation of the Bible

The New American Standard Version of the Bible